Images of Public Wealth or the Anatomy of Well-Being in Indigenous Amazonia

Images of Public Wealth or the Anatomy of Well-Being in Indigenous Amazonia

Edited by
FERNANDO SANTOS-GRANERO

THE UNIVERSITY OF
ARIZONA PRESS

TUCSON

To Olga F. Linares,
mentor, colleague, and dearest friend

The University of Arizona Press
www.uapress.arizona.edu

Printed in the United States of America
20 19 18 17 16 15 6 5 4 3 2 1

ISBN-13: 978-0-8165-3189-9 (cloth)

Jacket designed by Leigh McDonald
Jacket photo by Beth Conklin

Publication of this book is made possible in part by the proceeds of a permanent endowment created with the assistance of a Challenge Grant from the National Endowment for the Humanities, a federal agency.

Library of Congress Cataloging-in-Publication Data
Images of public wealth or the anatomy of well-being in indigenous Amazonia / edited by Fernando Santos-Granero.
pages cm
Includes bibliographical references and index.
ISBN 978-0-8165-3189-9 (cloth : alk. paper)
1. Indians of South America—Amazon River Region—Economic conditions. 2. Indians of South America—Amazon River Region—Social conditions. 3. Wealth—Amazon River Region. 4. Well-being—Amazon River Region. I. Santos-Granero, Fernando, 1955– editor. II. Title: Anatomy of well-being in indigenous Amazonia.
F2230.1.E25I57 2015
981'.1—dc23
2015005907

♾ This paper meets the requirements of ANSI/NISO Z39.48-1992 (Permanence of Paper).

CONTENTS

Introduction: Images of Public Wealth 3
FERNANDO SANTOS-GRANERO

I. HEALTH, VITALITY, AND EUPHORIA

1. It's Ear-y and Euphoric: Amazonian Music and the Performance of Public Wealth Among the Suyá/Kïsêdjê 37
ANTHONY SEEGER

2. Biopolitics of Health as Wealth in the Original Risk Society 60
BETH A. CONKLIN

3. Public Wealth and the Yanesha Struggle for Vitality 89
FERNANDO SANTOS-GRANERO

II. LAND, MONEY, AND CARE

4. Amazonian Kichwa Leadership: The Circulation of Wealth and the Ambiguities of Mediation 117
MARÍA A. GUZMÁN-GALLEGOS

5. "It Makes Me Sad When They Say We Are Poor. We Are Rich!": Of Wealth and Public Wealth(s) in Indigenous Amazonia 139
JUAN PABLO SARMIENTO BARLETTI

6. Divine Banknote: The Translation of Project Money into Public Wealth 161
GIOVANNA MICARELLI

III. LIVING WELL

7. Clashing Concepts of the "Good Life": Beauty, Knowledge, and Vision Versus National Wealth in Amazonian Ecuador 191
NORMAN E. WHITTEN, JR., AND DOROTHEA SCOTT WHITTEN

Contributors 217

Index 221

Images of Public Wealth or the Anatomy of Well-Being in Indigenous Amazonia

Introduction

Images of Public Wealth

FERNANDO SANTOS-GRANERO

This volume is devoted to exploring local notions of public wealth in indigenous Amazonia. It deliberately appropriates a concept that classical political economists developed to understand wealth accumulation in emergent capitalist nation-states with the intention of denaturalizing it and assessing its applicability in noncapitalist, kin-based societies. Its basic premise is that through the decolonization and indigenization of the classical concept of public wealth it is possible to grasp the uniqueness of indigenous images of personal and collective wealth. It further contends that the study of public wealth provides an exceptional opportunity to apprehend indigenous notions of *well-being* and the *good life*, in other words, to engage in an anatomy of well-being as it is conceived by indigenous Amazonian peoples.

This is a worthy and timely pursuit for three interrelated reasons. The first has to do with the profound financial crisis that has afflicted first-world economies since 2007. This crisis, which only now (2014) begins to show some signs of abatement, has generated widespread discontent. And, above all, it questions the efficacy and sustainability of capitalism as an economic order, as well as a way of life. This crisis has shown that whereas capitalism has been extremely successful in increasing the production and consumption of private goods, it has been much less efficient in taking care of and ensuring the quality of such public goods as education, health, equality of opportunities, and the environment. More importantly, the crisis has shown that John Maynard Keynes (1963) was only half right when he predicted, in the midst of the 1930 world economic crisis, that in a hundred years capitalism would greatly increase the standard of living of its members and enter an "age of leisure and abundance" in which, freed from the worries of the struggle for subsistence, human beings would be able to engage in what he called the "art of life" and learn "how to live wisely and agreeably and well" (Keynes 1963, 367). The present crisis has revealed that the emperor is quite simply naked. The discontented, organized in decentralized and loosely structured popular movements, charge the system—politicians, bankers, corporations, and their wealthy patrons—with making the rich richer and the poor poorer (#OccupyTogether 2012), with driving the planet into financial crisis out of sheer selfishness and a reckless pursuit of profit (Movimiento 15M 2013), with granting money and corporations the inalienable rights that belong to the people (Move to Amend 2012), and with using taxpayers' monies to bail out irresponsible and greedy financial institutions (#OccupyWallStreet 2011). Through their novel and often spectacular actions these transgressive movements have called attention to the strained relation between personal interest and the common good, corporate profit and state duties, and private gain and public wealth. In his controversial *Capital in the Twenty-First Century*, Thomas Piketty (2014) argued that higher rates of return on capital combined with lower rates of economic growth have led, since the end of World War II, to extreme inequalities in the distribution of wealth in capitalist societies, which has intensified the feeling that something is wrong with "millennial capitalism" (Comaroff and Comaroff 2001). By discussing radically foreign understandings of public wealth, this volume provides new referents on which to rethink conventional viewpoints and everyday practices and with them—may we dare hope—formulates, as Beth Conklin (chapter 2) suggests, "healthier life-politics and more equitable, inclusive economies."

The second reason, though more academic, is no less important. As a result of the increasing awareness that millennial capitalism has not only been unable to secure a sustainable growth but has also promoted a frantic consumerist lifestyle that has led to the rapid depletion of natural resources, the contamination of the environment, the disappearance of thousands of animal and plant species, the warming of the earth's temperatures, the overcrowding and pollution of cities, and a general diminution of the quality of life of human beings—always pressed to work more and become more indebted in order to spend more and acquire more material goods—there has been a renewed global interest on the topics of well-being, "happiness," and the good life. This is particularly noticeable in the popular media. Books on the subject of happiness have steadily increased in number from 50 in 2000 to 4,000 in 2008 (Paredes 2012, 5). Anthropology was slower to pick up on this trend, but when it did, it did so massively. At the 2011 Annual Meeting of the American Anthropological Association (AAA), 112 of the papers presented had the word *well-being* in either their titles or their abstracts, 31 had the word *happiness*, and 11 had the phrase *good life*. Echoing this increased interest, the AAA organized the Vital Topics Forum, On Happiness, whose proceedings were published in their flagship journal *American Anthropologist* in 2012 with Barbara Rose Johnston as guest editor. *Anthropology News*, the AAA's monthly newsletter, also devoted its March 2012 issue to the topic of Health, Well-Being and Happiness. Doubtless, this growing academic interest has deep roots in a widespread feeling of dissatisfaction with postindustrial societies and a generalized craving for alternative models to achieve happiness and well-being (see Atherton, Graham, and Steedman 2011; Ferry 2005; Fischer 2014; Jackson 2011). Yet, as Mathews and Izquierdo (2009, 1) have pointed out, "there is no unambiguously single pursuit of happiness—rather, there are multiple 'pursuits of happiness.'" Through a survey of the varied meanings of well-being, happiness, and the good life in indigenous Amazonian societies, this volume engages with and contributes to this burgeoning new theoretical field.

Finally, the academic interest on this topic goes hand-in-hand with a political reexamination of what should be the aim of governments and intergovernmental organizations in regard to the well-being of the people they represent. What may be considered a good life in contemporary societies? Is it possible to measure well-being and happiness? This trend began in 1990 when Pakistani and Indian economists, Mahbub ul Haq and Amartya Sen, designed for the United Nations Development Program a new way of measuring development intended to shift policy makers' attention from economic factors to human well-being. Combining three indicators—life expectancy, average years of schooling, and per capita gross national income—the new measurement, known as the Human Development Index (HDI), replaced older indicators based mostly on material aspects, such as per capita gross domestic product and standard of living. Although the HDI represented a vast improvement in regard to previous economists' perspectives, it has been criticized for relying on traditional indicators and for omitting other material and immaterial aspects of human well-being, such as environmental, emotional, and moral factors (Caplan 2009). As a consequence, new indices have been devised, such as the Economist Intelligence Unit's 2005 Quality of Life Index, which takes into consideration a combination of economic and social indicators. Another is the New Economics Foundation's 2006 Happy Planet Index, which is based on indicators of well-being and environmental impact. Gallup's 2009 Happiness Index focuses on individuals' overall satisfaction with their lives. The topic of how to measure happiness, health, or well-being has also drawn much academic interest as manifested in the host of new books addressing the subject (see Grosse 2011; Harvey and Taylor 2013; Scott 2012).

Others have gone a step farther in search not of new ways of measuring well-being but of radically new models of well-being. The main question for those involved in this quest is not so much how to strike a balance between the economic and noneconomic factors of well-being but, rather, to envision new paradigms of well-being that can become an alternative to the current global model of production and consumption. In Bolivia and Ecuador, presidents Evo Morales and Rafael Correa have sought to achieve this by resorting to ancestral indigenous notions of well-being. The new Bolivian (2006) and Ecuadorian (2008) constitutions, which recognize these countries as plurinational and multicultural, have enshrined the right to a good life taking as referents the Aymara and Quichua notions of *suma qamaña* and *sumak kawsay*. Translated into Spanish as *buen vivir* (living well or good life), these notions have been hailed as an autochthonous response to colonialism and neoliberal economic principles. In the words of an advocate of this process, "now it is the periphery . . . that rethinks development, that rescues ancestral ideas so as not to repeat the same errors, that bets for balance, for another kind of development—sustained and sustainable, that dares to remove the theories from the academies to put them into practice, that talks about the Good Life and inserts it into their constitutions—so that there is no doubt, as an objective to be pursued" (Chato 2011, my translation). Defenders of the notion of buen vivir have been better, however, at stating what the concept is as opposed to specifying what it stands for. They are vague as to its content, and—adopting what can only be characterized as an indigenous neocolonialist stance—they assume that what is true for the Quichua and Aymara indigenous majorities must be valid for all other indigenous peoples. More importantly, as Norman and Dorothea Whitten (chapter 7) state, in the process of appropriating these indigenous notions, national governments have profoundly modified their meaning by infusing them with neoliberal notions of capitalist wealth accumulation. Contributors to this book seek to rectify this situation by providing detailed ethnographic information about how well-being is conceived of by a diversity of indigenous Amazonian societies.

This volume is based on papers presented in a homonymous panel at the 54th International Congress of Americanists (Vienna, July 15–20, 2012). It deals with seven tropical forest peoples of Ecuador, Colombia, Peru, and Brazil (see Map 1) and explores indigenous Amazonian notions of public wealth and well-being. At the same time it places particular

MAP 1. Location of the indigenous Amazonian peoples discussed in this volume. Map by Fernando Santos-Granero.

emphasis on how these notions—based on the abundance of intangibles such as vitality, biopower, good health, and convivial feelings—differ substantially from those entertained in capitalist societies, which are more inclined toward the accumulation of material goods. In so doing, this volume elucidates five important connections.

Firstly, this volume explores the connection between public wealth and social and symbolic production. Is public wealth internally generated through long-term convivial relations between like people, or is it an external creation derived from predatory relations with radically different Others? In other words, is it an embodied aspect of a community's self, or an instance of incorporation of foreign substances, bodies, and artifacts? Secondly, the authors herein examine the connection between public wealth and indigenous notions of ownership and property. Is public wealth synonymous with collective property? Can items of personal property be considered to be part of collective wealth? Can public wealth be considered a form of collective, inalienable "patrimony"? Thirdly, we examine the connection between public wealth and personhood. What is the role of public wealth in the making of people—women and men—and, thus, in the reproduction of local collectivities? Are items of public wealth "figurations" of collective subjectivities or "materializations" of collective capacities? How does public wealth shape personal and collective identities? Fourthly, these chapters analyze the connection between public wealth and leadership in their various manifestations. Does control over public wealth reinforce positions of leadership? Or is public wealth a means through which collectivities control their leadership? Is leadership a function of public wealth? Or are leaders themselves items of public wealth? Finally, it looks at the connection between public wealth and well-being, and between public wealth and poverty. How does public wealth contribute to individual and collective well-being? Is public wealth an expression of, or a precondition for, collective well-being? How do indigenous Amazonian peoples conceive of states of poverty?

In the following pages, I first discuss the origin and development of the notion of public wealth in classical and neoclassical economics and make the case for why it may be fruitfully applied to the study of noncapitalist, kin-based societies. I then examine the nature of indigenous Amazonian public wealth as defined by contributors to this volume and address the sets of questions that oriented panel discussions and the volume's contributions. Finally, I summarize some of the general conclusions arrived at by the contributors to this volume and, following Whitten and Whitten (chapter 7), call attention to the transformative power that derives from confronting radically divergent notions of public wealth, well-being, and the good life.

Origin and Development of the Notion of Public Wealth

The life history of the notion of public wealth involves, among other things, the uneasy marriage between a Middle English word of West Germanic ancestry (*wealth*) and the Roman term *public*, whose root goes back to the origins of the Latin people and is somewhat convoluted. Its beginning is inextricably linked to the emergence of capitalism and the birth of political economy, as well as the social sciences. It is also attached to a work that until now has been considered the theoretical foundation of classical political economy: Adam Smith's 1776 *An Inquiry into the Nature and Causes of the Wealth of Nations*. In this work, Smith (1776, 212) defines "national wealth" as the "whole annual produce of the land and labor of every country." The wealth of a country, in his view, is composed of three elements: "the rent of land, the wages of labor, and the profits of stock." In other words, the main sources of wealth are land, labor, and capital (Smith 1776, 212). Although Smith (1776, 668) subsumed public and private riches under the notion of national wealth, he was aware of the difference between both, and he defined public wealth as the mass of assets that are indispensable to "defray not only the expense of defending the society and of supporting the dignity of the chief magistrate but all the other necessary expenses of government, for which the constitution of the state has not provided any particular revenue." Public wealth, in Smith's view, is constituted by three components: the public lands and public stock that belong to the "sovereign or commonwealth" and the public revenue obtained from taxation of the main sources of wealth, which are rent, wages, and profit.

It was not, however, until the publication in 1804 of *An Inquiry into the Nature and Origin of Public Wealth and into the Means and Causes of its Increase*, written by James Maitland, 8th Earl of Lauderdale, that the notion of public wealth acquired the character of a distinct economic concept. Maitland (1819 [1804], 6–7) questioned Smith's definition of national wealth as "the sum total of the riches of those who form the community." He showed how increases in personal riches often lead to a decrease in national wealth, whereas an increase in national wealth often results in a decrease of personal riches. This finding—which came to be known as the Lauderdale Paradox—led Maitland to distinguish public from private wealth and to limit the scope of the notion of national wealth to include only public wealth. Whereas he defined public wealth as "all that man desires, as useful or delightful to him," he restricted the notion of private wealth to "all that man desires as useful or delightful to him, which exists in a degree of scarcity" (Maitland 1819 [1804], 56–57).

The crucial difference between public and private wealth would, thus, be whether the items in question are scarce or not, which is tantamount to saying whether or not they have exchange value. In this view, all items "that man desires as useful or delightful" and that are found in nature in abundance have use value and form part of a nation's public wealth. In contrast, private wealth consists mainly of commodities—scarce natural resources, which when transformed through the action of labor or capital, acquire exchange value. Maitland was not as specific as Smith with respect to what exactly formed part of public wealth. He mentions "the whole of the fruits of the earth, as well as the produce of mines and fisheries" and certain kinds of specialized or skilled labor, such as that of artists (Maitland 1819 [1804], 130, 144). What is important here, however, is that in his view the use value inherent to items of public wealth was as crucial to human welfare as the exchange value of commodities.

This changed drastically with the publication of John Stuart Mill's *Principles of Political Economy* in 1848. In this popular economic textbook—which was revised and re-edited several times during Mill's life—Mill asserts that wealth is "everything . . . which serves any human purpose, and which nature does not afford gratuitously" (Mill 1848, 8). "Everything forms therefore a part of wealth"—he went on to say—"which has a power of purchasing; for which anything useful or agreeable would be given in exchange. *Things for which nothing could be obtained in exchange, however useful or necessary they may be, are not wealth in the sense in which the term is used in Political Economy*" (Mill 1848, 8; my emphasis). With these extraordinary words Mill dispensed with the ancient meaning of the term *wealth* and paved the way for the emergence of neoclassical economics.

The meaning of "wealth," according to 1974 *The Oxford Universal Dictionary*, derives from the thirteenth-century Middle English word *welthe*. In its origins it had a double meaning: "the condition of being happy and prosperous, well-being," and "prosperity consisting in abundance of possessions, riches, [and] affluence." Four centuries later, however, the term acquired a more collective dimension signifying "abundance of possessions or of valuable products, as characteristic of a people, country, or region, [and] the collective riches of a people or country." The term public wealth, coined by Maitland, was thus an exercise in redundancy, since the term public, which is derived from Old Latin's *poplicus* and means "pertaining to the people," did not add anything new to the meaning of wealth, which already had the connotation of belonging to a collectivity. By restricting the term wealth to commodities, or things that have exchange value, Mill essentially privatized the term and deprived it of its collective dimension. In this view, that which is common by virtue of its natural abundance cannot be considered as wealth. More importantly, by detaching natural resources that are abundant and which nature affords gratuitously from the definition of wealth, Mill helped—perhaps unwittingly, since in later editions of his book he manifested doubts about the perception that capitalism can grow indefinitely without destroying its natural base—to cloak nature's contribution to the production of wealth and made it easier for neoclassical economists to deny the existence of nature or assume that it can be completely subordinated to the narrow interests of profit making.

This theoretical shift had another critical consequence: it restricted the production of "real wealth" to state societies. According to Mill (1848), nonstate societies, incapable of producing commodities, are incapable of producing wealth. Mill's reflections on this matter had such a long-term influence on Western views of noncapitalist, kin-based societies that it is worth quoting him at length:

> There is perhaps, no people or community, now existing, which subsists entirely on the spontaneous produce of vegetation. But many tribes still live exclusively, or almost exclusively, on wild animals, the produce of hunting or fishing. Their clothing are skins; their habitations, huts rudely formed of logs or boughs of trees, and abandoned at an hour's notice. The food they use being little susceptible of storing up, they have no accumulation of it, and are often exposed to great privations. The wealth of such a community consists solely of the skins they wear; a few ornaments, the taste for which exists among most savages; some rude utensils; the weapons with which they kill their game, or fight against hostile competitors for the means of subsistence; canoes for crossing rivers and lakes, or fishing in the sea; and perhaps some furs or other productions of the wilderness, collected to be exchanged with civilized people for blankets, brandy, and tobacco; of which foreign produce also there may be some unconsumed portion in store. To this scanty inventory of material wealth, ought to be added their land; an instrument of production of which they make slender use, compared with more settled communities, but which is still the source of their subsistence, and which has a marketable value if there be any agricultural community in the neighborhood requiring more land than it possesses. This is the state of greatest poverty in which any entire community of human beings is known to exist; though there are much richer communities in which portions of the inhabitants are in a condition, as to subsistence and comfort, as little enviable as that of the savage. (Mill 1848, 11–12)

By comparing the paucity of material wealth in nonstate, "tribal" societies to the material deprivation of the urban and rural poor of modern capitalist societies, Mill misses entirely the point that wealth is a cultural construct and that, as such, it assumes different meanings in different times and places. Contributors to this volume question the notion that indigenous peoples are wealthless and live in a "state of greatest poverty." They subscribe to the idea that wealth is in the eye of the beholder and that, therefore, closer attention must be paid when indigenous people say, like Joel, the Ashaninka man quoted by Sarmiento Barletti (chapter 5), "we are not poor. We are rich!!" When indigenous people make such assertions, the image of wealth they have in mind is closer to the archaic meaning of the Middle English term—"the condition of being happy and prosperous; well-being"—than to Mill's narrower understanding of wealth as the totality of scarce items possessing exchange value. Indigenous perceptions are also closer to the seventeenth-century acceptation of the term wealth with its connotation of "the collective riches of a people or country" than to the more individualized meaning of contemporary usages of the term, which places emphasis on the individual accumulation of "a large amount of money and valuable material possessions."

Here we have deliberately adopted Maitland's redundant term "public wealth," so as to restore to the notion of wealth, the collective dimension of which it was deprived since Mill's times. We have not, however, restricted this notion to items that are naturally abundant and only possess use value. By wealth we understand an abundance of material or immaterial items that are highly valued due to their centrality in the sustenance and well-being of individuals and communities. In turn, we understand public wealth as the sum total of items of wealth over which a given collectivity has rights of property or usufruct. In other words, public wealth, in accordance with *The Oxford Universal Dictionary*'s definition of public, means that it "is open to, may be used by, or may or must be shared by, all members of the community." We are aware, however, that, as a result of their increasing participation in market activities, ethnopolitical organizations, and national politics, indigenous Amazonian peoples have engaged in a dynamic of interethnic relations and interculturality in which their understandings of public wealth, well-being, happiness, and the good life have come to compete with other—sometimes complementary, sometimes contrasting—understandings. As Whitten and Whitten argue in chapter 7, such a dynamic has not always resulted in an irreducible opposition of concepts but has provided the grounds for fertile intercultural deliberation and negotiation.

The Nature of Public Wealth

The contributors to this volume—and especially Sarmiento Barletti (chapter 5)—have pointed out the difficulty in determining what the sphere of the public is in indigenous Amazonian societies, particularly in contexts of increasing involvement in market activities, ethnopolitics, and national legal systems, which have given rise to new models of "community." Based on the notion of community as a legally defined geopolitical space containing related and unrelated people, these new models often clash with traditional ones founded on a more restricted notion of community as a space of everyday-life, kin-based relations. Though overlapping, the two models impose different kinds of obligations, excite different forms of allegiance, and propitiate different kinds of *sensus communitas* (sense of community). Other authors suggest that the public is tightly linked to collective action and that there are as many public spheres as sociocosmological domains of action recognized by any given indigenous Amazonian people (see Whitten and Whitten and Santos-Granero, chapters 7 and 3, respectively, on the Canelos Quichua and Yanesha). In either case, authors seem to agree that there is no single public sphere but a variety of public spheres that give rise to different forms of public wealth.

Contributors have also drawn attention to the fact that the notion of wealth is socially constructed and, as such, cannot be defined a priori. The meaning of wealth may vary spatially, from people to people, and temporally from time to time. By paying attention to ethnographic detail and assuming a historical perspective, the studies in this volume reveal important changes in indigenous Amazonian constructions of public wealth. This explains, for instance, why the Wari', a people living in western Brazil within a large national park where land is still abundant, do not consider land as public wealth (see Conklin, chapter 2), whereas the Amazonian Kichwa, who live in heavily colonized areas of eastern Ecuador where land is now scarce and the object of fierce competition, do (see Guzmán-Gallegos, chapter 4). It is therefore important to note that what may appear as significant differences in the way indigenous Amazonian peoples conceive of public wealth are often an artifact of the historical transformations brought about by their greater interaction with the encompassing national societies. However, given that the studies gathered in this volume do not have great historical depth, we cannot be sure that the "images of public wealth" conjured by them correspond to those extant at a time when many indigenous Amazonians lived in larger, more complex societies that were characterized by greater population density, more centralized forms of authority, life in urban centers, construction of earthworks, and the subjection of slaves and other subordinate populations (Heckenberger 2003; Iriarte, Gillam, and Marozzi 2008; Rostain 2008; Santos-Granero 2009). The study of indigenous Amazonian forms of public wealth in pre-European times remains, thus, a pending task.

Contributors also note that wealth, as several scholars have proposed (Graeber 2001; Gregory 1997; Strathern 1992; Turner 2003), is first and foremost a question of "value" and a notion much discussed in classical anthropology that has commanded renewed attention in recent times. In a special issue on Value *as* Theory in *HAU: The Journal of Ethnographic Theory*, the editors, Ton Otto and Rane Willerslev (2013), asked whether it is useful or even possible to develop an anthropological theory of value. Otto believed it was; Willerslev believed that it wasn't. Both agreed nonetheless that there have been two main lines of research on value. On the one hand, values are the set of ideal, normative understandings that characterize particular worldviews or cultural systems. On the other hand, value is the worth of things in economic transactions or exchange relationships. In either case, they coincided that value cannot be determined outside of its cultural and ethnographic context, and it is always relational, embedded as it is in the totality of relations of production and reproduction. The works gathered in this volume propose that indigenous Amazonian understandings of wealth place greater emphasis on shared cultural values than on notions of worth and exchange. This does not mean that items of public wealth in Amazonian societies are devoid of exchange value, but that even when owned by individuals such items acquire the condition of public wealth when they are shared rather than exchanged. In these societies wealth is measured by the success in securing such values rather than on the exchange value of that which a collectivity is able to amass. What are these values? And why are they so important?

Despite the variability in the way indigenous Amazonians conceive of public wealth—richly manifested in the chapters that compose this volume—there are several recurring traits that suggest the existence of a regional, Amazonian logic of public wealth. First, and in stark contrast with present-day Western understandings, most authors point out that wealth in indigenous Amazonia is seldom associated with the accumulation of material objects. Seeger (chapter 1) contends in highly evocative terms that to comprehend public wealth in indigenous Amazonia, "it is essential to remove the blinders of materialist definitions of wealth . . . and recognize that wealth can be as intangible as air and as fleeting as a reverberation, gesture, or emotional response yet be powerful and enduring in its effects." In a similar vein, Conklin (chapter 2) alludes to the "traditional disinterest in material wealth" characteristic of Wari' and other Amazonian societies. Although other authors have called attention to the greater prominence that material objects have acquired in recent times in the form of motorboats, trucks, and cattle bought with development project funds, or schools, health posts, and soccer fields built with the earnings obtained from selling communal resources or as compensation from oil companies, they all coincide, as Sarmiento Barletti (chapter 5) states: "indigenous Amazonian conceptions of wealth and value have little to do with individual material accumulation."

This brings us to the second point. Whereas Western conceptions of wealth call to mind images of hoarding tangible objects with high exchange value—as Scrooge McDuck's emblematic piles of gold coins—in indigenous Amazonia wealth evokes images of abundance of mostly intangible things with little exchange value: music, songs, and the moods they excite (Seeger, chapter 1); food, children, and social relations (Conklin, chapter 2), land, productive capacities, and people (Guzmán-Gallegos, chapter 4), or natural resources, convivial relations, and life-giving knowledge (Santos-Granero, chapter 3). None of these items can be accumulated as is the case of money, cars, houses, works of art, or bonds, and as we shall see, they find their realization only when they are shared or put to the service of others.

The appearance of money, vehicles, machinery, cattle, and other costly material objects in contemporary indigenous Amazonian societies has radically altered their capacity for wealth accumulation. It has not, however, changed how indigenous people perceive material accumulation, especially when it does not go hand-in-hand with an attitude of generosity, care, and compassion—that is, when it is not shared. In such cases, material wealth comes to be regarded as antisocial, and the selfish hoarders are punished through shaming, ostracism, and in extreme cases, even witchcraft attacks (see Sarmiento Barletti, chapter 5). This is especially true in the case of community leaders who have been perceived to accumulate undue amounts of money, goods, and opportunities obtained from the white world and who have refused to share them with their followers. Such leaders are thought to have turned into greedy white people and are harshly criticized until they change their attitude or are abandoned altogether (see Guzmán-Gallegos, chapter 4). In other cases, the selfish and unproductive accumulation of "hot" development project money in the hands of a few leaders is believed to produce a kind of "overheating" that liberates its pathogenic forces under the form of "development illness" (see Micarelli, chapter 6). The takeaway message in all these situations is that in indigenous Amazonia wealth has no value if it is not shared with others.

This leads us to the discussion of the nature of public wealth. Although the contributors to this volume mention a variety of tangible and intangible items as key components of contemporary forms of public wealth, there is a general consensus that public wealth in indigenous Amazonia is, in the last analysis, associated with the abundance of vitality. Whether conceived of as life-giving substances, health, beautiful life force, biopower, generative capacities, or productive skills, such vitality is regarded as the ultimate expression of public wealth and the key to collective well-being. Authors vary, however, on whether vitality *is* public wealth or just a *prerequisite* for the production of the *real* public wealth: people. In other words, they differ on whether the scarce resource in indigenous political economies is vitality or people. Such differences, I suggest, are an artifact of whether they place greater emphasis on the human or cosmic dimensions of the social production of wealth.

By placing emphasis on human sociality and the realm of internal group relations, Sarmiento Barletti and Conklin (in their individual chapters of this volume) regard vitality as a means in the making of "proper" human beings. They suggest that "human capital," that is, healthy, hardworking, moral people endowed with productive capacities and transformative skills, constitute the real public wealth in indigenous Amazonian societies. While negating neither the competition for life forces nor the circulation of vitality as key elements in the production of public wealth, they consider that people, the real public wealth among the Ashaninka and Wari', are the product of the caring, nurturing, and hard work of parents, kin, and friends.

In contrast, by focusing on the broader dimension of interspecific sociality—the network of relations encompassing humans, as well as plants, animals, objects and spirits, conceived as nonhuman people—I regard vitality as a scarce resource and a much-coveted cosmic substance that shapes the exchanges between all living beings (Santos-Granero 2009 and this volume). It is indispensable for the reproduction of all aspects of human, social, and cosmic life. Although I argue that generative forms of public wealth among the Yanesha of central Peru are made up of vitality, as well as the life-giving knowledge and ritual techniques of shamans, priests, and chiefly leaders—and even of these specialists themselves—I propose that the acquisition of vitality from alien Others is a multipurpose goal that goes far beyond the mere production of people. While a crucial component in processes of people-making, vitality is also used by priests to ensure the increase of plants and animals, as well as to feed the creator gods; it is used by shamans to cure people and protect them from enemy jaguars and spirits; and it is employed by settlement leaders to guarantee the access to resources in a juncture of increasing encroachment by Andean settlers.

Guzmán-Gallegos and Micarelli (chapters 4 and 6, respectively), adopt an intermediate position. They summarize the above differences as an opposition between Rivière's (1984) and Fausto's (2001) stances, which is that since labor is the scarcest resource indigenous Amazonian societies are ultimately *political economies of people*, and my own (Santos-Granero 2009), which contends that because vitality is the main object of strife among all living beings, these societies should be characterized as *political economies of life*. Although there are some important conceptual differences between these two positions—which I explore elsewhere—such differences do not significantly affect the way in which contributors to this volume understand how indigenous Amazonian forms of public wealth are produced, owned, and deployed.

The Production of Public Wealth

All contributors are quite clear that in indigenous Amazonia, public wealth—whether under the form of abstract vitality or concrete bodies—is always the combined product of internal relations of conviviality, mutual cooperation and caring, and external relations of competition involving alternate relations of predation, appeasement, seduction, or friendship. Seeger (chapter 1), for instance, sees ceremonies and the states of happiness and euphoria they produce as the main form of public wealth among the Kïsêdjê of Brazilian Mato Grosso. He stresses the fact that such ceremonies do not acquire the character of public wealth unless all members of the community participate in the event, "each according to his or her specific identity by gender, age, and name set." It is only when everybody sings, dances, and eats that a state of happiness/euphoria, which both vitalizes participants and reaffirms their sensus communitas, is achieved. Seeger is clear, however, in that this form of public wealth also requires engaging in relations "with other kinds of humans, other species, or spirits."

Likewise, Whitten and Whitten (chapter 7) note that among the Canelos Quichua of eastern Ecuador the concept of *sumaj causai*, which they translate as *beautiful life* or *beautiful life force*, is based on notions of community, conviviality, and kinship. But they make it clear that Canelos shamans and master potters insist that "one cannot understand one's own people's perceptions without understanding something of the lifeways and thought processes of other peoples." In other words, the achievement of a beautiful life requires engaging with *shuj shimita yachai* (the cultural knowledge of others).

This is not always an easy task. Guzmán-Gallegos (chapter 4) affirms that the Amazonian Kichwa "relate notions of public wealth and well-being to access and control of resources originating in the multiple worlds that, in their view, make up the cosmos." This can only be attained through interaction with a host of human and spirit beings that are at best ambiguous and at worse plain dangerous. The alien resources—including vital force—wrested from these ambiguous Others are crucial for the production of people and the reproduction of society. But so are land and other forest resources, which when transformed into means of subsistence and life force through the productive capacities and acts of caring of skilled men and women are also crucial in this process. Guzmán-Gallegos thus concludes that Amazonian Kichwa public wealth and well-being depend as much on relations of mutual predation with alien Others as on relations of cooperation and conviviality with neighbors and kin.

Although in this volume I distinguish convivial from generative forms of public wealth as produced by different agents and in different spheres of social action, I concur with other authors in that both types of wealth are interdependent and equally important for achieving a state of well-being. Whereas convivial wealth is produced internally and "consists of the totality of harmonious relations that members of a given collectivity establish with other people within and without their village by virtue of being . . . generous, loving, caring, and compassionate," generative wealth is produced externally and "encompasses everything that an individual obtains from powerful Others to ensure the life, good health, and reproduction of the members of the collectivity to which he or she belongs."

These are not, however, separate or unrelated spheres. As Micarelli (chapter 6) suggests when analyzing how the People of the Center of southeastern Colombia deal with the dangerous properties of development project funds, "money is the linchpin where the external world of radical alterity (*lo de afuera*) and internal world of shared substances (*lo de adentro*) swing into each other." People of the Center engage with the world of the whites, who are thought to control potentially dangerous substances essential for human existence, in the hope of "hunting" money in the form of development project funds. At the same time, however, they strive to cool off the hot nature of money by transforming it first into exchangeable products and then into work. Thus captured and transformed, money can be absorbed into the internal circuits of production, reciprocity, and commensality and contribute to the domestic process of people-making. The same could be said of other alien substances obtained from dangerous Others. For instance, the spirit blood or health-enhancing substance that Wari' warriors obtained in the past from slain enemies, when ritually transformed, could be transmitted to all those who had witnessed the killing, making them "grow fatter, stronger, and more courageous" (see Conklin, chapter 2).

Ownership and Public Wealth

Whether a means or an end, externally or internally produced, vitality and its material expression—the strong, healthy, and beautiful bodies of men, women, and children—occupy a central place in indigenous Amazonian notions of public wealth. These and other, more tangible assets, such as land, forest resources, trucks, buildings, machinery, and cattle, constitute important items of public wealth insofar as they are meant to serve the collectivity. But are they owned by the collectivity? Is public wealth synonymous with collective property? Most contributors to this volume would answer this question with a categorical no, arguing, on the one hand, that in indigenous Amazonia certain forms of personal or private wealth can be considered as part of a group's public wealth and, on the other hand, that the "public" dimension of public wealth is defined more by rights of usufruct than by property rights.

Among the Kïsêdjê, according to Seeger (chapter 1), certain songs and dances may be the property of a given name set or moiety. But when performed in a collective ceremony, they "constitute and produce a kind of insufficiently recognized public wealth." This is so for the *kandé* (owners/controllers of such songs and dances), who may determine the way in which these are used, but they do not "have the right to refuse to share them, which would [be] immoral in any event and could lead to accusations of being a *wayangá* (witch)." This resonates with the Yanesha and Wari' cases. I note in chapter 3 of this volume that the life-giving knowledge obtained by priests, shamans, and chiefs from a variety of alien Others—including gods, the spirit owners of animals and plants, and the less-than-human white people—is considered to be their personal property insofar as they have caused such knowledge to materialize through their ritual practices, political acumen, or the power of their thoughts. At the same time, however, I argue that these specialists' life-giving knowledge is also considered to be "an important component of [Yanesha] public wealth, for it acquires its full value when used on their behalf, *allohuenacop*, that is, 'for everybody.'" In turn, Conklin, in chapter 2, discusses one of the Wari's few exceptions—the stone quarry that belonged to the Oro Eo' kin group—to disinterest in owning material property. She suggests that whereas the quarry was acknowledged as the property of the Oro Eo', the Wari' "managed their uniquely scarce resource by facilitating its distribution to others," thus transforming what was clearly an item of private property into a constituent of public wealth.

Authors also agree that usufruct rather than property rights is the key element defining public wealth in indigenous Amazonia. The Ashaninka of eastern Peru consider that the mere fact of belonging to a community endows members with usufruct rights over items of public wealth: the materials they receive from nongovernmental organizations, state projects, or oil and timber companies, as well as the public buildings and spaces built with monies obtained from these sources (Sarmiento Barletti, chapter 5). Such rights are, however, informed by Ashaninka notions of ownership, which involve moral relations of care between owners and owned. Like the owners/masters of animal species, who protect and take care of the animals they give life to, the Ashaninka are expected to take care of items of public wealth, since that is the only way in which these are "able to function properly and look beautiful."

The Amazonian Kichwa also consider that members of a community have usufruct rights over communal lands (Guzmán-Gallegos, chapter 4). Such rights derive from membership in a given community and the relations of care established within a given space. As Amazonian Kichwa men and women have the productive capacities to create and recreate relations by caring for their children and spouses and entering into relations of symmetrical reciprocity with their kinfolk, they also have the capacities to "transform the forest into well-tended gardens and family places." These productive and transformational capacities constitute Amazonian Kichwa men and women into *amu* (owners) of the persons, objects, and places they have contributed to create. Rights of usufruct over public wealth—especially land and forest resources—are thus conducive to temporary ownership through transformational acts and relations of care.

Work is also a key element in People of the Center's notions of ownership and public wealth (Micarelli, chapter 6). Since public wealth is conceived of as composed of all those things "entrusted to people by the ultimate owner of all things with the condition that people put it to good use," it cannot be appropriated privately. However, as Micarelli argues here, public wealth is not synonymous with collective, inalienable property. On the contrary, through work, understood as the "transformative knowledge and capacities needed to materialize the creator's dream in daily life," People of the Center appropriate public resources that are indispensable for the sustenance of their individual families and the collective as a whole. In this sense, it could be argued that public wealth among People of the Center "can be considered as a form of collective, but *alienable*, patrimony" (original emphasis).

In all these cases, people have rights of usufruct rather than property rights over public wealth insofar as this kind of wealth was created for everybody or, being the product of collective efforts, is meant to be shared with everybody. For this reason, I suggest (chapter 3) that public wealth may be defined as "the totality of valued things—whether material or not—over which a collectivity claims to have rights of usufruct." Although through the transformative dimension of work items of public wealth may be appropriated by individuals and family groups, in indigenous Amazonia that which is public can never be fully privatized. And as soon as a person ceases to transform and take care of a given space through his or her work, the appropriated land and resources return to the public domain.

Public Wealth and People-Making

One of the central themes of this volume is the crucial role that public wealth plays in the fabrication of people and collectivities. This may assume a variety of forms. Among the Kïsêdjê, wealth is achieved through public ceremonies that involve elaborate musical performances and dance (Seeger, chapter 1). These ceremonies are central for the production of people as social beings; the ritual initiation of Kïsêdjê boys and girls into adulthood is the most prominent of such people-making ceremonies. At the same time, Seeger points out, "the intensity and duration of the final phases of Kïsêdjê rituals created euphoria, and they also created social life as it should be, with every position in society performing its appropriate roles."

Among the Yanesha, Amazonian Kichwa, Ashaninka, Wari', and People of the Center, where vitality constitutes a key component of public wealth, the making of social persons is achieved through transfers of life-giving substances obtained either from the gods, the masters/owners of plants and animals, or from parents, kinsmen, and friends. In all these cases, this becomes possible when the acquired vitality is transformed either through ritual means by specialists or through habitual acts of love, care, and nurturing; in other words, when it is transformed through productive work/knowledge.

In chapter 3, I describe how Yanesha generative forms of public wealth involve a variety of life-giving and fertilizing elements: the healing arts and ritual protection techniques obtained by tobacco shamans through interaction with a variety of spirit worlds; the vitalizing substances acquired by priestly leaders through prayers, vigils, fasts, and an attitude of suffering expectation; and the goods, documents, and knowledge obtained by settlement chiefs from the dangerous white people's world. Appeased and transformed through the intervention of these specialists, and in conjunction with environmental and convivial forms of wealth, generative wealth "guarantees, on the one hand, the nourishment, good health, moral formation, and productive capacities of Yanesha individuals and, on the other hand, a beautiful, harmonious and tranquil life conducive to the perpetuation of the collectivity as a whole."

Similar views are found among the Amazonian Kichwa and the Ashaninka. Guzmán-Gallegos (chapter 4) affirms that among the Amazonian Kichwa "public wealth and well-being are crucially related to the production of Kichwa men and women as persons and as a people." In her view people-making "is mainly related to the transmission of productive capacities and to the acquisition and maintenance of life forces." This is partly achieved through the transfer of *samai* (breath, vital force, or will) from parents and other adult relatives to children. Such transfers strengthen the recipient physically and spiritually, endowing him or her with the donors' capacities, moral virtues, and affects. However, the making of proper people and strong collectivities also requires the incorporation of alien substances, vitalities, and identities. Only the systematic transmission of domestic and foreign sources of vitality makes possible "the production of strong, gendered persons endowed with life-giving substances and transformative capacities."

In consonance with the Ashaninka dual understanding of "the public," Sarmiento Barletti (chapter 5) proposes that "access to public wealth in the *comunidad* [community] creates an identity as *comuneros* [community members] with equal rights and responsibilities, whereas the use and care of items of public wealth is intrinsic to the process of creating an *Ashaninkasanori* [real Ashaninka person] identity." In either case, competition for life forces and the circulation of vitality and other public goods are thought to be critical in the fabrication of real human beings—strong bodies and happy faces—and kinship. This, however, can only be attained through hard work and relations of care, that is, "through the morality of labor and wealth."

In their chapters, Conklin and Micarelli (chapters 2 and 6, respectively) each attribute even greater importance to work as the force that makes possible the transformation of abstract vitality into healthy, beautiful bodies and cohesive, moral communities. Among the Wari', hard work is believed to strengthen the heart. At the same time, maize and meat, the products of female and male productive endeavors, are believed to build strong blood. Thus, through hard work, strong and healthy Wari' men and women produce the necessary means for the fabrication of more strong and healthy individuals. Similarly, the vitality or blood-spirit obtained from slain enemies in the past was thought to be tamed through ritual seclusion and the ingestion of sweet manioc beer made by women, making the killer and those who witnessed his kill stronger and healthier. When these men came out of their ritual seclusion, they transmitted the enemy's tamed vitality to women through transfers of semen in sexual acts. Conklin concludes that Wari' people "conceive of primal life-vitality as the product of interdependent, cross-sex cooperation and circulation" that places value "not in individual possession, but in the collective production and circulation of vitality."

In turn, Micarelli notes that among People of the Center "the source and purpose of life hinge on the dynamic exchange between seemingly contrasting forces." Such exchange "fertilizes the constant flow and transformation of vital energy." Like Conklin, however, Micarelli suggests, firstly, that although public wealth is often acquired through acts of predation, it also requires "sustained curing and transformation of the substances obtained through such predatory acts." And, secondly, that for energy—whether under the form of vitality or money—to flow, people must work; for "work is the source from which not only the human body, identity, and society, but also life and the cosmos are continuously recreated."

Leadership and Public Wealth

According to the contributors, public wealth is critical for the production of proper human beings and prosperous collectivities. It also plays a key role in the production of leadership—at least in those societies where leadership is present (see Conklin, chapter 2, on Wari' reluctance to have leaders). Although not all contributors address this relation, those who do note that there is a close connection—almost an interdependence—between public wealth and leadership. By leaders, these authors mean not only settlement or village chiefs, but also a diversity of other specialists, who, due to their charisma or prestigious activities, exert some kind of moral or political authority over people that extend beyond the boundaries of their own kinship groups. Such leaders have an important mediating role in the production of public wealth. At the same time, they are as much producers as the product of public wealth.

I argue in chapter 3 that among the Yanesha, true leaders are those who have "the capacities to deal with alien Others and obtain from them things that are indispensable for his or her followers' survival." The most important such leaders are settlement chiefs known as "strong men," priestly leaders, and tobacco shamans. As we have seen, what defines them as leaders is the fact that they periodically enter into contact with powerful, sometimes dangerous, Others with the objective to acquire vitality, as well as life-giving knowledge and ritual techniques. Despite their status as personal property, these substances, techniques, and knowledge become part of the public wealth of the collectivities they have helped to produce and to which they belong, insofar as they share them constantly and generously. In the process, however, the leaders themselves turn into items of public wealth, becoming, as it were, a side product of the production of public wealth. This remains true as long as they continue to share their wisdom and capacities with their followers. As soon as they are thought to be acting selfishly, they are ignored, which among Yanesha people is the highest form of social death.

Amazonian Kichwa leaders are also mediators whose activities grant "access to vital resources originating in the human and spirit worlds and their transference into the world of the Kichwa" where they become part of a group's public wealth (Guzmán-Gallegos, chapter 4). They secure "their followers' life conditions and the need to balance relations of sameness and otherness throughout this process." As such, they are viewed as genitors, whose main tasks are to take proper care of their children. And as the "head and heart" of their ethnic organization—the Organization of Indigenous Peoples of Pastaza—they are conceived of as a human body. The mediating role of Amazonian Kichwa leaders is not, however, unproblematic. By being in close contact with perilous Others on behalf of their followers, they run the risk of turning into the Other, that is, of adopting attitudes and social practices that are contrary to Amazonian Kichwa lifeways. In relation to the world of the white people, this is expressed in the undue accumulation of wealth, which is regarded as a selfish way of "appropriating what people have created [thus] depriving them of their possibilities to achieve a good life."

The notion that leaders mediate between this and other worlds and that relations between them are often predatory is beautifully expressed in the People of the Center's view that leaders "'hunt' development money with the power of coca and, above all, of tobacco" (Micarelli, chapter 6). They conceive the world of the white people as a forest "where exogenous and potentially pathogenic substances that are nonetheless indispensable to human life are controlled by powerful Others." Such Others are "tricky and dangerous, but also seducible." People of the Center's leaders require "powerful mental vision, as well as technical skills" in order to hunt for money. Through tobacco dreaming they set on their prey in such a way that "what they call forth is the materialization of their thought, which they will feed to people." It is these materializations of the leaders' thoughts that become an important part of People of the Center's public wealth. However, in order to keep wealth from "going bad," leaders must ensure that it is properly distributed, generating abundance for all. To accomplish this, leaders appease "the energy of what they predatorily got from the outside and feed it to the exchange networks that guarantee the constant circulation of vital energy." If leaders go after money motivated by personal gain, do not work hard to obtain it, or fail to channel it into "the vital circuits of reproduction," they fail their followers and generate the conditions for their own demise.

In brief, indigenous Amazonian leaders have a central role in the production of public wealth. But if they act morally and succeed in creating public wealth and in sharing it generously, thus creating abundance for all and avoiding antisocial accumulation, they themselves come to be regarded as items of public wealth. To paraphrase British philosopher Samuel Butler, who noted that a chicken is just a way an egg makes another egg, it could be said that in indigenous Amazonia leaders are the way public wealth produces more public wealth.

The Anatomy of Well-Being (and Poverty)

Contributors to this volume agree that in indigenous Amazonia, the meaning of wealth, and particularly of public wealth, is closer to the Middle Ages acceptation of the condition of being happy and prosperous, than to more recent definitions regarding wealth as an abundance of riches. They observe that in these societies there is a close connection between the abundance of public wealth and a generalized state of well-being. Some authors view public wealth as a prerequisite of well-being. Others seem to suggest that these conditions are interdependent, so that the one cannot exist without the other. In this region of the world the notion of well-being is often expressed through terms that might be translated as *good life*, *beautiful life*, or *living well*. As we shall see, despite some variations, indigenous Amazonians seem to agree to a large extent on what they consider to be a good life. The same is true of its opposite, the notion of poverty, which is often equated with a lack of vitality and social relations epitomized by the figure of the solitary, undernourished orphan.

Wari' people understand collective well-being as a state defined by "the local abundance of food, the group's productivity, vitality, and fertility, and their capacity to mobilize in collective activities, especially to host gatherings for other communities" (Conklin, chapter 2). Impoverishment, in turn, is characterized "by food insecurity, ill health, and lack of social support." Like other indigenous Amazonian peoples, Wari' view the health and vitality of the members of a community as a kind of public wealth. As Conklin observes, in this context "biosocial well-being, strength, fertility, and thriving are indices of affluence and [are] the most essential human capital." This kind of well-being can only be attained, however, through an "ethos that identifies affluence with collective thriving and accords status to promoting the physical and emotional well-being of others," an ethos, in other words, that "treat[s] care as the prime value."

Care is also central to Amazonian Kichwa notions of well-being (Guzmán-Gallegos, chapter 2). Kichwa people establish "a close connection between access to land, forest, and rivers, their ability to transform the products these provide into proper food, the production of kinship relations and thereby people, and the possibility of achieving wealth and well-being." The epitome of the wealthy person is the *amu* (owner), a person "who has control over that which she has produced, and who can make her family achieve a good and wealthy life." The opposite is the *wakcha* (orphan), who lacks "appropriate productive capacities and is thus unable to produce valued objects or to create and maintain significant social relations." Poverty for the Amazonian Kichwa has little to do with material possessions. It is a condition resulting from social, moral, or personal lacks. As a result, wakchas are unable to produce public wealth. In contrast, through acts of care and love, people who are considered to be *amu* are able not only to ensure "the well-being of their close kin but also the maintenance of [Amazonian Kichwa] ways of life."

The lack of importance of material possessions in indigenous definitions of wealth and poverty is patently depicted by the Ashaninka case.

According to Sarmiento Barletti (chapter 5), "public wealth [is] a precondition for 'living well,' but this kind of wealth can only be understood within the relations of care encompassed by the notion of *kametsa asaiki*." This latter notion, which Sarmiento Barletti translates as "to live well/beautifully/peacefully," constitutes a personal and collective pursuit. It is sustained by the production of "real Ashaninka persons" through three interconnected sets of knowledge: control of antisocial emotions, promotion of an ethos of hard work, and celebration of relationships of care. Real wealth can only be produced and constituted by real Ashaninka people. The Ashaninka "relational ethos" explains why materially wealthy people who work hard, feel sorrow for others, and share their wealth and labor are regarded with admiration. Whereas those who amass material possessions but are lazy, dishonest, and stingy are despised and considered to be "poor." Such people, it is said, "do not know how to live well," for they "lack the ability to produce and relate to others following kametsa asaiki practices."

People of the Center's notions of public wealth and well-being are informed by what elders call "the principle of origin," which is the notion that the flow and transformation of vital energy can only be guaranteed through the dynamic exchange between contrasting forces. In this context, well-being is perceived as "emplaced in, and dependent on, a web of life properly tended by ritual experts." However, according to Micarelli, neither public wealth can be reduced to the abundance of life, nor is it synonymous with well-being. Public wealth is, above all, "a matter of the transformative knowledge and capacities that make the good life possible, the skills needed to maintain a constant exchange of vital energy, and restoration of the healthy fabric of abundant life on a permanent basis." As one of Micarelli's informants put it, "the knowledge of the creator to live on this world . . . this is the real wealth." Although among People of the Center poverty is generally associated with the state of being an orphan, the real poor are not orphans—who, at least in mythology, are depicted as "being endowed with the capacity to materialize a life of abundance"—but lazy people. Such are those who are deprived of social relations because they lack the "bodily affects and dispositions for nurturing exchange with other humans, nature, and the spirit world."

Feelings of happiness under the form of collective euphoria or rejoicing are an important dimension of indigenous Amazonian understandings of well-being, as shown by the Kïsêdjê and Yanesha cases. Seeger (chapter 1) observes that "there is a clear relationship between public wealth and individually experienced feelings of happiness, euphoria, and well-being." Through the performance of large collective ceremonies in which all members of the community are involved according to their gender, age, and name set and are conceived of as the maximum expression of public wealth, the Kïsêdjê attain a sense of satisfaction expressed by the term *kin*. This sentiment, which Seeger translates as "happiness/ euphoria," is often used to refer to Kïsêdjê collective ceremonies as "our happiness/euphoria." These sentiments are connected to the abundance of vitality and the achievement of a good life, *aji betxi pa*, which can be glossed as "we live morally good or beautifully together" and is conceived of as an opposition between a state of harmonious relations and a state of witchcraft and conflict.

In turn, among the Yanesha, environmental, convivial, and generative forms of public wealth are said to "constitute the pillars of well-being and *cohuen corramñats* (a good life)" (Santos-Granero, chapter 3). In this society, the acquisition of vitality is the most important component of a collectivity's well-being, whereas a good life is that in which food and drink abounds, children grow healthily, and people live peacefully in large, beautiful settlements. For the Yanesha, one of the most important material expressions of a good life is *coshame'teñets*, the act of rejoicing in celebration of the creator divinities through collective dancing and singing. The joy produced by such collective action, which Yanesha people associate with public wealth and well-being, is the opposite of their notion of poverty, which they equate with the condition of being an orphan; a condition in which the affected are "deprived of parents (leaders) who might support them, of a social network on which to rely for sustenance, and of the ritual means that are crucial to survive and thrive in a context of generalized struggle for vitality."

Among the Canelos Quichua, according to Whitten and Whitten (chapter 7), "concepts of community, conviviality, kinship, integration with nature and supernature, and a shunning of capitalist wealth accumulation" are all subsumed under the rubric of sumaj causai, the notion that, as has been noted, translates as beautiful life or beautiful life force. This beauty, created in mythical times for the enjoyment of humans by the lovely "red woman" (*Bixa orellana*), "black woman" (*Genipa americana*), and the power that emanates from them, is considered the main expression of Canelos Quichua public wealth. Today, not all Canelos are fortunate enough to lead a life that they and others would characterize as sumaj causai, but most would agree that they have an *alli causai* (good life). The opposite of this is the concept of *manalli*, a state of existence characterized by evil and bad situations, which Whitten and Whitten equate with the conditions of orphanhood and poverty. The term *waccha*, which is applied to orphans, widows, and widowers denotes "the condition of being without crucial aspects of a minimal social unit." Deprived of meaningful social relations, they and those who have been bewitched, cursed, or ensorcelled are manalli and, thus, are in a condition of poverty.

It is clear from the above that, in indigenous Amazonia, notions of wealth, well-being, and poverty have little to do with the possession or accumulation of material goods. Public wealth and well-being are conceived of as the product of the conjoined efforts of its members—efforts that involve relations of love, care, and concern for the well-being of others. Well-being attains it maximum expression in the sentiments of happiness, beauty, and rejoicing aroused by collective action. Poverty is universally regarded as a lack of social relations or of the moral qualities required to create and sustain such interpersonal relations.

Conclusion

It is clear that the notion of public wealth in contemporary capitalist societies is as far removed as possible from indigenous Amazonian conceptions. The capitalist notion of public wealth places emphasis on the possession and accumulation of material goods with high exchange value: real estate, natural resources, infrastructure, machinery, armament, works of art, fixtures and inventories, cash, gold reserves, stocks, securities, and notes among others. In contrast, indigenous Amazonian understandings of public wealth allude to mostly intangible goods with high use value, such as vitality, conviviality, health, happiness, and the knowledge to ensure them, which cannot be accumulated and over which people have usufruct rather than property rights. This explains why in capitalist societies public wealth may be privatized in the name of free markets—as exemplified by the wave of privatizations carried out in the past decades throughout the world as the result of the implementation of neoliberal policies backed by the International Monetary Fund. In contrast, in indigenous Amazonia public wealth can only be appropriated temporarily through the transformative dimension of work, and it always devolves into the public domain.

These distinctions do not imply, however, that indigenous Amazonian forms of wealth, characterized by their high use value, are less valuable than capitalist forms based on commodities with high exchange value. Nor does it mean, as Mill (1848) would have it, that because indigenous peoples tend not to produce and amass scarce resources with high exchange value, they are wealthless or poor. What these distinctions reveal is the existence of starkly different standards of value: on the one hand, a capitalist standard of value that underscores money and quantitative relations and, on the other, an indigenous standard that places greater emphasis on intangible, qualitative aspects and which is rooted in particular kinds of social relations. However, as a result of the tremendous social and political power that supports the capitalist standard of value

(Gregory 1997), indigenous wealth values are placed in a subaltern position, forcing Amazonian peoples to fight for the survival of their values within the capitalist societies of which they form a part.

The emphasis on usufruct and the idea that wealth has no value unless it is shared with others also explains why, in indigenous Amazonia, items of personal wealth may be considered as part of the public wealth of a given group, whereas in capitalist societies this would be inconceivable unless a person specifically bequeaths part of his or her wealth as a gift to the nation. Whereas the capitalist system promotes the disproportionate accumulation of personal wealth—sending *Forbes* magazine into paroxysms of delight when publishing their annual list of the superrich—indigenous Amazonian societies favor the generous distribution of wealth and punish selfish accumulation with ostracism, shaming, and witchcraft attacks. In indigenous Amazonia, personal and public wealth is only meaningful when put to the service of the common good. In contrast, in capitalist societies the accumulation of wealth is an end in itself that is celebrated by the media with great fanfare regardless of the sheer extravagance of the amounts amassed. This is evident in the following headlines: "Koch Brothers Net Worth Tops $100 Billion as TV Warfare Escalates" (http://dailyfirstpages.com/koch-brothers-net-worth-tops-100-billion-as-tv-warfare-escalates/) and "Warren Buffett Made $1 Billion in First 22 Hours of March Madness" (http://www.forbes.com/sites/danalexander/2014/03/21/warren-buffett-had-already-made-1-billion-22-hours-into-march-madness/). Madness indeed.

In indigenous Amazonia, the egalitarian distribution of public wealth and the generous sharing of personal wealth ensure equal opportunities and prevent the rise of rampant social and economic inequalities. Capitalist societies, with their enshrinement of personal accumulation and the increasing privatization of important segments of what was previously considered public wealth, multiply such inequalities exponentially. This constitutes, as Secretary General Ban Ki-moon warned at the 67th General Assembly of the United Nations in 2012, a "reproach to the promise of the United Nations Charter."

Capitalist economies are based on the premise that economic growth is unlimited and that all obstacles to growth may be surmounted through competition and technological ingenuity; permanent growth is indispensable for the system's survival. While there is no doubt that such premises have led to colossal material progress—at least for some—the price we have had to pay has been awfully high. A consumerist lifestyle that fosters constant dissatisfaction and high levels of indebtedness forces the great majority to live to work rather than work to live. At the same time a massive waste of resources (depleted aquifers and rivers; desertification and salinization of agricultural lands; devastated rainforests;

contamination of air, water, and land; loss of biodiversity; and large-scale climate change) puts at risk human health and the environment. These are some of the many "ilths" or negative effects that derive from capitalist economic activities (see Conklin, chapter 2). In contrast, although indigenous Amazonian political economies are also based on competition—this time a competition for vitality between all living beings—they do not function on the assumption that growth can be unlimited. On the contrary, sustained on the premise that all life forms are interconnected through the circulation of vitality and that vitality itself is finite, or at least unevenly distributed, they advocate moderation in the use of resources, particularly land, plants, and animals. This is based on the belief that excessive predation produces imbalances that will be avenged by the owners/masters of the overexploited resources through supernatural attacks.

In both systems, hard work is attributed a central role in the production of wealth, whereas in capitalist economies this work ethic is associated with the individual. In indigenous Amazonian economies the amassing of personal wealth is regarded as a means through which individuals may contribute to the production of socially constructive wealth. As Sarmiento Barletti (chapter 5) observes, in such economies, "wealth and labor are only valuable when deployed relationally." In other words, this happens when personal and public wealth are shared rather than hoarded, used to fulfil social obligations rather than attain personal profit, and employed to promote the common good rather than personal interest.

Although the pursuit of such key social values as health, happiness, and a good life are not unique to indigenous Amazonian peoples, the mode in which this is achieved differs substantially from the capitalist way. Whereas in indigenous societies this quest is conceived of as a project that can only be completed collectively through personal acts of generosity, love/compassion, and mutual caring, in capitalist societies it assumes the form of an individual task entailing competition, material accumulation, and hyperconsumption. In such societies the achievement of collective welfare is believed to be only possible through individual entrepreneurship.

These important distinctions do not derive from radical differences in the nature of indigenous Amazonians, who are endowed with the same virtues and failings that characterize all human beings. If indigenous Amazonians are more generous, caring, and solidary than members of capitalist societies, it is not because they are inherently so, but it is because their economic systems respond to different cosmologies and operate under very different premises than the capitalist system. It is thus not a matter of an opposition between Rousseau's altruistic "noble savage" and the rational, self-interested "homo economicus" of neoclassical economics but rather one of contrasting economic systems and standards of value that foster and reward widely different moral principles and social behaviors.

Today, when indigenous Amazonian peoples are becoming more engaged in market activities and national politics, these two ways of conceiving the world, society, and the good life are in route to a collision. As most authors in this volume have noted, the result of such a clash is not necessarily the replacement of indigenous Amazonian by capitalist notions. Rather, as Whitten and Whitten argue, although the difference in indigenous and capitalist notions of well-being and the good life has engendered "escalating misunderstanding and open conflict" between indigenous peoples and national governments, it has also opened up new intercultural spaces of reflection and discussion that are crucial to define the future of indigenous Amazonian peoples. The transformative power of such a clash of ideas is manifest in indigenous Amazonia. But it has also been gaining ground in global political debates as revealed by Uruguayan president José Mujica in his controversial speech at the Rio+20 Summit on Sustainable Development in June 2012. After evoking Epicurus, Seneca, and the Aymara people and condemning the consumerism, greediness, and wastefulness of capitalist economies, Mujica (2012; my translation) stated, "today, man does not govern the forces it has unleashed, but rather, it is these forces that govern man and life. We do not come into this planet to 'develop' in general terms. We come to life striving to be happy. Because life is short and it slips away from us. And no good is as valuable as life. This is what is fundamental." President Mujica went on to affirm that the ilths generated by the capitalist system are not economic but political in nature, and they are indicators that it is a good time "to reexamine our way of living" and "start fighting for a different culture." This resonates with Graeber's (2001, xi) call, which states that "now that it has become obvious that 'structural forces' alone are not likely themselves [to] produce something we particularly like, we are left with the prospect of coming up with some actual alternatives." It is therefore hoped that more and more people will actively adopt the simple premises advocated by indigenous Amazonians and espoused by President Mujica as guiding life principles. Otherwise, we run the risk of witnessing the collapse of the present system brought down by its own (our own) failures and excesses.

Acknowledgments

I wish to thank the late Olga F. Linares for revising this introduction and my chapter in order to polish—like always—my English. She was a gifted scholar, talented editor, and a great colleague and friend. I will miss her greatly.

References

Atherton, John, Elaine Graham, and Ian Steedman, eds. 2011. *The Practices of Happiness: Political Economy, Religion, and Wellbeing*. New York: Routledge.

Caplan, Bryan. 2009. "Against the Human Development Index." Library of Economics and Liberty (May 22). Accessed August 2012. http://econlog.econlib.org/archives/2009/05/against_the_hum.html.

Chato, Pilar. 2011. "El Buen Vivir, repensar el desarrollo." Otramérica, April 12, 2011. Accessed August 2012. http://otramerica.com/temas/el-buen-vivir-repensar-el-desarrollo/40.

Comaroff, Jean, and John L. Comaroff, eds. 2001. *Millennial Capitalism and the Culture of Neoliberalism*. Durham and London: Duke University Press.

Fausto, Carlos. 2001. *Inimigos fiéis: História, guerra e xamanismo na Amazônia*. São Paulo: Editora da Universidade de São Paulo.

Ferry, Luc. 2005. *What is the Good Life?* Chicago: University of Chicago Press.

Fischer, Edward F. 2014. *The Good Life: Aspiration, Dignity, and the Anthropology of Wellbeing*. Stanford: Stanford University Press.

Graeber, David. 2001. *Toward an Anthropological Theory of Value: The False Coin of Our Own Dreams*. New York: Palgrave.

Gregory, Chris. 1997. *Savage Money: The Anthropology and Politics of Commodity Exchange*. Amsterdam: Harwood Academic.

Grosse, Melanie. 2011. *Measurement of Trends in Wellbeing, Poverty, and Inequality with Case Studies from Bolivia and Colombia*. Frankfurt am Main: P. Lang.

Harvey, John, and Vicki Taylor, eds. 2013. *Measuring Health and Wellbeing*. Thousand Oaks: Sage Publications.

Heckenberger, Michael J. 2003. "The Enigma of the Great Cities: Body and State in Amazonia." *Tipití: Journal of the Society for the Anthropology of Lowland South America* 1(1):27–58.

Iriarte, José, J. Christopher Gillam, and Oscar Marozzi. 2008. "Monumental Burials and Memorial Feasting: An Example from the Southern Brazilian Highlands." *Antiquity* 83:947–61.

Jackson, Michael D. 2011. *Life Within Limits: Wellbeing in a World of Want*. Durham: Duke University Press.

Johnston, Barbara Rose, ed. 2012. "Vital Topics Forum 'On Happiness.'" *American Anthropologist* 114(1):6–18.

Keynes, John Maynard. 1963. "Economic Possibilities for our Grandchildren." In *Essays in Persuasion*, John Maynard Keynes, 358–73. New York: W. W. Norton and Co.

Maitland, James. 1819 [1804]. *An Inquiry into the Nature and Origin of Public Wealth and into the Means and Causes of its Increase*. Edinburgh: Archibald Constable and Co. Accessed July 2010. http://ideas.repec.org/b/hay/hetboo/lauderdale1819.html.

Mathews, Gordon, and Carolina Izquierdo. 2009. *Pursuits of Happiness: Wellbeing in Anthropological Perspective*. New York and Oxford: Berghahn Books.

Mill, John Stuart. 1848. *Principles of Political Economy*. London: John W. Parker, West Strand.

Move to Amend. 2012. "We the People, Not We the Corporations." Accessed August 2012. http://www.movetoamend.org/.

Movimiento 15M. 2013. "Movimiento 15M." Accessed April 2015. http://www.movimiento15m.org/.

Mujica, José. 2012. *Human Happiness and the Environment—Address by Uruguayan President José Mujica*. The Wander Life (Travel Think Tank). Accessed April 2014. http://thewanderlife.com/human-happiness-and-the-environment-address-by-uruguayan-president-jose-mujica-at-rio-20-summit/.

#OccupyTogether. 2012. "The #Occupy Movement." Accessed August 2012. http://www.occupytogether.org/aboutoccupy/#background.

#OccupyWallStreet. 2011. "Declaration of the Occupation of New York City." Accessed August 2012. http://www.nycga.net/resources/declaration/.

Paredes, J. Anthony. 2012. "Happiness Anthropology Redux." *Anthropology News* 53(3):5.

Piketty, Thomas. 2014. *Capital in the Twenty-First Century*. Cambridge: Harvard University Press.

Otto, Ton, and Rane Willerslev. 2013. "Introduction: 'Value *as* Theory' Comparison, Cultural Critique, and Guerilla Ethnographic Theory." *HAU: Journal of Ethnographic Theory* 3(1):1–20.

Rivière, Peter. 1984. *Individual and Society in Guiana: A Comparative Study of Amerindian Social Organization*. Cambridge: Cambridge University Press.

Rostain, Stéphen. 2008. "Agricultural Earthworks on the French Guiana coast." In *Handbook of South American Archaeology*, edited by Helaine Silverman and William Isbell, 217–34. New York: Springer/Kluwer/Plenum.

Santos-Granero, Fernando. 2009. *Vital Enemies: Slavery, Predation, and the Amerindian Political Economy of Life*. Austin: University of Texas Press.

Scott, Karen. 2012. *Measuring Wellbeing: Towards Sustainability?* New York: Routledge.

Smith, Adam. 1776. *An Inquiry into the Nature and Causes of the Wealth of Nations*. The Electronic Classics Series. The Pennsylvania State University. Accessed July, 2010. http://www2.hn.psu.edu/faculty/jmanis/adam-smith/Wealth-Nations.pdf.

Strathern, Marilyn. 1992. "Qualified Value: The Perspective of Gift Exchange." In *Barter, Exchange, and Value: An Anthropological Approach*, edited by

Caroline Humphrey and Stephen Hugh-Jones, 169–91. Cambridge: Cambridge University Press.

Turner, Terence. 2003. "The Beautiful and the Common: Inequalities of Value and Revolving Hierarchy Among the Kayapó." *Tipití: Journal of the Society for the Anthropology of Lowland South America* 1(1):11–26.

PART ONE

Health, Vitality, and Euphoria

CHAPTER ONE

It's Ear-y and Euphoric

Amazonian Music and the Performance of Public Wealth Among the Suyá/Kïsêdjê

ANTHONY SEEGER

Prologue: A Moment of Indigenous Polyphony in Sound and Movement

To understand the importance of musical sound in Lowland South America, think for a moment of its opposite: silence and the quiet of daily life. I do not refer to the complete silence of an anechoic chamber, but to the silence of a raiding or hunting party or what you would hear on a quiet riverbank with scattered children playing, canoes beaching, and families bathing and talking. If you have never been in such a place, think of a walk on a quiet night when you hear snatches of the conversations of passersby, wind, traffic, dogs barking, and the chance sounds of place and moment.

Then consider a recording made in the final hours of the Kïsêdjê (formerly known as the Suyá) *Bee Ceremony* (track 10 on the CD accompanying Seeger [2004]).[1] The excerpt begins with low-pitched, unison male voices chanting a song learned from the bees, shaking their *piqui-pit* rattles, and stamping rhythmically inside one of the residential houses. Each man's woven palm-leaf headdress indicates the seasonal ceremonial moiety to which he belongs. Standing still just outside that house, without stamping his feet or moving his body, a young man sings a loud high-pitched, solo-shouted song with wider tonal variation and longer sustained notes than the unison song. He sings without coordinating the pitch or rhythm of his solo song to the rattles and stamping of the unison singers inside the house. The contrast between the deep-voiced unison chanting and the higher-pitched solo is dramatic. A short time later an old man inside the house begins to give a very loud falsetto cry on a single note (*kuá, kuá*) that is the prerogative only of old men during ceremonies, and it contributes to the excitement and euphoria of the singers and the listening audience of women and children. The old man's shouts are not fully coordinated with either the solo singer or the stamping and rattle of the unison dancers, but they have a tendency to begin on the beat or the off-beat of the chant. So far all the sound is masculine. Eventually, the men end their unison song with a characteristic melodic formula and final line, after which they rush out of the house and run to another house where they will sing a different unison song learned from the bees. As they emerge, women who have been standing outside listening and watching begin to shout excitedly, adding more timbres to the night air. The men also shout as they run like a swarm of bees to another house. The four distinct and identifiable vocal ranges, performance styles, intervals, and rhythms are a kind of polyphony whose multilayered sound is characteristic of moments of musical intensity and euphoria in Kïsêdjê ceremonies.

Introduction: Anthropology, Sound, and the Public Good

Most anthropologists who have studied the indigenous peoples of the Americas have carefully measured village sites, expounded on hunting practices, counted calories, analyzed kinship, examined political power, considered the impact of the invasion of indigenous lands and the degradation of their environment, and argued over the significance and nature of private wealth. Most anthropologists have paid far too little attention to the sounds of oratory and music and to the movement of bodies through space while making those sounds. It is essential to remove the blinders of materialist definitions of wealth—ably accomplished in the chapters of this volume and with particular care by Whitten and Whitten in chapter 7—and recognize that wealth can be as intangible as air and as fleeting as a reverberation, gesture, or emotional response yet be powerful and enduring in its effects. In this chapter I argue that Lowland South American indigenous performances of music and dance are complex constructions that simultaneously showcase certain forms of private wealth in their performance and in themselves constitute and produce a kind of insufficiently recognized public wealth. Ignored or misrepresented in economic theories of wealth, Lowland South American indigenous peoples contribute the lesson that one kind of public wealth may be sought in the structures of and emotional responses to the performance of collective music and dance.

This chapter uses data and insights gained during long-term research among the Kïsêdjê people in Mato Grosso, Brazil, to address the five connections mentioned in Santos-Granero's introduction to this volume. I argue that: 1) public wealth is not necessarily synonymous with collective property, and it may be passed from generation to generation; 2) public wealth can be generated through internal relations, as well as external relations (with other kinds of humans, other species, or spirits), and it may be public through its inclusion of all genders, most ages, and often several types of beings; 3) public wealth is a key component of the creation of the person as a social being, which is achieved through public ceremonies; 4) some leaders are more involved with public wealth than others; and 5) there is a clear relationship between public wealth and individually experienced feelings of happiness, euphoria, and well-being. This chapter begins with a brief introduction to the Kïsêdjê, then moves to a discussion about the concept of *kandé* (ownership and control), next examines ceremonies as a form of public wealth, and finally advances to a series of conclusions based on some of the issues raised by Santos-Granero in his introduction and the contributions of the other authors in this volume.

In parts of indigenous Lowland South America music and dance performances are as grandly and carefully structured as the large thatched houses, plazas, and interconnected villages of pre-Columbian settlements described by Michael Heckenberger (2003). In some Lowland South American societies large public collective musical performances constitute and stimulate a highly desired kind of public wealth, which Maitland (1819 [1804], 56–57) famously defined as "all that man desires as useful or delightful for him"—in the form of collective happiness and euphoria. The large circular plazas surrounded by the uxorilocal houses of Kïsêdjê villages are at once a theater in the round, a concert hall, a space transcending narrow kinship relations, and a place of interaction with other beings and states of being (figure 1.1). This village design focuses attention on performers and audiences and concentrates sounds from different sources, human and nonhuman. Thatched or upright log walls are not barriers to sound. The unison singers, soloist, old man, and women in the example I described in the prologue may not be able to see one another perfectly, but they hear each other, and their combined sounds

FIGURE 1.1. Kïsêdjê men singing a dry-season unison song in the center of the plaza in front of the men's house (right), while women watch from the shadow of a residential house. Photo by Anthony Seeger.

intensify their experiences as the sounds mingle in the air and in the ears of all of them. In addition to sound, body movement is part of most musical performances in Lowland South America. The words for *song* and the movements accompanying it may be the same, as they are among the Kïsêdjê. The rhythmic movements of the singers inside the house contrast with the stasis of the male soloist and the stillness of the women waiting for the men to swarm out of the house. Old men often intone their falsetto shout sitting stationary in their hammocks or on their platform beds where their cries carry through the walls and across the village plaza. The plaza itself is defined by movements of musicians/dancers around its perimeter and from its center to its periphery. The movement and stasis, and the sounds and the silence bring the community members together and make them euphoric. Before the arrival of combustion engines, shotguns, and electronic sound reproduction, no sound was louder in Kïsêdjê society than the collective singing and associated sounds of large communal ceremonies except occasional bursts of thunder during storms. All daily life was quiet by contrast; and it became so as soon as the ceremony ended.

These large public performances are complex arenas for the representation of several kinds of personal and collective wealth, as well as the expression and experience of public wealth. To a certain extent Kïsêdjê society is an orchestra; different ages, genders, and ceremonial groups are expected to contribute distinctive sounds to the whole. The resulting polyphony is part of what makes people happy or euphoric. Kïsêdjê society is an orchestra without a conductor, however. There is no attempt to keep all the performers to a single beat or a harmonically related pitch. The cacophonous and polyphonic sounds described in the prologue are typical of the musical intensification that occurs toward the end of most Kïsêdjê ceremonies, as well as in many other ceremonies reported on in indigenous South America. In this brief moment, simultaneous sonic contributions present a rich texture and reestablish specific relationships between ceremonial groups, genders, and ages, as well as with spirits, space, and time. Descriptions of music and dance that portray their contribution to the experience of the emotions of happiness, euphoria, or ecstasy have been inadequately theorized and rarely recognized for their significance. The emotions generated through public performance song and dance in South America call for a renewed attention to the now obsolete Middle Ages meaning of wealth: "the condition of being happy, prosperous; well-being" (*Compact Edition Oxford English Dictionary* 1971, 3718). Being happy is probably related to the "good life" in Ecuador, as authors in this volume describe in several chapters, and to concepts of life among the Yanesha (Santos-Granero in chapter 3). I hope that, by calling attention to sonic structures, kinesthetic constructions, and emotional responses, I stimulate some thinking on music and dance by all readers, even if they have never considered music and dance performance to be a significant part of social life or indigenous experience.

The Grandeur and Significance of Indigenous Structures of Music and Dance

Around the same time that Michael Heckenberger (2003) began to reveal the large-scale networks of pre-Columbian settlements in the Upper Xingu region in Mato Grosso, Brazil, which defied most previous anthropological thinking about settlement size in the region, Rafael José de Menezes Bastos and Acácio Piedade began to detail a complex level and scale of musical organization in the same region that also had been previously largely ignored (though presciently observed by Ellen Basso [1985, 249]). Menezes Bastos transcribed and analyzed in great detail the music of an entire eleven-day ceremony of the Kamayurá. His is probably the most extensive transcription undertaken of any Amerindian music (Menezes Bastos 2013). His careful analysis revealed complex relationships among the many distinct musical pieces performed during the eleven days. In a similar fashion, Piedade demonstrated that the flute pieces of the Wauja (another Upper Xingu community) are organized by the performers into complex suites (Piedade 2004, 2011), while most ethnomusicological attention previously was focused on individual short "pieces." Menezes Bastos suggests that "a notable characteristic of the music of Lowland South America . . . can be summarized under the heading of 'sequentiality.' . . . Everything appears to indicate that isolated pieces of music do not make much sense in the region" (Menezes Bastos 2006, 8). Instead, most individual pieces of music made sense by their part in a much larger sequence, or set of interlocking sequences of a size and grandeur not previously imagined. The size and complexity of the relationships of musical pieces to one another in these large units sonically resemble the physical structures Heckenberger (2003) describes in his work on pre-Columbian Upper Xingu groups of settlements.

The reasons scholars did not recognize the larger units before is because of European ideas about the "primitiveness" of the communities, their own decidedly primitive recording equipment, and an inability for European listeners to hear—or lack of interest in—the (to us) subtle similarities and differences among pieces (brilliantly discussed in Fausto, Franchetto, and Montagnani [2011]). Very often Amerindian music has been dismissed as boring and repetitious. It appears that in many cases we simply do not hear what is being varied or understand its novelty and significance. Careful analysis has revealed that there are music/dance structures of a size previously unperceived in the Upper Xingu and among the central and northern Gê-speaking societies, who also live in central Brazil. This has yet to be demonstrated for other areas, but possibly only because no one has been looking for them. Also, in many parts of the Amazon, researchers had only arrived after the disappearance of the large religious festivals in the communities they studied and thus had to rely on memories of past events.

Nearly as important as sequence is the emotion elicited through simultaneous performance of different kinds of sounds—a characteristic of much indigenous music from the highland, as well as lowland regions of South America. Ellen Basso (1985) indicates that the Kalapalo (a Carib-speaking Upper Xingu community) have the verb *-ail-* to describe their experience of communal performance. According to Basso, this verb is most often used to speak of rituals in which several types of musical performances occur simultaneously, and it refers to a sense of satisfaction that she suggests is a South American version of Victor Turner's communitas—the unstructured state in which members of a collectivity share a common experience as equals. She writes that "applied to musical ritual -ail- expresses the joy of experiencing communal action" (Basso 1985, 255). She describes musical ritual as giving a "wonderful power of community emerging from group performance" (Basso 1985, 252).

In sum, careful analysis of the sonic structures and intensive work with indigenous music specialists reveals that the sounds and probably the movements of at least the Upper Xingu and Gê music and dance are subtle, highly structured, extensive, and emotion-filled events.

Ethnographic Background: The Kïsêdjê Within Lowland South America

Like most of the other chapters in this volume, I focus on a specific ethnographic case as a forum through which to address some more general issues. Most of us only know one indigenous language and have done the majority of our research in one place, and I am no exception. Like the others, most of my comparative remarks appear at the end of the chapter. I began my research with a group, then called the Suyá, in 1971. My most recent visit to this group, which, now calls itself Kïsêdjê, was in 2010.[2]

Two of the most important things about the Kïsêdjê in the context of the present discussion is that, among the groups discussed in this volume, they are unusual in how recently (1959) they made peaceful enduring contact with Brazilians and in their continuing refusal to convert to Christianity or allow missionaries into their village. Thus, I decided to do research among them because their lives would have been relatively unaffected by media, Christianity, and capitalism, which made them a good group to study the relationships between musical performance, cosmology, and social organization. Another difference between the Kïsêdjê and most of the other groups discussed in this volume is that they do not have a tradition of shamans, although they may consult the shamans of other groups when they are ill.

The Kïsêdjê are a Gê-speaking society in northern Mato Grosso that is linguistically related to the northern Kayapó and the Timbira groups. They appear to have originally been part of a single group with the Tapayuna, but they separated from them in the 1800s and moved to the headwaters of the Xingu River where they encountered the Upper Xingu network (described by Heckenberger [2003]; see also Franchetto and Heckenberger [2001]). For the past one hundred and seventy or so years the Kïsêdjê have been intermittently part of the Upper Xingu network and are the only Gê-speaking members of that network. Their relations with the other groups varied. At times they intermarried, participated in intertribal ceremonies, and adopted many items of material culture, cuisine, and ceremonial life. At other times they raided some villages and took women and children as captives as retaliation for deaths they said were caused by Upper Xingu witches. They were selective in their adaptations of Upper Xingu material culture. They did not adopt important components of Upper Xingu musical culture and religious beliefs, such as wind instruments (described in Menezes Bastos [1999a] and Piedade [2011]) and major death rituals, like the Kuarup. They did adopt the Upper Xingu women's ceremony, Iamuricumã (Mello 2005), which they have performed regularly since at least the 1940s. In addition, they absorbed members of the Manitsauá and the Iarumá indigenous groups in the late nineteenth and early twentieth centuries. Since 1959, a number of Kïsêdjê have married Trumai, (another group somewhat marginal to the Upper Xingu network), Mehinaku, Yudjá (formerly called Juruna), Kaiabi, and Tapayuna. Their complex interethnic history during the past one hundred and seventy years has resulted in a community that has displayed features of Upper Xingu communities and the northern Gê in their daily lives and in the ceremonies and music/dance they have performed. At times the Kïsêdjê emphasized their Gê-ness (especially after the arrival of the surviving Tapayuna in 1970); at other times they emphasized their Xinguano features and relationships.[3] I will at times reference ethnographic research in the Upper Xingu, since some of it is very relevant to the Kïsêdjê as well. I witnessed and recorded a number of performances of several Upper Xingu rituals, as well as a number of Timbira ceremonies based on a northern Gê-style naming system and crosscutting moieties that resembled rituals described by Curt Nimuendaju (1946), Julio Cesar Melatti (1978), and William Crocker (1990).

I have elsewhere characterized Kïsêdjê social life as alternating between two poles: one based on kinship groups (and affines) in residential houses and the other on ceremonial groups engaged in ceremonial activities in the village plaza (Seeger 2004, 6). Each of these poles had its characteristic features. Kinship was based on a kind of "corporeal identity" of substance that united siblings, their parents, and their children. Ceremonial life was based on activities involving relationships through shared names. Kinship also formed the basis of most political factions, the sharing of utilitarian belongings, and access to certain subsistence resources (old gardens, fruit tree stands, etc.). Name sets and their associated moiety and ceremonial group affiliations crosscut kinship. Name set members (those who use one of a number of personal names that are identified as a single set of names) were all ceremonially identical. They had the same moiety and ritual group affiliations, body paint, special ornaments, and they shared specific rights and obligations regarding ritual paraphernalia and certain songs (figure 1.2). The moieties were only visible and operative during ceremonies. There were two pairs of moieties whose membership was crosscutting; name sets in two different moieties in one pair could be in the same moiety in the other pair. Name groups and the moieties comprised of them were not the basis for political factions or marriage arrangements. Kinship groups generally acted for the "private"

FIGURE 1.2. Two members of a Kïsêdjê name set, identically painted and ornamented, singing over their young name receiver, seated in his grandmother's lap, during the Mouse Ceremony. Photo by Anthony Seeger.

good; ceremonies were performed for the public good. For generations there had been multiple faction leaders and only a single owner/controller, or master of collective ceremonies. Ceremonies were essential for social reproduction; a child became a man or woman through rites of passage involving music and dance. Ceremonial life was part of public wealth after death, while affinity appeared to virtually disappear in the village of the dead. The village of the dead described to me by the Kïsêdjê was one of music, dance, euphoria, and social stasis; everyone was young, they did not age or give birth, and they all sang and danced and were happy.

Is there private property in Kïsêdjê public spaces? The Kïsêdjê built quite a few new villages over the decades but retained the basic structure of a circle of uxorilocal houses with certain named houses in fixed positions with respect to the others (see Seeger [1981, 72–74] on house names). Women were called the kandé (owner/controllers) of the residential houses. The meeting place of the men was in the exact center of the plaza where imaginary lines from opposing houses intersected. Adult men normally sat in the center directly in front of their residential houses (with their backs to them), thus to a certain extent they reiterated the spatial relations of the houses in their nightly gatherings. The plaza was the primary location for collective singing and dancing of both genders, although parts of most ceremonies were performed in the residential houses, the men's house, and/or outside the village but usually within earshot of it. The space in front of each of the residential houses was used by its residents in a number of ways. During the afternoon families sat in front of their houses (or to the side if the front was in the direct sun) and watched the events in the plaza. The residents of each house were responsible for keeping the part of the plaza in front of their houses clear and swept. This was taken seriously before ceremonies when residents used hoes to remove all vegetation from between their house and the center of the plaza and between theirs and neighboring houses. When visiting a village it was possible to immediately see the amount of ritual activity going on. If grass was growing in the plaza except for in paths running from each house to the center, it was a clear sign that there had been no ceremonies. One explanation given for doing such a careful job of clearing and sweeping was so the dancers would not hurt themselves by stepping on fish bones and sharp trash as they danced around the village plaza in the dark, but the clearing was also an aesthetic and moral statement. Individual houses took responsibility for contributing to the public good of ritual space by clearing the plaza in front of their houses. The ritual spaces were shared, but each residential house had a responsibility for clearing part of it.

Property: Owners/Controllers and Wealth

Concepts of ownership and property are central to discussions of private and public wealth, including music and dance. Property and ownership are knotty concepts, and in any given society they are profoundly integrated with other concepts and institutions. One of the things that initially impressed me about Kïsêdjê society in 1971 was how widely food was distributed, how much material culture was shared, and how no one ever said no when another person asked them for something. When I finally learned to speak functionally, one of my teachers said "Tony, it's time to stop speaking like a child. Only children say '*i-ngoi*' (my pot); it is OK when young children say that, but adults say '*aji iõ ngoi*' (our pot)." The pot in question was one I had traded for, ate out of every day, and washed in the river; it was a very personal item. In a sense, I had the usufruct of the pot, but it was not completely identified with me but with a residential group. I could change my way of speaking, but it took me longer to figure out what "possession" meant and who "we" were.

The answers varied considerably for different kinds of things. If at first Kïsêdjê society seemed like a society where most people had the same belongings, and sharing was ubiquitous, I later came to see it was not that simple. Ownership and control were central concepts for a proper understanding of daily life, as well as political and ceremonial activity. As noted earlier, the Kïsêdjê word *kandé* can be translated as "owner/controller." Lévi-Strauss (1969) glossed a similar relationship as "master" for other groups. It was a word central not only to material objects but also to social roles, such as political and ritual leaders and to certain kinds of knowledge (Seeger 1981, 180–83; see Fausto [2008] for an excellent and extensive discussion of the subject).[4]

I have used the gloss *owner/controller* for the Kïsêdjê word *kandé* because the kandé's right to control how something would be used was a crucial element to understanding the concept. If you had a thing, or knowledge, or a certain right, you had the right to share it, give it away, or determine how it could be used. But you did not necessarily have the right to refuse to share it, which would have been immoral in any event and could have led to accusations of being a *wayangá* (witch). This restriction on rights made the concept of kandé very different from international property law.

There were multiple kandé of music and dance. First, all music and dance was said to come from outside the village; there were no Kïsêdjê composers, no writers of protest or love songs, and no experimental choreographers. Every song, dance, and ceremony had an original kandé from whom the Kïsêdjê had learned it. They could be animals or animal spirits, monsters, Kïsêdjê transformed into animal/human mixes, mythical and current enemies (indigenous and nonindigenous), or captives and the occasional anthropologist. These outside beings were called the kandé of the ceremonies or songs and dances learned from them. The Kïsêdjê who learned the songs and dances and introduced them to everyone else were not their kandé. In the 1970s, an individually performed song learned from a tree and taught by a specialist to a person who would then sing it in a ceremony "belonged" to the tree in one sense but it also belonged to the person who sang it aloud for the first time, not to the person who learned it from the tree and taught it. Thus, the first person, or group, that sang a given song so that a large public could hear it was its human kandé. When I asked what it meant to be the kandé of a song I had been taught and had sung aloud for the first time, I was told "it means that when you hear someone else singing it you can say, 'hey, don't mess around (*atarakwechi*); sing it well!'" I couldn't prevent a person from singing it, but they would have to sing it seriously.[5]

The kandé of ceremonies was further complicated by the dual influences on Kïsêdjê ceremonies: the northern Gê practices and the music learned from the Upper Xingu and other indigenous peoples. There was a difference in who controls the ceremonies between the Upper Xingu traditions performed by the Kïsêdjê and their Gê traditions. In the Upper Xingu an individual and certain ancestors and descendants are the kandé of specific rituals, and knowledge is passed consciously in exchange for prestigious goods (described in Fausto, Franchetto, and Montagnani [2011]). The major Upper Xingu ceremonies among the Kïsêdjê had individual owners/controllers who passed them from generation to generation. The rest of the adult men as a group would need to ask the kandé of the specific Upper Xingu ceremony for permission to perform it. This was almost always granted (with the stricture to do it seriously and well), and the kandé and his relatives would provide food. The rest of the village, in turn, might build the owner a house and would dance the ceremony for him. The ritual owners were called *meropakandé*, which translated as "owner/controller of the village." They only held the status if the village performed their ceremonies for them. Upper Xingu ceremonies almost never involved the name-based moieties and other Gê-style ceremonial groups and relationships.

The ceremonies the Kïsêdjê say they learned during the period when they "slept on the ground and drank only water" (like the other northern Gê), rather than in hammocks and drinking water with manioc mixed in it like the Upper Xingu indigenous peoples, were controlled either by a moiety or another ceremonial group. Certain name-based groups were the kandé of certain songs that should only be performed *by* those groups, and the moieties are owner/controllers of certain ceremonies that they had to give permission for the other moiety to perform. The rights the moieties had over "their" ceremonies were basically to give permission to each other to perform them and to tell each to take their ceremony seriously and perform it well (figure 1.3).[6]

FIGURE 1.3. The two Kïsêdjê moieties standing by the log where they will simultaneously sing their respective moiety songs. After the singing, an elder will cut the thick link between the halves of the log, and the moieties will run a relay race carrying them into the village. Photo by Anthony Seeger.

Repertoire and performance styles were the prerogative of specific groups determined by name set, gender, and age. For example, when performing songs as a group, one moiety was supposed to sing faster than the other and had a repertoire of songs naming different animals. Some songs were supposed to be performed by men and others by women. Only in Upper Xingu ceremonies did men and women sing the same song together at the same time. In some cases, the members of a single name set had a ritual act to perform and specific sounds to perform it to. One name set, for example, had the right/obligation to call the rest of the performers into the village during the Mouse Ceremony and employed a specific whistle to do so. Individuals made sounds or sang according to their name, gender, and age. Each gender and age contributed characteristic sounds to large public ceremonies through individual songs, cries, shouts, or silence. Although parts might belong to certain name sets or moieties, the older Gê ceremonies, as a whole, were created collectively and might be characterized as a kind of public wealth.

Public spaces were very important in ceremonies and could be considered public wealth during performances that used and, to a certain extent, created them. The two most important spaces were the village plaza—the open space created by the circle of matrilocal houses controlled by women—and the men's house, built somewhat to the west of the village center (the two moieties usually sat at different ends of a single men's house, but at certain times they each built a separate house). The village plaza was the public space *par excellence*. Although cleared by individual houses it was the location of most music and dance performance and of all kinds of public events, including soccer games. Maitland describes a system of roads as an example of public wealth; for the Kïsêdjê, a cleared plaza could be similarly characterized.

The circle of residential houses surrounding the plaza belonged to the women who lived in them with their uxorilocally residing husbands, their parents, and their children. Most houses were built by groups of kinsmen. Houses figured importantly in certain ceremonies and were one of the places where music was made. Singing in the houses was usually done between the front door and the back door and between the two central large posts that supported the roof (or around the single central post if there was only one), but these house spaces were not public in the same sense as the plaza. The space immediately in back of the houses was a private domain for women, children, families, and activities that people did not want to perform publically for the entire village. In most cases only close kin visited one another in the back of each other's houses. The space was also called the "dead zone" or the "quiet zone"; music and nonkinship-based activities were never performed there. A village—three or more houses with a central space between them—was, thus, essential for having a public space; having enough people of different name sets and moiety membership was absolutely essential for performing ceremonies.

In sum, the Kïsêdjê present a case of collective or public control over ritual performances, which were themselves a form of public wealth. A group must desire to perform a ceremony enough to ask for permission to do so. Patrons were either individuals for the Upper Xingu ceremonies or moieties and other name-based ceremonial groups for at least some of the Gê ceremonies. But neither patron could order the others to perform their ceremony; they had to be asked for permission to do so.

Why Music? Toward the Good Life, Collective Euphoria, and Well-Being

On what basis can I argue that music and dance are significant forms of public wealth? Menezes Bastos (1999b) has argued for the importance of what he calls *world hearing* for Lowland South American indigenous societies. He suggests that hearing and sound production are more important modalities than most anthropologists have recognized. A number of essays in the edited volume *Burst of Breath* (Hill and Chaumeil 2011) support or modify this to a degree, but there is no question that the performance of certain sound qualities and structures are important means through which meaningful events are created and experienced throughout the region.

In addition to what Menezes Bastos has proposed, I suggest two other aspects of music/dance performance: the importance of the emotions created through music and dance performances and the significance of space established through the movements of musicians and dancers through space. Music does not consist only of structures and qualities of sounds, it is also associated with specific emotions; it is sentiment as well as sound (as Steven Feld [1982] so eloquently demonstrated in his study of the Kaluli in Papua New Guinea). This sentiment is something that separates musical performance from weaving, body painting, architecture, garden layouts, and many other human constructions.

The Kïsêdjê have a word for the sentiment aroused by collective performances of music and dance: *kin*. A general gloss would be "happy" or "euphoric." The word has a variety of uses. It means "to like" and "to be happy" versus *kin-kitili*, to "not like." Thus, it was used to evaluate—I like this, and I don't like that—and to denote an emotion. The word denotes a kind of euphoria, especially when the suffix *kumeni* (really) is appended to it. This kind of euphoria is elicited by and results in music and dance. The word kin has another use. The Kïsêdjê sometimes use it to refer to their ceremonies as a group, such as *wa kini* (our happiness/euphoria). One man described the feeling as a feedback loop that increases. He said, "when we are happy/euphoric we sing; when we sing we are happy/euphoric." For a performance to create euphoria, however, everyone in the community had to participate according to his or her proper role (defined by gender, age, moiety affiliation, name set, etc.). When someone was angry, discontented, or in mourning, he or she demonstrated that by silence, stasis, and nonparticipation in collective events. This often made the other participants less happy and could result in a performance judged to be bad or ugly.

Kïsêdjê song and dance were performed to express and to create a specific emotion that I have translated as happiness or euphoria. Music and dance are associated with emotions in many parts of the world. One needs to look no farther than the vernacular music in the United States to find them (electronica and blues). Reaching euphoric states in Kïsêdjê ceremonies required, however, more than a few people singing together. Many factors contributed to this feeling of euphoria, including food ("when we sing, we eat," observed one elder about ceremonies), universal participation ("when everyone sings, it is beautiful or good; when some people are silent it is ugly or bad," said another), and the observance of specific interpersonal relationships. Mother's brother/sister's son joking relationships were always enacted with more enthusiasm during ceremonies, as were relationships between a man and his sisters (and a sister and her brothers), and among members of a name set. Laughter and excitement were also part of collective euphoria. The intensity and duration of the final phases of Kïsêdjê rituals created euphoria, and it also created social life as it should be with every position in society performing its appropriate roles—roles that would continue after their death in the villages of the living, as well as the dead.

When the Kïsêdjê described the importance of euphoria in their ceremonies, I was reminded of Emile Durkheim's description of the importance of "collective exaltation" in Aranda ceremonies in *The Elementary Forms of the Religious Life* (Durkheim 1965 [1915], 245–62). I do not think my analysis is Durkheimian, but there is no question that "collective exaltation" was an important part of Kïsêdjê ceremonies. All Lowland South American ceremonies are complex events that certainly include aspects of hierarchy, status, and power. But among many indigenous peoples, the experience of collective performance is central to their happiness and the existence of society. In her analysis of Kalapalo speech and ceremony, Ellen Basso (1985, 245) suggests the mechanism through which such emotion is aroused.

> By collectively performing music, [the Kalapalo] not only model themselves upon their images of powerful beings, but they feel the worth of these models by experiencing the transformative powers inherent in human musicality. Unlike trance states or those of alternative, illusionary states of consciousness, these transcendent powers unite within a heightened state of sensual consciousness [and] bodily feelings of great intensity, transforming for a time the meanings given to the personal self and to the collectivity, as well as to the environmental setting.

Later in the same chapter she suggests that "for the Kalapalo (and perhaps other central Brazilian peoples who devote much of their lives to collectively performing musical ritual) it is music as an enacted symbol that communicates and at the same time creates an experience of communitas" (Basso 1985, 252). While Victor Turner (1967) initially identified the experience of *communitas* with rites of passage, a more recent book by his widow Edith Turner (2012), *Communitas: The Anthropology of Collective Joy*, suggests a much broader interpretation of the term to include emotional responses to the music, dance, and laughter of many kinds of collective activities. The term thus even better applies to the joy of collective community action Basso describes for the Kalapalo and the euphoric happiness of the Kïsêdjê. This intense joy of engaging in community music and movement may well extend to other indigenous peoples in central Brazil and far beyond.

Public Wealth: Happiness and Euphoria Through Collective Performance.

In his classic inquiry into the nature and origin of public wealth, Maitland (1819 [1804], 56) suggests that public wealth may be said "to consist of all that man desires, as useful or delightful to him" without the condition of scarcity that defines private wealth. The euphoria experienced by the Kïsêdjê in performance fits his definition well; it was not a limited good or restricted to any specific person or group. While private property (involving a condition of scarcity or restriction) could be found in performances, there was an overwhelming public significance that—in the Kïsêdjê case—appears to be part of the nature and experience of society itself.

In his introduction to this volume, Santos-Granero suggests that the study of public wealth in indigenous South America is important because the nonmaterial ways of thinking about public wealth may help us rethink the definition of public wealth and society. This was certainly true of the Kïsêdjê, who neither sold their labor nor purchased goods during the early years of my research but valued the sound and euphoria produced in public ceremonies. Like a number of other groups discussed in this volume, they were living an alternative to capitalism. The idea of public wealth—and of its sonic expression and experience—is important because it helps us understand these societies today and in the interpretation of the archaeological record. The large public spaces Heckenberger (2003) described were not required by shamanism but were required by and created for public festivities of which sound and movement were major parts. The indigenous understandings of public good apparently have a long history in the region and are not simply a response to colonialism and neoliberal capitalism.

One example of an indigenous expression of public good, *ben vivir*, is discussed in a number of the other chapters in this volume. The Kïsêdjê have a term and concept of the ideal state of society that is somewhat similar to ben vivir, although I do not remember any extensive discussions of the term during my stays with the Kïsêdjê between 1971 and 1982 that resembled the descriptions of indigenous groups in western Amazonia today (see Whitten and Whitten, chapter 7, Sarmiento Barletti, chapter 5, and others in this volume). I recall that the phrase *aji betxi pa* (we live morally good or beautifully together) was largely used in public oratory and exhortations.[7] It was also used as the imperative *aya betxi pa* (you [should] live morally good or beautifully together) and was addressed to others—often the audience listening to the orator. On the occasions I remember it being used, the "goodness and beauty" largely appeared to be a contrast between a lack of conflict (good) and witchcraft and conflict (bad). I do not recall the concept being discussed outside of the context of formal speech. The phrase did not develop in response to the Brazilians they had met or the frontier society in Mato Grosso because their experience with them was very limited when I first heard it. The Kïsêdjê might someday use the term as part of a broader indigenous discourse or to define more clearly what it means to be Kïsêdjê. It might someday be used in a conscious reformulation of themselves—something the Kïsêdjê have already done with respect to their dual Upper Xingu and northern Gê ritual heritage in the early 1970s. By 2012, when soybean plantations had deforested most of the land right up to the borders of their territory, the Kïsêdjê had developed a consciousness of the rapacity of agribusiness and its effects on their environment. In a ten-minute video message to the Rio + 20 conference on YouTube (Amne Adji Kapẽrẽ Mba—Carta Kĩsêdjê para a Rio+20,https://www.youtube.com/watch?v =FU2O9RNNTx8), the speakers vigorously condemn the damage that unchecked agribusiness is doing to them, but they do not use the phrase *aji betxi pa*. Yet the basic idea of valuing community life is certainly as significant for the Kïsêdjê as it is for many of the other groups described.

A significant contrast between the Kïsêdjê and some communities in the Upper Amazon described in this book is that I have not encountered the idea that energy and game are a limited good.[8] The Gê-speaking societies in central Brazil moved their villages fairly frequently. Some groups migrated long distances over time. Precontact Kïsêdjê villages were also often partially abandoned during parts of the year as family groups hunted and gathered on treks. I never heard any statement that hunters should not kill as many as possible of an animal species. The Kïsêdjê seemed to eat as many of a species considered edible as they could catch and kill. They also sometimes cut down small wild fruit trees and gathered honey from wild nests. I never heard of sickness couched in a language of "energy loss." Some of the groups in western Amazonia seem to have remained in the same location for a long time and appear to have developed strategies of energy control the Gê did not. The public good of the Kïsêdjê may, therefore, differ somewhat from the forms of public good described by other authors in this volume.

Based on the previous discussion of ownership and control of things and events, as well as on the importance of euphoria and happiness, as essential components of the ceremonies of cosmological and social reproduction, I return now to address some of the issues on which this volume is focused. This chapter contributes to discussions of the good life by other contributors in this volume and shows that ideas of a good life may be expressed and experienced through sound and movement involving the collaboration of the whole society. Public wealth can endure through generations, but the methods of its transmission vary. The method of intergenerational transmission over time varied according to whether the ceremony was learned from the Upper Xingu (a patrilineal succession of kandé, who gained prestige through the performance of their ceremonies), or a Gê-style ceremony that was passed by name transmission (an equally effective method) through an unrelated group of name-set holders. These are two very different kinds of transmission—one based on kinship and the other on a system of naming relations that were parts of complex name exchanges. The enactments of public ceremonies may be brief and ephemeral; the sounds disperse; the dancing stops; the body paint is washed off; and material culture used in the ceremonies is destroyed or otherwise disposed of, repurposed, or hidden after their conclusion, and communities return to silence.[9] But ceremonies can be reexperienced through repeated performances and also in oral narratives that include the songs and the remembering and recounting of past performances. It is this quiet transmission that enables some indigenous peoples today to perform once again long-abandoned ceremonies that are now reappearing throughout Lowland South America after a generation or more of suppression or the lack of energy to perform. A kind of oral/aural archive persists for some time after a certain ritual life has been abandoned. Thus, the public good may be invisible for long periods of time yet still be significant and renewable.

Public wealth in the form of euphoria and happiness as part of large public music and dance performances was generated through internal relations among Kïsêdjê in a given performance but relied on external relations—relations of Kïsêdjê with other indigenous peoples, monsters, various animal and plant species, or spirits from whom they learned the ceremonies and songs. Every performance was a restatement or reenactment of the earlier relationships among species and groups of people. But every performance involved a changing cast of living Kïsêdjê organized into groups by gender, age, and name-set affiliation.

Where might we find the equivalent of the large public spaces and high degree of collective engagement with emotion in the large urban centers of Latin America today? One place that comes to mind is the large sports stadiums to be found in most cities where fans affiliate themselves with one or another team, sometimes move and shout together in unison, and experience intense emotional engagement as fans and supporters. Even more than most Christian calendrical celebrations, the intense experience of attending soccer matches might be compared with the kind of valued public experience of the ceremonies I have described for the Kïsêdjê.

Public wealth through song and dance can be a key component of social reproduction. I described a naming ceremony at some length in *Why Suyá Sing* (Seeger 2004 [1987]), and long initiation rituals are found among northern Gê groups and in the Upper Xingu. Kïsêdjê initiation rituals of the Upper Xingu and Gê types required complex transformations through song, dance, and body ornamentation that involved public wealth, as well as private wealth. This may be less the case in indigenous societies where shamans are key figures in social transformations or in groups where conversion to Christianity places more weight on Christ's life than that of the good life of individual believers (after baptism and before the funeral).

Music and dance, and their accompanying definition of and enactment in time, physical space, and sonic dimensions are enduring evidence of the grandeur and public wealth of many Lowland South American societies. They can tell us things we may fail to see if we look only for tangible remains in archaeological sites or at the information granted to anthropologists in the language-centric domain of the ethnographic interview, generally carried out in the quietness of individual interaction in domestic spaces. The acoustic spaces and experiences created through elaborate and extended performances of music and dance may be one of the best places to look for public wealth in indigenous South America.

Notes

1. Given the Kïsêdjê reluctance to have their music made available on the Internet, the only places the excerpt may be heard are on the referenced CD and at the Indiana University Archives of Traditional Music. I have done my best to describe the sounds with words, but any such attempt is always a failure. They have produced an excellent video of a different ceremony that conveys the sights, sounds, and emotions of these events (Kïsêdjê 2012).

2. I use the past tense to refer to the period between 1971 and 1982 when I did most of my field research. I am greatly indebted to the anthropologist Marcela Stockler Coelho de Souza at the University of Brasília for many contributions to my understanding of what has been happening since she began research with the Kïsêdjê around 2006. My more than forty years of involvement with the Kïsêdjê (see Seeger 2008 on long-term fieldwork) have been considerably enriched by her thoughtful comments and her publications (see Coelho de Souza 2010, 2012).

3. The difference between Amadeu Lanna's description of the Kïsêdjê from his short 1962 visit to their village (Lanna 1967) and my encounter with them in 1971 were striking. Lanna described them as an impoverished version of Upper

Xingu societies; I encountered a group emphasizing their Gê heritage following the arrival of the related Tapayuna in their village. We were both correct, and the Kïsêdjê move from Upper Xingu to Gê and then back to a middle position over the decades is a striking example of remaking processes.

4. Fausto's (2008) extremely thoughtful discussion of a large South American literature on "masters" (the relationship of master to the objects mastered) places more emphasis on filiation and predation than the Kïsêdjê case would appear to warrant; but the Gê-speaking groups often seem very different from their Arawak, Tupi, and Carib neighbors. While some generalizations may hold for much of the region, in other ways the Lowland South American societies appear to be very different from one another.

5. Needless to say, the Kïsêdjê 1970s concepts of music ownership were not at all congruent with Brazilian copyright law or WIPO best practices, and thus any rights they would have under national law were moot. The ownership of music and dance (as well as intangible and tangible heritage) is an area undergoing very rapid change. Aspects of this have been very well described for the Kïsêdjê in the first decade of the twenty-first century in Coelho de Souza (2010, 2012) and more generally in Seeger (2004 [1987]).

6. In at least one case the last moiety to request permission to perform it from the other then became the moiety that needed to be asked. The "control over permission" shifted with each performance (Kïsêdjê [2012] soundtrack).

7. This phrase might be broken down as adji=we (plural subject usually referring to an identifiable group); betxi=good/beautiful; pa=are together in a group. The Kïsêdjê word for "village" is *patà* (place where we are together as a group).

8. I must add a caveat. It is always difficult to say with any certainty what does not exist in any community, since the fact that I did not note it does not mean it might not have existed.

9. The title of Thomas Turino's 1993 book about Andean music in Peru, *Moving Away from Silence* nicely expresses the importance of music as a moving away from silence and daily life as a return to it.

References

Basso, Ellen B. 1985. *A Musical View of the Universe: Kalapalo Myth and Ritual Performance*. Philadelphia: University of Pennsylvania Press.

Coelho de Souza, Marcela S. 2010. "A vida material das coisas intangíveis." In *Conhecimento e cultura: Práticas de transformação no mundo indígena*, edited by Marcela Coelho de Souza and E. Coffaci de Lima, 97–118. Brasília: Athalaia Gráfica e Editora.

———. 2012. "A Pintura esquecida e o desenho roubado: Contrato, troca, e criatividade entre os Kïsêdjê." *Revista de Antropologia* 55(1):209–53.

Crocker, William C. 1990. "The Canela (Eastern Timbira) I: An Ethnographic Introduction." *Smithsonian Contributions to Anthropology* 33. Washington, DC: Smithsonian Institution Press.

Durkheim, Emile. 1965 [1915]. *The Elementary Forms of the Religious Life*. New York: Free Press.

Fausto, Carlos. 2008. "Donos demais: Maestria e domínio na Amazônia." *Mana* 14(2):329–66.

Fausto, Carlos, Bruna Franchetto, and Tommaso Montagnani. 2011. "Les formes de la mémoire: Art verbal et musique chez les Kuikuru du Haut-Xingu (Brésil)." *L'Homme* 197:44–70.

Feld, Steven. 1982. *Sound and Sentiment: Birds, Weeping, Poetics, and Song in Kaluli Expression*. Philadelphia: University of Pennsylvania Press.

Franchetto, Bruna, and Michael Heckenberger, eds. 2001. *Os povos do Alto Xingu: História e cultura*. Rio de Janeiro: Editora UFRJ.

Heckenberger, Michael J. 2003. "The Enigma of the Great Cities: Body and State in Amazonia." *Tipití: Journal of the Society for the Anthropology of Lowland South America* 1(1):27–58.

Hill, Jonathan D., and Jean-Pierre Chaumeil, eds. 2011. *Burst of Breath: Indigenous Ritual Wind Instruments in Lowland South America*. Lincoln: University of Nebraska Press.

Kïsêdjê. 2012. "Festa do rato." In the DVD *Cineastas indígenas Kïsêdjê*. Olinda, Brazil: Video nas Aldeias.

Lanna, Amadeu. 1967. "La division sexuelle du travail chez les Suyá du Brésil Central." *L'Homme* 8:67–72.

Lévi-Strauss. Claude. 1969. *The Raw and the Cooked*. London: Jonathan Cape.

Maitland, James. 1819 [1804]. *Inquiry into the Nature and Origin of Public Wealth and into the Means and Causes of its Increase*. Edinburgh: Archibald Constable and Co. http://ideas.repec.org/b/hay/hetboo/lauderdale1819.html.

Melatti, Julio Cesar. 1978. *Ritos de uma tribo Timbira*. São Paulo: Ática.

Mello, Maria Ignez Cruz. 2005. "Iamurikuma: Música, Mito e Ritual entre os Wauja do Alto Xingu." PhD dissertation, Universidade Federal de Santa Catarina (UFSC).

Menezes Bastos, Rafael José de. 1999a. *A musicológica Kamayurá: Para uma antropologia da communicação no Alto Xingu*. Florianópolis: Editora da UFSC.

———. 1999b. "Apuap World Hearing: On the Kamayurá Phono-auditory System and Anthropological Concept of Culture." *World of Music* 41:85–96.

———. 2006. "Música nas terras baixas da América do Sul: Estado da arte (Primeira parte)." *Antropologia em Primeira Mão* 86:4–20.

———. 2013. *A festa da Jaguaritirica, uma partitura crítico-interpretativa*. Florianópolis: UFSC.

Nimuendaju, Curt. 1946. *The Eastern Timbira*. University of California Publications in Archaeology and Ethnology, Vol. XLI. Berkeley: University of California Press.

Piedade, Acácio Tadeu de Camargo. 2004. "O canto de Kawoká: Música, cosmologia, e filosofia entre os Wauja do Alto Xingu." PhD dissertation, Universidade Federal do Santa Catarina.

———. 2011. "From Musical Poetics to Deep Language: The Ritual of the Wauja Sacred Flutes." In *Burst of Breath: Indigenous Ritual Wind Instruments in Lowland South America*, edited by Jonathan D. Hill and Jean-Pierre Chaumeil, 239–55. Lincoln: University of Nebraska Press.

Seeger, Anthony. 1981. *Nature and Society in Central Brazil: The Suyá Indians of Mato Grosso.* Cambridge MA: Harvard University Press.

———. 2004 [1987]. *Why Suyá Sing with Accompanying CD.* 2nd edition. Champaign: University of Illinois Press.

———. 2008. "Long-Term Field Research in Ethnomusicology in the 21st-Century." *Pauta, Porto Alegre* 19(32–33):3–20. http://www.seer.ufrgs.br/EmPauta/article/download/10742/6366.

Turino, Thomas. 1993. *Moving Away from Silence: Music of the Peruvian Altiplano and the Experience of Urban Migration.* Chicago: University of Chicago Press.

Turner, Edith 2012. *Communitas: The Anthropology of Collective Joy.* New York: Palgrave Macmillan.

Turner, Victor W. 1967. "Betwixt and Between: The Liminal Period in *Rites de Passage.*" In *Forest of Symbols*, edited by Victor W. Turner, 93–111. Ithaca: Cornell University Press.

CHAPTER TWO

Biopolitics of Health as Wealth in the Original Risk Society

BETH A. CONKLIN

It is health that is real wealth and not pieces of gold and silver.
—*Mahatma Gandhi*

Introduction

Across time and cultures, one of the few universals in human life may be that people everywhere recognize health as a key element in personal well-being. Sickness and debility undermine enjoyment of even the greatest riches; happiness research shows close links between individual health and life satisfaction. Health and wealth interact in many obvious ways. More affluent people can get better food and medical care; the economic consequences of disability are more devastating for the poor. At the societal level, economists have long recognized that productivity depends on the nutritional status and physical vitality of the labor force.

Is health a form of public wealth? Though health is widely viewed as a social good, cultural systems differ markedly in the relative value, rewards, and resources devoted to cultivating health versus accumulating wealth. They differ also in whether health is seen as a private or public good and as a personal or public responsibility. In Lowland South America, many native people treat the vitality of the members of a community as a kind of public wealth. Biosocial well-being, strength, fertility, and thriving are indices of affluence and the most essential human capital. This chapter explores *health as wealth* among the Wari', a population of about 4,000 Chapakuran-speaking people who live in indigenous reserves in the western Brazilian municipality of Guajará-Mirim, Rondônia. If wealth is measured in money, material possessions, or property, then Wari' have little. Nor do they have durable sacred objects, sacred sites, or inheritable ritual paraphernalia. There is, in fact, little inheritance at all; for when someone dies, Wari' destroy all his or her possessions, crops, and house. In the analysis that follows, I explore Wari' traditional disinterest in material wealth and the corresponding emphasis on collective health. I further examine how this fits the biopolitical priorities of past generations and their cultural logics of property, personhood, relational biology, leadership, and status.

The Wari' language has no explicit terms for wealth, poverty, or the good life, but Wari' do express strong judgments about relative affluence and impoverishment and about better-off and worse-off individuals, families, and groups. Personal well-being revolves around three factors: having abundant, high-quality food (especially game, fish, fruit, honey, and maize, which is the traditional staple crop); having many children and kin living nearby; and having the social support one needs. Conversely, impoverishment is defined by food insecurity, ill health, and lack of social support. At the community level, Wari' judge affluence in similar terms, by the local abundance of food, the group's productivity, vitality, and fertility, and their capacity to mobilize in collective activities, especially to host gatherings for other communities.

Throughout South America (and the world), a search is on among thoughtful citizens, activists, and intellectuals to develop healthier life politics and more equitable, inclusive economies. My goal is to identify aspects of Wari' experience that speak to that search. A major question pertains to how people can be motivated to find status and satisfaction in less damaging practices of material consumption. Indigenous cultures offer no ready-made models. But examples like the Wari' do show how generations have lived meaningful lives oriented to the pursuit of collective well-being and investments in human and social capital rather than money or material wealth.

I examine the Wari' case from a historical perspective that resonates with issues at stake in the risk society thesis, one of the most influential theories of contemporary society. Ulrich Beck (1992), Anthony Giddens (1991), and others have observed that postindustrial society is undergoing a shift from wealth to risk as a determinant of subjectivity, identity, status, and politics. Beck's model, on which I focus, sees insecurity fostering broad social trends toward *flexibilization*, *individualization*, and fragmented "*subpolitics*." These trends are reflected in neoliberal privatization of formerly public goods and the retreat from commitments to use public wealth to improve public services.

The Wari' offer a counter example of a different kind of risk society. Building on classic models of egalitarianism developed by Marshall Sahlins (1972) and Pierre Clastres (1987 [1974], 2010), which highlight the benefits of eschewing property accumulation, ownership, and inequalities of power, I explore how practices based in an egalitarian health-not-wealth orientation helped Wari' survive in a context of pervasive risk from epidemics and interethnic violence. I use this conversation between Wari' ethnography and the risk society thesis methodologically to illuminate parallel dynamics, as well as contrasting values and practices. As in postindustrial risk societies, geosocial flexibility and mobility were Wari' priorities. But in contrast to the individualizing, socially fragmenting tendencies that Beck and Giddens see emerging in response to insecurity, Wari' orientations to fostering collective health channel aspirations and agency toward a socially integrative ethos of productivity, responsibility, and practices of care.

Health, Wealth, and Ilth

The value that native Amazonians place on health prefigures challenges to conventional economics and development policies. Since the 1970s, scholars and policy makers concerned with global poverty have advocated that health should be taken into account in measures of development. The *capabilities approach* developed by Amartya Sen (1985), Martha Nussbaum (2011), and economist James Foster (2011) emphasizes that individual dignity, freedoms, and agency to fulfill basic needs and pursue aspirations are fundamental to self-realization. The United Nations has adopted alternative measures, such as the Human Development Index (HDI). The HDI includes quality of life indices, such as literacy, longevity, health, and infant mortality as an alternative to the narrow measures of economic output defined by the gross domestic product ([GDP] cf. Fischer 2014, 9–12).

Health is a distinct kind of social good. Valuing health foregrounds inequities and vulnerabilities in ways that wealth-focused economics does not. Whereas property can be privately owned, individual health is inseparable from public health. Social, political, and environmental conditions affect food, water, medical care and exposure to infection, toxins, danger, and stress. Health data are powerful tools for policy reform because they are quantifiable; life expectancy, infant mortality, and disease rates can be compared across populations. And health statistics illuminate inequities that remain hidden in calculations based on wealth alone. The GDP can mask large differences between wealthy elites and impoverished masses, but health statistics count each individual alike and thus shed light on disparities within populations. For example, the United States ranks first among the world's nations in GDP but is thirtieth in infant mortality between Poland and Slovakia (McDorman and Mathews 2009).

Cultural logics of health and wealth are closely linked to treatments of *ilths*. Ilth is a term coined by progressive economists to describe negative effects of economic activities. In conventional calculations of wealth output, such as GDP, cancer, oil spills, disastrous hurricanes, and crime contribute positively to the economy, by increasing spending on health care, environmental cleanup, reconstruction, and prisons. Pollution, species extinction, stress, and suffering are *externalities*, side effects excluded from the economic calculus. Critics like ecological economist Herman Daly (2003), a former senior economist at the World Bank, emphasize the need to count ilths, as well as wealth, social "bads" as well as goods, risk as well as riches.

As a broader concept than poverty, ilths encompass harm and diminished resilience: factors that hurt people in the present and that degrade future capacities (human capital and natural/ecological capital) to cope with change. Like health, a focus on ilths calls attention to negative and uneven consequences of economic arrangements. Whereas wealth is the axis around which orthodox economic cosmology revolves, ilths are a twin focus for those concerned with social and environmental justice.

Ilths generated by global capitalism are at the center of risk society theory. Beck (1992) observes that class society in the earlier, industrial economy was based on unequal accumulation of wealth. Politics centered on negotiating the distribution of wealth among groups differentiated by occupation and property ownership. In postindustrial society, the ability to avoid risk is a growing basis for status differentiation and politics. With rapid technological change and the global integration of labor and finance markets, jobs come and go, local conditions change, and insecurity spreads. At the same time, "manufactured risks"—nuclear, chemical, environmental, and genetic dangers created by humans—proliferate and often affect entire populations, regardless of class (Beck 1992, 19–50). Spreading risk affects identity formation, consciousness, and politics (Mythen 2004, 2). These increasingly are determined not only by material/monetary wealth, but also by the ability to avoid risk. Education, access to information, and social networks—that is, human capital and social capital, not just occupation and property—increasingly differentiate the haves and have-nots.[1]

Flexibilization, individualization, fragmented politics, and reflexive consciousness are broad trends in risk society. Coping with insecurity and change requires adaptability on many fronts, geographic, social, political, and psychological. Old identities and solidarities wane. Formerly class-based party politics are displaced by subpolitics, in which people come together temporarily around specific issues and interests, such as indigenous rights activism and environmentalism in Amazonia (cf. Conklin and Graham 1995). With neoliberalism's ascendancy, formerly public resources and responsibilities are privatized and responsibility is individualized. The consumer replaces the citizen in many arenas. "Choice" becomes central in the construction of personal identities. With the knowledge that other choices always are possible, self-questioning and heightened reflexivity become a mode of modern life (Giddens 1991).

Risk society is nothing new in Amazonia. In a cogent critique of the Eurocentrism in Beck's social history, Stephen Nugent (2000, 239) observes that the experience of modernization, which in South America arguably began with the European invasion five centuries ago, "has been precisely that of a risk society." Nonelite Amazonians' lives historically took shape against imperatives to manage the risks of disease, violence, enslavement, and dispossession that accompanied expanding states and market economies. Nugent suggests that rather than forging new ground, Europe and North America may be undergoing a "third worldization," as affluent economies become the risk societies that capitalism and colonialism created in places like Amazonia.

Public Wealth and Ilth in Amazonia

Amazonia is a case study in how "wealth" and "the public" can be defined and deployed by nation-states in ways that impoverish people and resource-rich environments. The history of the past five centuries can be read as a series of encounters between different systems of value and life-politics that treat some human lives as more worthy of consideration than others.

In earlier eras, notions of savagery and civilization provided conquerors, colonizers, and capitalists with moral justification to take over native peoples' lands and resources. Today, claims about public wealth often play similar roles. Under neoliberalism, the slippery concept of the public has been hijacked to equate with government control. States in thrall to elites and corporations use claims about public wealth (and ignore realities of public ilths) to undermine indigenous peoples' rights to their own territories and resources.

In the name of national patrimony, South American governments repeatedly turn to Amazonia to appropriate resources. Ignoring the presence of hundreds of native communities, in 1970 Brazil's dictatorship declared the Amazon "a land without men, for men without land" and initiated development programs that transferred large amounts of "public" land to settlers, ranchers, and logging and mining corporations. In 2013, Ecuador's president Rafael Correa opened Yasuni National Park, said to be the most biodiverse place on earth (Wallace 2013), to oil drilling under Huaorani and Kichwa lands. Correa cited the need to invest this national wealth in public goods (hospitals, clinics, and schools). An unspoken factor was the flip side of public wealth—public debt. This oil money was needed to repay China for the Ecuadorian state's borrowing in the name of the nation.

Downstream from the Wari', on the Amazon's largest tributary, the Rio Madeira, Brazil has begun construction on the first two of sixty dams that will reengineer Amazonia and harness the national wealth of its hydropower. With nearly a thousand species of fish, the Madeira is the world's most biodiverse river. In 2012, the start-up of the first dam, Santo Antônio, launched a series of technical debacles. Weeks of raging waves wiped out the municipal port and homes in Porto Velho, the state capital; upriver, there were massive fish die offs in water black as coffee. In 2013, exploding turbines injured dam workers. In 2014, the dams' environmentally unsound design combined with record rainfall and deforestation in the Andes flooded more than 5,000 families' homes and caused over $200 million in damage (Hurwitz 2014; Osava 2014). Rondônia needs electricity, but all of this energy is exported a thousand miles south to power industries in São Paulo state (cf. Aranha 2013).

One reason why Amazonia's forests, minerals, and untamed waters still exist in relative abundance today is that native people historically did not see these as wealth to exploit for profit. With the expansion of capitalist frontiers, things that native people did not consider to be useful, scarce, or appropriate to own or exchange—land, trees, minerals, rivers, biogenetic material from plants and human bodies—were redefined (Conklin 2002). Transformed into property and commodities, these became wealth resources for outsiders to claim, occupy, steal, buy, compensate, or protect. Much of the violence of Amazonian history is the story of invasion and conflict driven by state societies' drive to appropriate from indigenous people's lands the wealth resources that states have already used up in their own lands (Bodley 1982, 3–7).

The consequences of divergent native and national notions of wealth can be read not only in history books, but in the landscape itself. Viewed from above in satellite photos, Rondônia is a patchwork of contrasting expanses of brown and green, many divided by sharp, straight borders. The green expanses are protected forests—indigenous reserves, biosphere reserves, extractive reserves, and national parks—that have been used mostly by native people and *caboclos*, forest dwellers who use the forest in similarly sustainable ways. The brown areas are deforested and degraded, tangible evidence of the national society's quest for wealth and poverty of imagination to envision healthier paths for collective well-being.

The Wari'

Some two hundred miles upstream from the new Madeira dams, in one of those still-mostly green expanses, live people who call themselves Wari'. Known to outsiders as the Pakaas Novos, they historically controlled the forests of western Rondônia north, east, and south of the town of Guajará-Mirim along the right-bank tributaries of the Mamoré and Madeira rivers, which form Brazil's border with Bolivia.

One November morning at the height of the drought of 2010, I was drifting in a boat barely afloat on a few inches of water in the Rio Pakaas Novos. Benjamin Oro Eo', the young *chefe* (chief) of the village of Santo André, was piloting me and a first-time visitor upriver. The going was slow. The Pakaas Novos flows deep in the rainy season, but that year's dry season had left the river lower than any elder could remember. It was arduous navigating around the exposed river bottom and masses of vegetation clogging the shallow water. Benjamin cut the engine to take a break, and his visitor took the opportunity to pose a question whose bluntness startled me. "So, is life better or worse now than in the old days?"

What an impossible question, I thought. There are too many factors to weigh, so many trade-offs in how Wari' life has changed in the half-century since they came under the sway of Brazil's government and market economy (which happened in stages in the 1950s and 1960s). To me, this seemed too complicated to categorize as better or worse. But Benjamin answered immediately. "Things are better now. In the old days, white people (*wijam*) ordered everything. They had the money, the schools, the medicine, the boats. Wijam told Wari' what to do. Now we are in charge. We have our own things. We have food. We have lots of children, many old people. Wari' are strong (*hwara opa'*). We are strong and we run things ourselves. We tell white people what to do."

Benjamin's response encapsulated two, inextricably linked Wari' values: autonomy and biosocial well-being. His time frame was his own life experience—the past two decades during which Wari' have gained more leverage in their relations with whites, with citizenship and the right to vote, indigenous organizations, bilingual schools, and community-staffed health clinics.

Hwara opa' is the Wari' term that comes closest to the Western concept of health. It connotes vitality, the strength that enables a person to do productive work. The physicality of hwara opa' is inseparable from its social and moral dimensions. The World Health Organization (WHO) defines health holistically as a "state of complete physical, mental and social well-being and not merely the absence of disease or infirmity" (WHO 1948, 1). Wari' go farther. Like many native people, they see health as the tangible manifestation of proper sociality and morality. People who are hwara opa' take initiative; they work to produce food and care for their family. The idea of being strong but lazy is unthinkable.

Feeding and being fed is what Nancy Munn (1986) calls a template of value. At the center of Wari' notions of vitality, being hwara opa' is about having agency: the ability to feed, protect, and nurture others. Men and women gain status and respect by demonstrating capacities to procure, produce, and share food (especially meat, fish, and maize), raise healthy children, protect their kin and coresidents from harm, and cultivate social ties. People lose status if they are lazy or irresponsible, unsupportive of kin, or sexually indiscreet in ways that generate conflict between families.

Prestige comes from bringing people together in coordinated activities—to host a festival, present a musical performance, roof a house, carry out a collective work project, or, in the old days, lead a war expedition. For a community, hosting parties (especially multiday festivals) for other communities is the highest prestige marker of communal productivity and affluence. Such gatherings are venues to explore, establish, and maintain amity among people from different locales who might intermarry or provide help in times of need. In the spiritual realm, the same parties mediate cosmological relations among living Wari', their ancestors, and animals.

Wari' have three kinds of traditional, intercommunity festivals: *tamara*, *hütop*, and *hüroroin*. These are distinguished, respectively, by increasing elaboration of roles, performances, and interactions between guests and hosts. Hüroroin is the most complex and involves a three-day festival for which the hosts must brew large quantities of maize chicha, which ferments in a vat made from a *pana* (huge hollow tree). Fresh (unfermented or lightly fermented) chicha is symbolically associated with blood, vitality, fertility, nurturance, and conviviality; in daily life, offering it is the essential gesture of hospitality. For parties, the chicha is strongly fermented, and producing and consuming it is a focus of competitive one-up-manship. For hüroroin, hosts vie to brew more chicha than their guests can possibly consume, and the male visitors who drink it vomit immediately so they can drink more. After a good party, the village plaza is a lake of golden liquid (figures 2.1 and 2.2).

Hütop and tamara are less elaborate but also require making lots of chicha. The ability to host a celebration depends on having surplus maize;

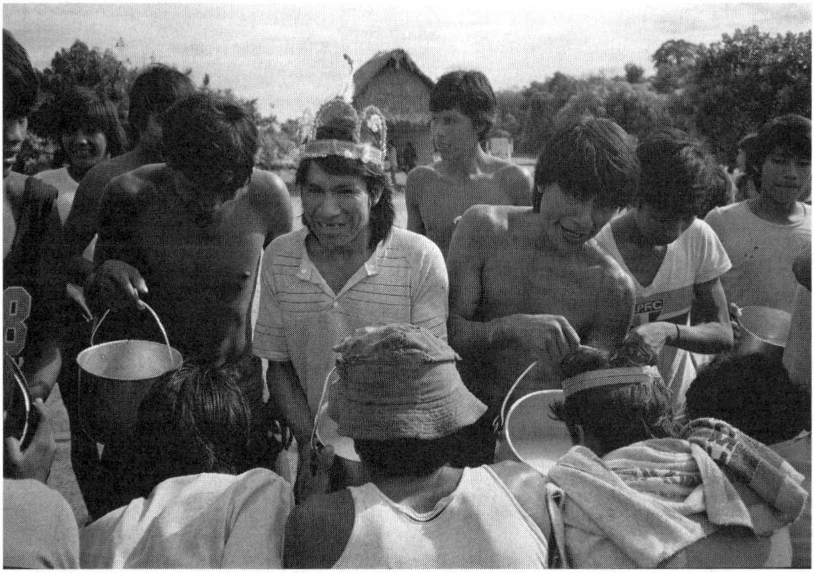

FIGURE 2.1. In a hüroroin festival at Santo André, hosts goad their guests to drink buckets of fermented maize chicha. Photo by Beth Conklin.

FIGURE 2.2. In the wake of a round of drinking and vomiting, a village shaman sits contemplatively, while in the background a disapproving missionary comes to survey the scene. Photo by Beth Conklin.

FIGURE 2.3. Musical performances in hüroroin parties are prime occasions when a community displays its public wealth of coordinated social energy. Photo by Beth Conklin.

socially ambitious families plant extra crops for this purpose. Chicha making also depends on the willingness of women and girls to spend many hours grinding maize. (In the past, before commercial sugar was available, women laboriously masticated the grain to break down its complex carbohydrates and sweeten the brew) A big communal pana, brimming with golden chicha, is a tangible sign of collective productivity and collaboration.

At intercommunity parties, the guests' roles are to perform for their hosts, singing, drumming, and dancing in same-sex or mixed-sex groups. Wari' performances emphasize coordination and repetition, singing the same melody over and over, and doing the same, simple dance step over and over. The beauty of many bodies, painted, adorned, and shining with oil, moving and singing in synchrony, is a prime Wari' aesthetic (figure 2.3). As Anthony Seeger (chapter 1) emphasizes, musical performances are prized forms of collective wealth throughout Amazonia. Today, Wari' hold fewer traditional parties but take pride in other, coordinated activities, such as church singing and intervillage soccer matches. As occasions to assert and assess a group's affluence, these events are as close as Wari' come to displays of public wealth.

Material Logics and Biologics

Land and fertile soil for farming are the most important subsistence resources, but these historically have not been scarce. And there has been little stress or competition over them. This lack of scarcity is key; elsewhere in Amazonia, as Guzmán-Gallegos (chapter 4) and Santos-Granero (chapter 3) point out in this volume, land has become an item of public wealth for many native groups as the result of land shortages due to intense colonization by migrants who claimed space for farms and pastures.

Wari' do not own land as private property. They treat landscape resources as commons/common wealth, with access open to all members of the group, or as common-pool resources whose use is regulated by local norms and available to whoever takes the initiative to work with them. Usufruct prevails; investing labor in clearing and burning to make a field or pasture, or felling a tree to gather fruit, establishes a loose, first right to use it in the short term in what Sarmiento Barletti (chapter 5) describes as a performative sense of property.

Wari' lost about two-thirds of their precontact territory when the Brazilian government defined legal reserves for them in the 1960s. But the epidemics that followed contact killed three-fifths of the population, so the land that remained was enough to support them for several decades.

With better medical care, the population recovered demographically; today there are more than 4,000 Wari' living in villages in the rural Postos Indígenas. As young people marry and start families, the rising generation will confront land shortages for the first time, and attitudes toward land use and ownership may change.

Until very recently all Wari' villagers produced most of their own food by farming, hunting, fishing, and gathering. Some earned small amounts of cash by selling rubber latex, crops, manioc flour, or crafts, but people generally had little money and few possessions. In what Sahlins (1972, 10) called "the democracy of property," Wari' manage basic resources with egalitarian access to the knowledge, skills, and local materials needed to fulfill subsistence needs. From a capabilities perspective, they rank high in freedoms and access to basic needs. As in similar indigenous societies, a host of explicit and implicit norms and rules for sharing, asking, giving, and receiving militate against major inequalities. Wari' share not because they are more altruistic than other people but because social approval rewards generosity and nonpossessiveness.

Attention to properties rather than property ownership means valuing the qualities of people and materials that can be directed, with intention and skills, to promote prosperity, agency, influence, and status. Terence Turner (1995) sees *production* as a primary principle that encompasses biological, social, and symbolic (re)production. He observes that where social identity is not constituted primarily through exchanges of goods (valuables, gifts, or commodities), the public circulation of symbolic tokens of valued aspects of persons (e.g., verbal performances and visual displays) and bodily modifications are primary communicators of identity and status. Carlos Fausto (1999, 2012) identifies production and consumption, and circulation and exchange, as two primary schemata that interactively pattern a host of external and internal dynamics across Amazonia.

Status and influence derive not from possessing things but from setting things in motion. The prestige associated with having an object derives from its social history and its possible social futures: from the relationships that constituted the object and the relations it can foster. Wari' see a large, well-built house not as wealth in itself but as evidence of the productivity (physical strength, industriousness, skill, and cooperation) of those who pooled their labor to build it and as a status-enhancing space that invites socializing where many people can gather.

Wari' prosperity is not a static condition or achievement but an activity with generative potential to pursue aspirations and cultivate resilience. This is an expansive notion of productivity in which dichotomies of tangible/material and intangible/social are irrelevant. Activities that orthodox economics would define as nonproductive—affective and performative acts of grooming, body painting, gift giving, conversation, storytelling, singing, or party giving—are valued as ways to foster the relations through which individuals and groups thrive. Affluence is the product of proper flows of human effort, creativity, materials, and care in relations of giving, receiving, and tending.

A key insight of medical anthropology is that cultural notions of persons as embodied beings are linked with sociopolitical ideas and practices. Biological thinking about life processes—cultural understandings of conception, birth, growth and maturation, health, debility, contamination, death, and decay—tends to reflect and reinforce ways of thinking about sociality, identity, belonging, and property. Capitalist emphases on individualism, ownership, and wealth accumulation resonate with germ theory views of the individual body-self as a private fortress to defend and shore up against invaders. The one-sperm/one-egg model of conception underpins notions of parental rights similar to property ownership.

The relational biologies of native Amazonia embrace more ecological models of human physiology that recognize body, mind, and spirit as interactive dimensions of the self.[2] This self is a relational self, interdependent with other bodies, beings, and spirits. Amazonian ethnography foregrounds the integration of social and material/bodily relations as a continuum of activities. Persons and bodies are always in transition, always being made, unmade, and modified. Different native Amazonian groups have different models of how this works. For some, *life* is the circulation of vital energies and substances (cf. Uzendoski 2005). Others emphasize appropriating vitality from outside the group. The Wari', like the Yanesha described by Santos-Granero (chapter 3), view both processes—circulation and appropriation—as central to maintain and enhance personal, as well as collective, life.

Wari' relational biology highlights the body's permeability and the bioactivity of fluids and other substances that pass among people in sex, cosleeping, commensality, and other interactions, and among people, animals, and spirits. In contrast to the Western belief that DNA defines a fixed identity and kin ties, Wari' hold a more complex model of how embodied processes modify identity and kinship during the course of one's life, which provides a conceptual frame to affirm changing affiliations (Conklin and Morgan 1996; Conklin 2001a, 2001b).

The emphasis on productivity is buttressed by the Wari' belief that hard work strengthens the heart, and maize and meat build strong blood. Inactivity slows blood circulation, which makes people weak and sick. The processual, relational making of persons and their capacities means that they also are fragile, vulnerable, and in need of constant attention and tending (see Guzmán-Gallegos, chapter 4, for similar ideas among the Amazonian Kichwa). Wari' models of mind-body physiology locate emotions in the heart; feelings of sadness, loneliness, anxiety, and insecurity constrict the heart, slow circulation, weaken blood, and lead to debility and illness. This biological model encourages attention to the well-being and emotions of others. Easing angst and suffering is not just kindness but essential to collective well-being.

Death is a moment when contrasts between Wari' and Western logics of property and prosperity appear starkest. In the West, inheritance is a prime concern; to whom will the dead person's wealth pass? How much will beneficiaries receive? Inheritance is a major factor that perpetuates inequalities of wealth and power. In contrast, many native Amazonians, especially in smaller, egalitarian societies, respond to death by destroying property. Wari' carry this to an extreme; they burn the houses of the dead and burn, destroy, or give away all their food, personal possessions, and any growing or harvested crops with which they worked. Unlike the famous potlatches of northwestern North America, these rites of public destruction are neither wealth displays nor status competitions. Rather, this is part of a practice of care for the emotions of others. Wari' believe that eradicating material traces of the deceased helps ease the grief of bereaved kin by removing tangible reminders that provoke sorrow (Conklin 2001a).

Destruction was not just loss; it produced new relations and forced the bereaved family to depend on kin for shelter and food thus renewing commitments and indebtedness. Especially for people who value food as much as Wari' do, destroying all of a household's crops and food stores was a radical act and testimony to the importance they ascribed to this remaking of mourners' worlds. Maize is the only food that Wari' traditionally stored in quantity, which was curated in carefully stacked, golden pyramids on platforms shielded by thatch. Whereas norms for sharing allow people to ask for (and expect to be given) almost anything they see in someone's home (which, not surprisingly leads to much hiding of possessions), maize and essential tools are private property that are off-limit to routine begging and borrowing.

In view of the care with which Wari' treat maize, its ritual wastage seems contradictory. Besides destroying maize after a death, most chicha consumed in hüroroin and hütop celebrations also is wasted when it is vomited on the spot. These practices could undercut food security, but the two rituals are linked in ways that partially counter this effect. Death imposes a hiatus in party giving; after someone has died, it is disrespectful to hold a party in the community for some time afterward (properly, a full year). Maize that would have gone into making (vomited) chicha is therefore available to be eaten as food. The rule against partying after a death means that when a celebration does take place, it is a tangible sign that the community is healthy—hwara opa'.

Politics of Egalitarianism

One of anthropology's most enduring ideas is Sahlins's (1972, 2) account of "a Zen road to affluence" among foragers (hunter-gatherers). Drawing on 1960s research on work time and quality of life, Sahlins argued that limiting desires for material possessions allows people to satisfy basic needs relatively easily and have substantially more time for leisure, socializing, and cultural activities than workers in Western societies. Sahlins emphasized the physical burdens of carrying possessions when food getting depends on flexibility to hunt and harvest wild plants at changing locations. "Mobility and property are in contradiction," he observed (Sahlins 1972, 12). As many a postindustrial householder knows, the more stuff you have, the harder it is to move.

Sahlins's model has been criticized for overgeneralizing and for the difficulty of testing its claims empirically (Bird-David 1992; Kaplan 2000; Solway 2006). But the core insight stands: affluence can be defined in terms of life satisfactions of sociality and skills, not material wealth and possessions. Sahlins's student, David Graeber, extended this perspective in his book *Debt: The First 5,000 Years*, which ends with a tribute to the "nonindustrious poor." "Insofar as the time they are taking off from work is being spent . . . enjoying and caring for those they love," Graeber (2011, 390) writes, they may be "pioneers of a new economic order that would not share our current one's penchant for self-destruction."

Clastres (2010, 189–208) took up Sahlins's model of foragers as the "original affluent society" to develop a complementary political analysis of the strategic uses of egalitarian values and practices that undercut hierarchy in small, bounded, subsistence-based societies (including horticulturalists like the Wari'). Drawing on his fieldwork with the Guayaki of Paraguay, Clastres (whose work first appeared in the 1970s) argued that some native people chose to live in leaderless, staunchly egalitarian societies in order to avoid control by the state and to prevent the rise of coercive power in their own societies. In these indigenous economies of power and desire, eschewing material accumulation, inequality, and political hierarchy protects autonomy and small groups' abilities to move away, split up, and form new allegiances and solidarities.

Clastres's model resonates with many dynamics of precontact Wari' society. The only social groups with which individuals identified, other than their household and residential community, were kin-based, named, territorial subgroups: the Oro Eo', Oro Nao', Oro At, Oro Mon, Oro Waram, and Oro Waram Xijein. These subgroups are loose affiliations with no formal political structure. Individuals can emphasize ties to their mother's or father's kin as they choose and shift, reformulate, and create new identities in response to life circumstances (see Vilaça 2010).

Wari' leadership is situational and ephemeral; they traditionally had no chiefs, no nobility, no age grades, or other internal social groupings. A man or woman who takes the lead in directing one activity (such as a musical performance, festival, collective hunt, war expedition, or move to a new site) often fades into the background in other contexts. No one coerces or orders anyone around; even within households, parents have only limited authority over their children (figure 2.4).

Outsiders have found this ambiguity of leadership maddening. For years, administrators from the National Indian Foundation (FUNAI) cajoled Wari' to name village chiefs. People at Santo André intuited, correctly, that administrators mainly wanted someone to enforce their dictates, and they evaded this issue for years. In 1987, they finally decided they had to comply, but this did not work out quite the way the bureaucrats had hoped. The community meeting to select Santo André's first chief was a raucous affair. FUNAI's regional director had sent a list of local men—all respected, responsible heads of household—whom he considered good candidates to be village chief. As the names were read one by one, people (including the nominees themselves) started laughing and cracking jokes. "He farts too much!" "He's too skinny!" "Not me, I'm going fishing!" "Not my brother, he smells like a monkey!" Laughter mounted as people called out new nominations: a six-year-old girl, the baby crawling across the floor, somebody's dog. Each was greeted with ridicule until one name was mentioned and suddenly, there was a chorus of agreement. "Yes, that's right; he's the one! Oron is our chief!" With instant consensus and a collective cheer, the meeting broke up and everyone departed in fine spirits. This made no sense to me. Oron was a genial young man who spoke good Portuguese but had little status in the community. Orphaned young, he had few close kin, and he was married but childless in a society where fatherhood is a prerequisite for full manhood. Why did everyone think he should be chief?

A couple of weeks later, I looked out my window and saw Oron and two of his wife's cousins, aged eight and ten years, laboring in the hot sun chopping weeds. An order had come from FUNAI to clean up the village plaza. This was onerous work that Wari' considered pointless. Instead of recruiting his constituents, their chief was doing the work himself assisted by the only followers he could muster. Then I understood; Oron was the ideal leader because he had no power.

The first chief did not last long. Doing FUNAI's bidding was tedious, and he went to live elsewhere for a while. Other men tried the chief's role, but the job had few perks; there was no salary and, unlike the situation described by Giovanna Micarelli (chapter 6), no "project money." Santo André's chief mostly just received orders from FUNAI and criticism from fellow Wari'. No one wanted to deal with this for long, and one man

FIGURE 2.4. In the ephemeral pattern of Wari' leadership, the woman who organizes and leads the musical performance by female guests who sing nonstop for days in a hüroroin festival is highly respected but has no formal influence in other contexts. Photo by Beth Conklin.

followed another in the role. The community tried a two-chief system with elders from the two largest kin groups. This did not work either. Eventually, they hit on the idea of having five chiefs simultaneously, chosen by five extended families. This arrangement lasted longer, but the individual chiefs did not. A man would serve for a few weeks or months, get annoyed, and quit. At any given moment, one or two leadership positions usually were vacant.

Wari' did not seem to mind unstable leadership but FUNAI did. They eventually returned to a single-chief model, and the role eventually settled on someone from one of the largest families: Benjamin, a young father who was hardworking, fair-minded, and diplomatic. Perhaps most importantly, he never ordered anyone to do anything.

Singing for Stone

Historically, there was one notable exception to the general pattern of Wari' disinterest in owning material property. In the entire territory known to their ancestors, the hard, fine-grained stone used to make axes and knives was found in only one place. This was a site called Kit, which means "knife" in the Wari' language. It is located on the lower flanks of the western Serra dos Pakaas Novos in the southern part of the Wari' homeland. The only archaeological survey of this site was done by Maria Dulce Gaspar of the Museu Nacional in Rio de Janeiro, in collaboration with anthropologist Aparecida Vilaça. Radiocarbon dating of a single sample from Gaspar's survey suggests this site has been used by native people for at least 2,500 years.

The stone at Kit was the kind of scarce, high-use/high-exchange value wealth resource on which great fortunes are built in market economies. The outcropping is small, and the quarry could have been regarded as private property. But Wari' treated it as the common property of an extended kin group and created means by which stone and tools could flow into the whole population.

As long ago as oral history recounts, Kit was occupied by the Oro Eo', a subgroup that lived around the Rio Ocaia. This was the mythological heart of Wari' society. Downriver from Kit, the culture hero Hujin confronted the giant, carnivorous Master of Animals spirit named Oro Tapan and bested him in a musical contest that gave birth to the intercommunity festivals that knit together their precontact society and cosmology.

The Oro Eo' who lived at Kit kept tight control over the quarry. Other Wari' villages stood empty part of the year; after planting maize in September, everyone left to spend the rest of the dry season camping in the forest, hunting, and living off palm hearts and other wild foods. As is common among swidden horticulturalists, villages relocated to new agricultural sites about every five years. Kit was the exception; its inhabitants never moved and never left it unoccupied.

The common-property regime by which Kit's people managed their quarry allowed usufruct rights to their kin; anyone related by birth or marriage could cut stone whenever they wanted. The Oro Eo' subgroup constituted the "public" with rights to this wealth. But Oro Eo' recognized that it was in their interest to share this scarce resource more widely, so they headed off theft and aggression by facilitating access for other Wari' under restricted, but not onerous, conditions. They did this by integrating stone into the politics of hospitality and the logic of the gift.

Kit was the cultural crossroads of precontact Wari' society. The Oro Eo' threw many parties; elders describe a village alive with singing and storytelling. Some parties were formal affairs to which they invited another community. The guests traveled as a group and performed for their hosts. After the party, when the visitors had gathered to leave, the people of Kit presented them with worked tools: axes and knives for men and women and little "honey-cutting" axes for the children.

Individual Wari' who wanted stone could show up at Kit uninvited and hope to be welcomed. Visitors shared news from home and often entertained their hosts with stories and songs; with amity affirmed, Oro Eo' let them cut stone. As owners of the site that drew people from all over, the Oro Eo' heard more stories, songs, news, and gossip than any other Wari'. To this day, they are remembered as the intellectuals and folklorists of the population—the information masters of their social universe.

Biopolitics in the Original Risk Society

Oro Eo' managed their uniquely scarce resource by facilitating its distribution to others in ways that enhanced their own social networks and influence (social capital) and knowledge (human capital). Why were these their priorities rather than the accumulation of property wealth? Thinking about this in light of the risk society thesis points to the salience of Beck's flexibilization as a response to pervasive risk. This intersects with Sahlins's and Clastres's insights into how nonaccumulative economics and resistance to hierarchy preserve flexibility and undercut oppression by centralized power. In an environment of danger and shifting opportunities, it makes sense to keep one's options open, geographically and socially.

Wari' residential groups move, split up, regroup, and shift allegiances. Unburdened by many material possessions, and without official positions or affiliations to tie them to one place or leader, families come and go.

They move to take advantage of resources (soil, fish, game, schools, and proximity to kin) or get away from an unhealthy situation, interpersonal conflict, painful memories of the dead, or as in the past, outsiders who brought violence and disease.

For at least a century before contact, Wari' pursued an isolationist foreign policy. They had no trade, no intermarriage, and no sustained, peaceful relations with any other humans, native or nonnative. They regarded wijam (non-Wari') with categorical hostility. Encounters with wijam brought disease, rape, kidnapping, attacks, and massacres that forced Wari' to flee and abandon their homes and crops. Geosocial self-isolation, flexibility to move when needed, and oversight of social/spatial boundaries and interactions with outsiders were life-preserving biopolitical strategies.

In the five centuries since the European invasion of South America began, infectious diseases exported from the Old World have been the single biggest threat to native people's lives and livelihoods. After government teams contacted Wari' in the 1950s and 1960s, wave after wave of measles, mumps, whooping cough, influenza, colds, and malaria killed 60 percent of the population—three out of every five people—within two or three years. This pattern of mass death is a story that has been repeated in every epidemiologically isolated people's encounter with larger, cosmopolitan populations. What is unusual about the Wari' is that they managed to survive, and thrive, so long in a region where most other native people had been devastated decades earlier. Their remarkable survival into the second half of the twentieth century as an intact, independent people derived in no small part from their attitudes toward wealth and health.

The importance of the epidemiological context cannot be overstated. Security depended on controlling interethnic boundaries. Smallpox, measles, mumps, whooping cough, polio, influenza, and colds spread through human-to-human contact; these could infect Wari' only in close encounters with outsiders, such as the rape of Wari' women and girls by mineral prospectors that caused an epidemic of respiratory illness in the Rio Lage area in the 1950s. Proximity to infected humans also mattered with malaria; the *Anopholes* mosquitos that transmit it have flight ranges of only a few kilometers (Araújo et al. 2013).[3] For a small population like the ancestral Wari', keeping away from outsiders was the best protection.

Hostility to wijam was a key to survival. Wari' saw wijam as nonpersons who could be killed with impunity; they controlled a large region of western Rondônia by shooting invaders and retaliating for attacks against their own people (Conklin 1997). Operating on a principle I have called *generalized revenge* (Conklin 2008), their guerrilla warfare terrorized the countryside. Their practices of bodily mutilation (victims' corpses were often found missing heads and limbs that were taken as trophies) fed a reputation as savage, cannibalistic warriors, which was highly effective at discouraging intruders. Anthropological analyses of Amazonian alterity have highlighted the symbolic power of self/other distinctions. Wari' history shows how radical alterity had life-and-death consequences.

Commodities and epidemics were intertwined factors in relations with wijam. Wari' knew about outsiders' diseases long before contact; experiences with limited, local epidemics may have encouraged their isolationism. One story tells of a Wari' man who married a Brazilian woman and went to live with her people. His Wari' kin made several trips to visit him, from which they returned with knives, metal pots, and clothing that they liked very much. Then after one trip, they got sick and several people died. After that, they avoided any more friendships with wijam.

Caution and self-quarantine were principles in Wari' sociality. Even today, visitors are treated warily. At Santo André parties, people express concern that someone might poison the chicha or hide poison in a wall or roof. The ritual structure of parties facilitates surveillance. Visitors sleep and eat separately, in a forest camp outside the village. They perform together while hosts watch, and male visitors drink fermented chicha while most of the hosts do not. Parties usually end in a spirit of conviviality, but relations can be quickly redefined. In the past, when sickness followed a visit by people from elsewhere, Wari' cut off relations with them and closed their village to all visitors until the sickness passed.

Circulating Vitality

The collective, biosocial productivity at the heart of Wari' notions of well-being coalesces in their vision of the most potent source of human vitality, which comes from slain enemies. One motivation for men to risk the dangers of going off to kill wijam was the idea that in doing so, they acquired this powerful, health-enhancing substance. Women cheered them on as they set out to acquire it, and the highest status a man could achieve was to become *napiri*, an enemy killer who had completed the ritual transformation that produced this vitalizing substance.

Wari' believe that the enemy's invisible spirit-blood passes into the bodies of everyone who witnesses the killing. This is initially a dangerous, alien substance, and the men and boys separated themselves from the community and went into ritual seclusion for several weeks in the men's house. Reclining in large, communal hammocks, they practiced strict bodily disciplines to control the alien element. They consumed only sweet chicha, which tamed and transformed the enemy blood-spirit, making it "become Wari." Enacting the "familiarizing" logic that Fausto (1999, 2012) describes, external vitality acquired by killing was turned into health-enhancing internal generativity.

In a process resonant with female reproductive imagery (Conklin 2001b), the bellies of the men and boys swelled as they drank pot after pot of chicha. The transformed enemy substance made boys grow taller and adult men grow fatter, stronger, and more courageous. Napiri were said to live long lives and be resistant to illness. This transformation was not just an individual male achievement, but a cross-sex collaboration. Wari' emphasize the essential contribution of women and girls who worked to make the copious quantities of chicha on which the warriors' self-realization depended. Santo André elders idealize this as a loving relation between a young man and his unmarried sister. When a napiri died, he was honored with special funeral rituals, and the same rites were performed for his sister when she died.

When ritual seclusion ended and the napiri emerged with their bodies plump, sleek, and strong, they were objects of erotic desire. When they had sex, the vitalizing substance passed in their semen to their female partners. These women, in turn, grew fatter, stronger, and resistant to illness. Wari' thus conceive of primal life-vitality as the product of interdependent, cross-sex cooperation and circulation. Uniting the two schemata of Amerindian social production identified by Fausto (1999, 2012), production and consumption flowed into circulation and exchange. Value was located not in individual possession, but in the collective production and circulation of vitality. This is a central aspect of what Santos-Granero ([2009] see also chapter 3) has called *political economies of life*.

Medicine, Money, and Desire

The weight that Wari' accord to health rather than material wealth is evident in the history of how epidemics and metal tools interacted to end their independent existence in the 1950s and 1960s. Far more efficient than stone, steel axes and machetes were objects of desire. In the early twentieth century, the growing rubber economy brought an influx of Brazilians who settled in and around Wari' territory in the rubber-rich forests near the Rio Ouro Preto. Wari' raided these wijam homesteads to steal metal tools in feats of courage that became a focus of male status competition.

The *sertanistas* (backwoodsmen), whom the Brazilian government hired to pacify Wari' and open their territory's rubber wealth to capitalist extraction, used "gifts" of machetes to lure Wari' into the friendly encounters that spread disease. Wari' first allowed government agents and missionaries to enter their villages only to bring penicillin, which worked like a miracle drug that saved one life after another in those early years. Some Wari' responded to the epidemics by rejecting all things wijam, including antibiotics. In the first-contact epidemics near Kit in 1961, many Oro Eo' fled deep into the forest where they tried to live independently for two more years. In the northern Lage/Ribeirão contacts the same year, thirty Oro Mon decamped to the Rio Formosa headwaters where they held out on their own until 1969. In both cases, it ultimately was desire to see their kin, not desire for Western goods that eventually drew them out of the forest and into the epidemiological maelstrom that swept them into the orbit of state power, dependency, and commodity relations.

In the new world of manufactured goods, the things Wari' wanted most were axes, machetes, shotguns and ammunition, fishing line and hooks, flashlights and batteries (for night hunting), blankets, mosquito nets, cooking pots, and sugar. For decades, Wari' had little ability to buy things, and commodities were a persistent focus of relations with FUNAI employees, missionaries, and anthropologists.

New sources of income entered Wari' life in the late 1990s when the government began to contract some young women and men as salaried bilingual teachers and nursing assistants. After Lula da Silva, the leader of Brazil's socialist Workers' Party, became president in 2003, poor families with children began to receive conditional cash payments under the Bolsa Familia poverty-reduction program, which essentially directed a portion of Brazilian public wealth into the pockets of the poor. Combined with other government benefits, including old-age pensions for elders and maternity payments for women, this gave Wari' households regular income for the first time. The amounts of money are small; few if any villagers make it into Brazil's middle class. But Wari' have new possibilities to buy things and invest in profit-making activities.

Popular culture often represents indigenous people as nonmaterialistic or even antimaterialistic (Conklin 2010). But anyone who has spent time with native Amazonians knows that many express avid interest in commercial goods. In the 2000s when Wari' received money to spend, they joined the rest of Brazilian society in a consumer spending spree.

Outsiders tend to equate indigenous desire for commercial goods with Western consumerism and see it as crass corruption of primitive purity. This is one of the biggest tensions in relations between indigenous people and even their most sympathetic supporters. One perspective for better understanding is to realize that much indigenous materialism is a different *kind* of materialism that is relational and implicated in very indigenous modes of sociality (cf. Ewart 2014; Fisher 2000). Wari' value goods for their productive capacities: to do work, produce food, share or exchange with others, and to cultivate future-oriented relationships. Acquiring consumer goods demonstrates one's capabilities: the intercultural knowledge, skills, and social connections to move through the town and stores, as well as the relations that constitute commerce.

At Santo André, the ways Wari' have chosen to spend their new income are revealing. Tools and transportation to facilitate food production have come first. In the mid-2000s, men bought chain saws to clear fields and trails, and .22-caliber rifles for hunting. Women bought fishing equipment and butane cooking stoves. In the later 2000s, families saved to buy 8 Hp rabeta boat motors, which can navigate the shallow streams where most fertile soil and groves of useful palms, fruit trees, and Brazil nuts are located in this region. By 2010, almost every household owned a motor, and most had traded their old dugout canoes for flat-bottomed aluminum boats.

Wari' buy more commercial food now than in the past, but (at least at Santo André) the great majority of families still rely mostly on farming, fishing, and hunting and gathering. The new money's most visible effect is dietary. With the motors and money to buy fuel, people can go farther away to fish at choice fishing spots up- and downriver that used to be too distant to visit often. The community is visibly better-nourished and teeming with babies and children. In these terms, as Benjamin said, "life is good."

Conclusion

This examination of Wari' biopolitics suggests several points for thinking about wealth-focused economics and alternatives. It highlights the cultural-historical specificity of the individualization, privatization, and social fragmentation that Beck and Giddens see emerging in postindustrial risk society. Wari' have found a different path through an insecure world in which they cultivate an ethos that identifies affluence with collective prosperity and accords status to the promotion of the physical and emotional well-being of others.

The indigenous notion of health as wealth is in tune with the capabilities approach's holistic understanding of human development and with feminist emphases on the value of care in domestic household labor and caregiving professions, such as child-care workers and home health aides (cf. Waring 2003). But the Wari' case highlights how neoliberal individualism and wealth-focused relations constrain even progressive imaginations. For Wari', attachments to others are fundamental to self-realization; an individual's capacities develop not only with freedoms and personal empowerment but also in connections and commitments to other people. And a Western approach that treats care and caregivers in a framework of class and identity politics, as just one more interest group to compensate monetarily, is more limited than the relational ontology of the Wari', who treat care as the prime value in a much wider range of activities that include parenting, gardening, hunting, enemy killing, party giving, and sheltering bereaved kin. Valuing interdependencies and solidarities requires recognizing shared vulnerabilities and responsibilities as part of human development.

For centuries, writers from Montaigne and Rousseau onward have found in native Lowland South America ideas and inspiration to reflect on Western ways and Western wants. The evidence that other, more humane and satisfying ways of life are possible inspires alternative visions. Reflecting on indigenous cultures from the perspective of 1960s and 1970s cultural criticism, Sahlins described a "Zen" path to affluence by limiting material desires. Clastres saw testimony to the possibility of freedom from hierarchical power, "conceptual embodiments of the thesis that another world is possible: that there is life beyond capitalism, as there is society outside of the State" (Viveiros de Castro 2010, 15).

Today, the reflexivity and questioning that is integral to modernity is challenged to grapple especially with global inequalities of wealth and health. Competing notions of well-being and claims about public wealth are at the center of the most consequential debates and struggles. The question of how we treat collective resources, risks, and responsibilities overflows the boundaries of economics and goes to the heart of how to imagine the world in which we want to live.

Notes

1. The risk society model has been criticized for downplaying the continuing power of wealth. Wealth clearly can reduce many risks; wealthier people insulate themselves in gated communities, buy air purifiers, move to cleaner environs, and pay for better medical care. However, there also is substantial evidence for the growing power of education, information, and new social networks as other bases for status and social differentiation.

2. Key works on Amazonian personhood, embodiment, and subjectivity available in English include Descola (1994); Ewart (2013); Gow (1991); Londoño Sulkin (2012); McCallum (2001); Overing and Passes (2001); Rival and Whitehead (2001); Santos-Granero (2009, 2012); Seeger (1981); Taylor (1992, 1996); Turner (1995); Vilaça (2002, 2005); Viveiros de Castro (1998, 2004); and articles in special issues of *Tipiti: Journal of the Society for the Anthropology of Lowland South America*, volume 3(2), edited by Laura Rival, and volume 4(1–2), edited by Fernando Santos-Granero and George Mentore.

3. It is unclear whether monkeys infected with malarial parasites can transmit the infection to other monkeys or humans (Araújo et al. 2013).

References

Aranha, Ana. 2013. "A Raging River. Eye on the Amazon, January 24." *Amazon Watch*. Accessed February 7, 2014. http://amazonwatch.org/news/2013/0124-a-raging-river.

Araújo, Maisa S., Mariluce R. Messias, Marivaldo R. Figueiró, Luiz Herman S. Gil, Christian M. Probst, Newton M. Vidal, Tony H. Katsuragawa, Marco A. Krieger, Luiz H. Pereira da Silva, and Luiz S. Ozaki. 2013. "Natural *Plasmodium* Infection in Monkeys in the State of Rondônia (Brazilian Western Amazon)." *Malaria Journal* 12:180. Accessed January 31, 2014. http://www.malariajournal.com/content/12/1/180.

Beck, Ulrich. 1992. *Risk Society: Towards a New Modernity*. Thousand Oaks, CA: Sage.

Bird-David, Nurit. 1992. "Beyond the Original Affluent Society: A Culturalist Reformulation." *Current Anthropology* 33(1):25–47.

Bodley, John H. 1982. *Victims of Progress*. Palo Alto, CA: Mayfield Publishing.

Clastres, Pierre. 1987 [1974]. *Society Against the State: Essays in Political Anthropology*. New York: Zone Books.

———. 2010. *Archaeology of Violence*. Los Angeles, CA: Semiotexte.

Conklin, Beth A. 1997. "Consuming Images: Representations of Cannibalism on the Amazonian Frontier." *Anthropological Quarterly* 702:68–78.

———. 2001a. *Consuming Grief: Compassionate Cannibalism in an Amazonian Society*. Austin, TX: University of Texas Press.

———. 2001b. "Women's Blood, Warriors' Blood, and the Conquest of Vitality in Amazonia and Melanesia." In *Gender in Amazonia and Melanesia: An Exploration of the Comparative Method*, edited by Thomas Gregor and Donald Tuzin, 141–74. Berkeley, CA: University of California Press.

———. 2002. "Shamans Versus Pirates in the Amazonian Treasure Box." *American Anthropologist* 1044:1050–61.

———. 2008. "Revenge and Reproduction: The Biopolitics of Caring and Killing in Native Amazonia." In *Revenge in the Cultures of Lowland South America*, edited by Stephen Beckerman and Paul Valentine, 10–21. Gainesville, FL: University of Florida Press.

———. 2010. "For Love or Money? Indigenous Materialism and Humanitarian Agendas." In *Editing Eden: Reconsideration of Identity, Politics, and Place in Amazonia*, edited by Frank Hutchins and Patrick Wilson, 127–50. Lincoln: University of Nebraska Press.

Conklin, Beth A., and Laura R. Graham. 1995. "The Shifting Middle Ground: Brazilian Indians and Eco-Politics." *American Anthropologist* 974:695–710.

Conklin, Beth A., and Lynn M. Morgan. 1996. "Babies, Bodies, and the Production of Personhood in North America and a Native Amazonian Society." *Ethos* 244:657–94.

Daly, Herman E. 2003. "The Ilth of Nations and the Fecklessness of Policy: An Ecological Economist's Perspective." *Post-Autistic Economics Review* 22, November 24, article 1. Accessed September 17, 2013. http://www.paecon.net/PAEReview/issue22/Daly22.htm.

Descola, Philippe. 1994. *In the Society of Nature: A Native Ecology in Amazonia*. New York: Cambridge University Press.

Ewart, Elizabeth. 2014. *Space and Society in Central Brazil: A Panará Ethnography*. London: Bloomsbury Academic.

Fausto, Carlos. 1999. "Of Enemies and Pets: Warfare and Shamanism in Amazonia." *American Ethnologist* 264:933–56.

———. 2012. *Warfare and Shamanism in Amazonia*. New York: Cambridge University Press.

Fischer, Edward F. 2014. *The Good Life: Aspiration, Dignity, and the Anthropology of Wellbeing*. Stanford, CA: Stanford University Press.

Fisher, William. 2000. *Rainforest Exchanges: Industry and Community on an Amazonian Frontier*. Washington, DC: Smithsonian.

Foster, James. 2011. "Freedom, Opportunity, and Wellbeing." *Handbook of Social Choice and Welfare* 2:687–28. Amsterdam: Elsevier.

Giddens, Anthony. 1991. *Modernity and Self-Identity: Self and Society in the Late Modern Age*. Palo Alto, CA: Stanford University Press.

Gow, Peter. 1991. *Of Mixed Blood: Kinship and History in Peruvian Amazonia*. Oxford: Clarendon Press.

Graeber, David. 2011. *Debt: The First 5,000 Years*. Brooklyn, NY: Melville House Publishing.

Hurwitz, Zachary. 2014. "Grab for Profits Pushes Madeira River Past Its Limits During Historic Floods." International Rivers, March 11, 2014. Accessed April 14, 2014. http://www.internationalrivers.org/blogs/258/grab-for-profits-pushes-madeira-river-past-its-limits-during-historic-floods.

Kaplan, David. 2000. "The Darker Side of the Original Affluent Society." *Journal of Anthropological Research* 563:301–24.

Londoño Sulkin, Carlos D. 2012. *People of Substance: An Ethnography of Morality in the Colombian Amazon*. Toronto: University of Toronto Press.

McCallum, C. 2001. *Gender and Sociality: How Real People Are Made*. Oxford: Berg.

McDorman, Marian F., and T. J. Mathews. 2009. "Behind International Rankings of Infant Mortality: How U.S. Compares With Europe." *National Center for Health Statistics*, Brief 23, November. Accessed February 8, 2014. http://www.cdc.gov/nchs/data/databriefs/db23.htm.

Munn, Nancy 1986. *The Fame of Gawa: A Symbolic Study of Value Transformation in a Massim (Papua New Guinea) Society*. New York: Cambridge University Press.

Mythen, Gabe. 2004. *Ulrich Beck: A Critical Introduction to the Risk Society*. London: Sterling Press.

Nugent, Stephen. 2000. "Good Risk, Bad Risk: Modernisation and Amazonia." In *Risk Revisited*, edited by Patricia Caplan, 226–48. London: Pluto Press.

Nussbaum, Martha. 2011. *Creating Capabilities: The Human Development Approach*. Cambridge, MA: Belknap Press.

Osava, Mario. 2014. "Deforestation in the Andes Triggers Amazon 'Tsunami.'" Inter Press Service, April 16, 2014. Accessed April 16, 2014. http://www.ipsnews.net/2014/04/deforestation-andes-triggers-amazon-tsunami/.

Overing, Joanna, and Alan Passes, eds. 2001. *The Anthropology of Love and Anger: The Aesthetics of Conviviality in Native Amazonia*. London: Routledge.

Rival, Laura, ed. 2005. "Special Section: The Body in Amazonia." *Tipiti: Journal of the Society for the Anthropology of Lowland South America* 3(2):105–95.

Rival, Laura, and Neil Whitehead, eds. 2001. *Beyond the Visible and the Material: The Amerindianization of Society in the Work of Peter Rivière*. New York: Oxford University Press.

Sahlins, Marshall. 1972. "The Original Affluent Society." In *Stone Age Economics*, Marshall Sahlins, 1–39. Chicago: Aldine.

Santos-Granero, Fernando, ed. 2009. *The Occult Life of Things: Native Amazonian Theories of Materiality and Personhood*. Tucson: University of Arizona Press.

———. 2012. "Beinghood and People-Making in Native Amazonia: A Constructional Approach with a Perspectival Coda." *HAU: Journal of Ethnographic Theory* 2(1):181–211.

Santos-Granero, Fernando, and George Mentore, eds. 2006. "In the World and about the World: Amerindian Modes of Knowledge." Special issue in honor of Prof. Joanna Overing. *Tipiti: Journal of the Society for the Anthropology of Lowland South America* 4(1–2).

Seeger, Anthony. 1981. *Nature and Society in Central Brazil: The Suyá Indians of Central Brazil*. Cambridge, MA: Harvard University Press.

Sen, Amartya. 1985. *Commodities and Capabilities*. Oxford: Oxford University Press.

Solway, Jacqueline. 2006. "'The Original Affluent Society': Four Decades On." In *The Politics of Egalitarianism: Theory and Practice*, edited by Jacqueline Solway, 66–77. New York: Berghann Books.

Taylor, Anne Christine. 1992. "Remembering to Forget: Identity, Memory, and Mourning among the Jívaro." *Man* 28(4):653–78.

———. 1996. "The Soul's Body and Its States: An Amazonian Perspective on Being Human." *Journal of the Royal Anthropological Institute* 2(2):201–15.

Turner, Terence. 1995. "Social Body and Embodied Subject: Bodiliness, Subjectivity, and Sociality among the Kayapo." *Cultural Anthropology* 10(2):1 43–53.

Uzendoski, Michael. 2005. *The Napo Runa of Amazonian Ecuador*. Champaign, IL: University of Illinois Press.

Vilaça, Aparecida. 2002. "Making Kin out of Others in Amazonia." *Journal of the Royal Anthropological Institute* 8(2):347–65.

———. 2005. "Chronically Unstable Bodies: Reflections on Amazonian Corporalities." *Journal of the Royal Anthropological Institute* 11(3):445–64.

———. 2010. *Strange Enemies: Indigenous Agency and Scenes of Encounter in Amazonia*. Durham, NC: Duke University Press.

Viveiros de Castro, Eduardo. 1998. "Cosmological Deixis and Amerindian Perspectivism." *Journal of the Royal Anthropological Institute* 4(3):469–88.

———. 2004. "Exchanging Perspectives: The Transformation of Objects into Subjects in Amerindian Ontologies." *Common Knowledge* 10(3):463–84.

———. 2010. "Introduction: The Untimely, Again." In *The Archaeology of Violence*, Pierre Clastres, 9–51. Los Angeles, CA: Semiotexte.

Wallace, Scott. 2013. "Rain Forest for Sale." *National Geographic* 223(1):82–119.

Waring, Marilyn. 2003. "Counting for Something! Recognising Women's Contribution to the Global Economy Through Alternative Accounting Systems." *Gender and Development* 111:35–43.

WHO (World Health Organization). 1948. "Preamble to the Constitution of the World Health Organization." *Official Records of the World Health Organization* 2, 100. http://www.who.int/governance/eb/who_constitution_en.pdf.

CHAPTER THREE

Public Wealth and the Yanesha Struggle for Vitality

FERNANDO SANTOS-GRANERO

During a long talk about land with Berna Pascual Coronel, founder of the settlement of Alto Yurinaki and last active Yanesha priestly leader, he said to me in a pensive but firm voice, "Dios ha dado vida para todos; ha dado tierras para todos; único falta marcar dónde para saber que uno ahí tiene" (God has given life to everybody; he has given land to everybody; the only thing we have to do is to mark where, so as to know that one has it there).[1] At the time, 1977, I was an undergraduate student heavily influenced by Marxist theory and mostly interested in the material aspects of the Yanesha people's increasing engagement in market-oriented activities. So I took Berna's statement as an instance of ideological shift from a traditional perspective in which land was viewed as everyone's to a more capitalist conception in which it became imperative to demarcate boundaries in order to secure ownership. It was only much later that I noticed in Berna's speech that "life" occupied a more prominent place than "land" as a godsent gift. And it took me even longer to realize that Yanesha political economy revolved around life as the scarcest resource.

When asserting that Yato' Yos, the creator god, had given life and land to humanity, Coronel used the Spanish expression *para todos*, a translation of the Yanesha term *allohuenacop*. This Yanesha term, meaning literally "for everybody," has, however, the double sense of something that is meant "for all" members of a given group and, at the same time, is "common" to all members of the group (see Duff-Tripp 1998, 62, 488). The term does not imply, however, that such common things necessarily "belong" to the collectivity or that they have the character of collective "property"; especially since Yanesha assert that people can only own what they have made with their own hands or what they have caused to be by means of their ritual practices or the power of their thoughts. Rather, it denotes that such things are available to, and can be used by, the members of the collectivity because they were created for everybody or are meant to be shared with everybody. Allohuenacop is, thus, the closest Yanesha equivalent of the Western notion of public wealth here understood not as public property or national wealth but rather as the totality of valued things—whether material or not—over which a collectivity claims to have rights of usufruct.

Among the Yanesha of the Selva Central region of Peru, public wealth can be generated at three levels. At the broad cosmological level public wealth consists of all the things and beings that Yato' Yos and the gods of *yompor* (our father) category have created for the benefit of their human creatures, the Yanesha. These creations include land, animals, plants, mountains, lakes, rivers, salt mines, clay deposits, and symbolically significant landmarks. In other words, these creations represent a kind of *environmental wealth* from which the Yanesha derive their sustenance and over which they consider to have exclusive rights of use as a collective. Especially important in this divinely produced type of wealth are land, game animals, and food plants, as well as those animals and plants that, despite not being edible, are attributed supernatural powers that can be harnessed for the benefit of human beings. Until recently, this kind of public wealth was relatively abundant, and it was taken for granted. It was only when colonization intensified and vast portions of the Yanesha traditional territory were occupied by foreign colonists that land and forest resources came to be regarded as crucial components of collective wealth at the local and supralocal levels.

At the more restricted level of interpersonal relations, public wealth consists of the totality of harmonious relations that members of a given collectivity establish with other people within and without their village by virtue of being *amueraña*, a personal attribute that comprises the qualities of being generous, loving, caring, and compassionate. The establishment of harmonious or friendly relations with strangers or with people with whom one has quarreled, described by the term *amo'tsteñets*, results in the creation of different ego-centered networks of sociality, the sum of which can be regarded as constituting the *convivial wealth* of a particular collectivity (Santos-Granero 1991, 43). In its narrowest sense, the term *yamo'tsesha'* encompasses a person's nuclear family and closest relatives; in its broadest sense, however, it can comprise all of the Yanesha as a big family and even beyond. This kind of wealth is considered to be the basis of a good, tranquil life, which is the Yanesha people's greatest aspiration. Today, the maximum expression of convivial wealth is a community's capacity to gather large numbers of people when celebrating a collective festivity, such as a soccer championship or the celebration of the community's foundation date. This resonates with the Kïsêdjê and Wari', who regard large collective musical performances in and of themselves as a form of public wealth (see Seeger, chapter 1, and Conklin, chapter 2).

At the intermediate local level public wealth encompasses everything that an individual obtains from powerful others to ensure the life, good health, and reproduction of the members of the collectivity to which he or she belongs. These powerful others include not only a large range of gods and spiritual beings but also other human collectivities that are believed to possess supernatural forms of knowledge and power. Whereas in principle this kind of *generative wealth* can be produced by any individual, most often it results from the efforts of three types of specialists: *cornesha'* (priests), *pa'llerr* (shamans), and settlement leaders or *am̃cha'tarẽt* (strong men). The prestige and power of these specialists is based on their possession of the necessary skills to obtain vitality and other life-giving assets from alien others that are thought to be indispensable for the survival of individuals and the collectivity. In the recent past, such assets have included life-giving prayers and offerings, sacred *cosham̃ñats* songs, and divine portents obtained by priests from the higher divinities; mystical techniques of healing and protection acquired by shamans from the masters/owners of a variety of animals, plants, and spirits; and life-ensuring extraordinary things, such as metal tools, land titles, health posts, and schools obtained by settlement leaders from white people.

Environmental, convivial, and generative forms of public wealth constitute the pillars of well-being and *cohuen corramñats* (a good life) as the Yanesha understand it. They are indispensable to guarantee the nourishment, good health, moral formation, and reproductive capacities of Yanesha individuals, as well as a beautiful, harmonious, and tranquil life conducive to the perpetuation of the collectivity as a whole. In other words, these three forms of public wealth are crucial to ensure Yanesha life. In a political economy in which life force is considered to be the scarcest resource, and competition for vitality between all living beings is rampant, the abundance of such forms of public wealth can only be accrued through the appeasement, containment, or predation of alien others. This is especially true of generative public wealth, which is the focus of the present chapter.

In this chapter, I examine the production of generative wealth among the Yanesha from a historical perspective focusing on the period between 1910 and the 1960s. This was a time when the Yanesha priest/temple complex still flourished, but massive colonization and increasing participation in the market had begun to transform Yanesha society. Most of the information used in this chapter comes from recorded interviews and unrecorded talks with a large number of Yanesha elders during my 1977 and 1983–1984 fieldwork. These men and women were young in the 1920s, 1930s, and 1940s when there were at least twenty ceremonial centers fully functioning in Yanesha territory, and they had firsthand knowledge of the activities of priests, shamans, and village headmen (Santos-Granero 1991, 242). In the first section, I discuss the main pillars of the Yanesha *political economy of life*. In the following three sections, I examine how priests, shamans, and chiefs engaged in a permanent quest for vitality on behalf of their respective followers. I focus on the lives of three renowned specialists: Santos Ortiz, priest of Palmaso; Valerio Ambrosio, master shaman from Pucharini; and Berna Pascual Coronel, founder and long-time headman of the settlement of Alto Yurinaki. I argue that their activities produced particular forms of knowledge that were indispensable to ensure the lives of their followers and that such life-giving knowledge was considered an important instance of public wealth. In the conclusion, I compare generative to environmental and convivial types of public wealth to call attention to its transient nature in a context of interspecific strife for vitality.

The Yanesha Political Economy of Life

The basis for the central role of vitality in Yanesha political economy and its importance as an essential component of Yanesha notions of public wealth is to be found in the Yanesha myth of creation. According to this myth, everything that exists today was created either by Yato' Yos, Our Grandfather Yos, or by his older classificatory brother, Yosoper (Smith 1976a, 84–85).[2] Yato' Yos's first creation was a flat earth that he created by mixing mud (some say excrements) with the breast milk of his mother (others say sister) and insufflating his divine breath into the mixture; it was under the one in which the divinities lived. As soon as he created this earth, however, his jealous brother took it over. Yato' Yos asked him for some mud, and with it, he created a second earth in between the one inhabited by the divinities and that taken over by Yosoper. He then went on to create, through the same procedure, humans, plants, animals, birds, fish, and all the beings that exist nowadays. But for every being that he created, Yosoper created many more in the same image. Some say that, angry with his meddling brother, Yato' Yos cursed each of these beings and turned them into noxious, venomous, or stinking species (Smith 1976a, 85). Others say that it was Yosoper who, out of meanness and ineptitude, transformed all of his brother's creations into harmful beings. In either case, Yato' Yos is credited for having created everything that is good, edible, and sublime, whereas Yosoper is attributed to the origin of all that is noxious, evil, or sorcerous.

At the beginning of time, all the beings created by Yato' Yos, including plants, animals, and even some objects, had a human shape. They were human persons endowed with a portion of the soul of the creator god. Yanesha myth tellers assert that Yato' Yos created the five-layered cosmos and all the beings that inhabit it by using his *parets* (divine power). This kind of power is shared by all divinities, who, for this reason, are known collectively as *partsesha'*, (the powerful ones). In creative acts, this generic divine power assumes material form as *pa'toreñ* (a divinity's vital breath). The related term, *a'toreñets*, has the double meaning of "to blow," as in blowing on a fire, and "to bless," in the sense of infusing something with divine vital breath.

Yanesha thinkers claim that the source of pa'toreñ is the soul of the creator god, known as *parets puecamqueñ* (divine powerful soul). They say that through the act of creation, which entailed the blowing of his vital breath, Yato' Yos infused a portion of his divine soul into all living beings. Accordingly, all living beings are believed to possess *camuequeñets* (a soul), which endows them with animacy, consciousness, will, and agency.[3] Yanesha people use to say "yecamquëñpa yecheñ ñeñt̃ yacrra'tene" (it is the soul that we have which gives us life). And they use the term *o'rrerrñats* to signify respiration, as well as life. For this reason, I have suggested elsewhere that the notion of vitality is a better translation for camuequeñets than "soul" (Santos-Granero 2006). Given that the camuequeñets of a person is an individual manifestation of *parets puecamqueñ*, the all-encompassing soul of the creator god, it is thought that when a person dies, his or her vitality rejoins that of the creator god in Yomporesho, the layer of the cosmos in which the higher divinities live.[4] A similar thing happens with plants and animals, whose vitalities, once they die, also rejoin that of the creator god. Thus, from a Yanesha point of view, vitalities are in constant circulation between the creator god and his living creatures, and between this earth, known as Rromuepatsro (the land of death), and Yomporesho (the land of the higher divinities).

It is believed that the vitality or vital breath of the creator god is unequally distributed among his living creatures, which would explain why some species are more abundant than others. But, according to Yanesha thinkers, it is also subject to important imbalances as the result of interspecies predation. In order to subsist, humans, animals, plants, spirits, and even certain objects must prey on other species. Predation may take a physical form, as when a jaguar kills a deer or a man kills a peccary.

Alternatively, it may assume a metaphysical form as when an animal steals the vitality of a human being, or white people magically deprive the Yanesha of game animals in order to starve them. In either case, interspecific predation causes life forces to be in permanent circulation. As long as members of different species or kinds of people maintain certain equilibrium in their mutual predation, imbalances in the distribution of vitality may be kept at bay. But as soon as members of one species are perceived as preying excessively on those of another, interspecific predation escalates, the distribution of vitality becomes even more skewed, and existing imbalances increase.

Yanesha people are very aware of the risks posed by mutual predation and the escalation of interspecific warfare. When boys are trained as hunters and fishermen, they are told repeatedly that they should avoid directing their efforts to only one species of game or fish lest they anger the *po'mo'ya'car* (spirit master/owner) of that species. In such situations, the angry spirit master/owner may appear to the transgressor as a giant form of the animal it owns in order to kill him, or it may steal a portion of the transgressor's vitality, which the latter experiences as a form of disease. Boys are also told not to always go to the same hunting or fishing spot so they do not overhunt or overfish them and offend the *mellañoteñ* spirit guardians of the animals living in those places. When this happens, the enraged guardians can also avenge themselves by depriving the greedy hunter or fisherman of part of their vitality. Animal master/owners, which are said to be the "mothers" or "fathers" of a given species, are similarly incensed when a hunter shoots one of its wards without killing it and leaves the wounded prey to bleed to death in the forest. Such acts are regarded as inexcusable wastes of precious life and are punished either by stealing the insensible hunter's soul, transforming him into an animal of the same species and thus compensating the original loss, or making him lose his way in the forest.

Girls being trained in gardening practices are told that when digging manioc tubers or harvesting maize, beans, or peanuts, they should collect all the produce of the plants they cut, dig up, or harvest. Otherwise, it is said that the spirit master/owners of these plants may avenge the wastefulness of the selfish gardener by stealing part of her vitality. Boys and girls are also taught that they should never throw animal or plant parts—bones, fish scales, peels, or seeds—into the fire because such an act destroys the vitalities of these beings, impairing their reproduction, and is regarded as hostile by their spirit master/owners. As a result, the latter may avenge the act by sending disease to the transgressor or making their wards barren—in the case of fruit trees, for instance—or scarce in the case of game animals and fish.

The struggle for vitality also involves conflicts between humans and certain classes of spirits. It is said that when a person or family draws too much water from a certain stream or river, the *pocoy* water spirits might take revenge on the children of the household by making them sick (Wise 1958, 8). Pocoy spirits, also called *sirenas* (mermaids) in Spanish, regard excessive drawing of water from their aquatic world as a threat to their life and survival. Unless they are propitiated through the mediation of a shaman or diviner, they are prone to attack those whom they feel have attacked them (Wise 1958, 8). The same happens if people bathe too much in a given stream. Other spirits, like *oneñeť*, *jo'*, and *pane* are malevolent and do not need to be provoked. Being followers of Yosoper, they are envious of the human creatures that Yato' Yos created and enjoy harassing and eating their vitalities.

The struggle for life force also involves other kinds of human beings. The ancient Inka, personified in Yanesha mythology as the figure Enc, and white people, known as *ocanesha'*, are considered to be extremely powerful nonhuman kinds of people (see Guzmán-Gallegos, chapter 4, and Conklin, chapter 2, for similar perceptions of white people among the Amazonian Kichwa and Wari', respectively). Enc and ocanesha' have a human shape, but they possess superhuman powers and lack the moral values that characterize "real" human people. According to myth, Enc was sent by the creator god to this earth to help his human creatures. But he turned into an exploitative, authoritarian, and abusive leader. He forced the Yanesha to work without reward, replaced legitimate Yanesha leaders as he wished, and imposed forms of sexual policing that were totally alien to Yanesha people. Worst of all, he ordered the killing of many Yanesha men and women for minor transgressions. White people, in turn, are considered to be children of Yosoper. They are said to have appeared in this earth due to the irresponsibility and arrogance of Enc, who carelessly opened the mystical doors that kept them shut in the underworld and did not bother to close them. White people are viewed as exploiters and oppressors who first killed Enc's followers to steal their riches, then invaded the lands of the Yanesha, and killed many of them. They forced the survivors to work for them. To make things worse, the white invaders stole Yompor Yompuer, the technological god, from the Yanesha. For this reason, it is said, nowadays white people are rich and multiply greatly (*mereñets*), whereas Yanesha people remain poor and do not increase as much. Inka and white people are considered to be *amtsañ* (great killers), and they are thought to use their supernatural powers to deprive the Yanesha of their life force and means of living. It is against this backdrop of generalized competition for vitality that Yanesha notions of generative wealth acquire full meaning.

Priestly Forms of Public Wealth: Santos Ortiz

The last cornesha' of the ceremonial center of Palmaso, Santos Ortiz, better known as Tsachopeñ, is remembered as a wise and astute leader. His house of worship, which was located in the valley of Oxapampa, functioned until the early 1920s. He and his followers worshipped the gods Yompor Yompere, Yachor Mamas, Yemonasheñ Senyac, and Nepañer Senyac, who were transformed into stone by the sun god before he ascended to the upper world (figure 3.1).[5]

Tsachopeñ lived at a time of great turmoil. In 1847, after one hundred years of relative isolation from white-mestizo society, following Juan Santos's 1742 messianic and anticolonial uprising, the Peruvian government began an aggressive project of reconquest of the Selva Central region. Its first phase entailed the occupation of the valley of Chanchamayo and the destruction of Yanesha—and Ashaninka—gardens, temples, and ironworks (Santos-Granero 1988). The second phase, begun in 1881, involved the occupation of the valley of Chorobamba after a combined epidemic of smallpox and yellow fever decimated the local Yanesha and weakened their resistance (Barclay and Santos 1980, 48). In the following years Peruvian and Tyrolese colonists gradually occupied most of the lands in this valley. The despoiling of Yanesha lands was not, however, achieved

FIGURE 3.1. Stone gods in the ancient site of Palmaso, valley of Oxapampa. Photo by Fernando Santos-Granero.

without resistance. In 1898, the local Yanesha united with their Palcazu neighbors and began a systematic attack of colonist homesteads aimed at expelling them from their territory (Orden Franciscana 1900). Unfortunately, the appearance of a new, unidentified epidemic changed the course of events. Arguing that the epidemic had been sent by white people in revenge for Yanesha hostility, Tsachopeñ, the priest of Palmaso, persuaded his followers to depose their arms (Smith 1976b, 28). He feared that the white people were set to exterminate the Yanesha and sought to appease them by putting an end to the hostilities.

What I know about Tsachopeñ and the temple of Palmaso derives mostly from interviews and talks that I had in 1984 with his grandson, Pedro Ortiz, and from a brief monograph that Father Manuel Navarro wrote in 1924. Pedro was born around 1904 and was a teenager in the years previous to the abandonment of the ceremonial center, which must have occurred around 1920. In his 1924 work Navarro (1967 [1924], 390) reports that the temple of Palmaso, known as Capilla de los Chunchos (Indians' Chapel), had only recently been abandoned. This was a critical time for the Yanesha of the Chorobamba Valley. They had been defeated and displaced from their lands, and they were in a clear process of demographic decline. Navarro (1967 [1924], 391) notes that by then Yanesha couples "barely [had] one or two children, and sometimes none. . . . And if to this, we add the ravages that any epidemic causes among them, it is easy to understand the extinction that is observable every day in the midst of this unfortunate tribe."

Yanesha people were convinced that the epidemics had been brought by the white people to decimate them and that this was the source of their demographic decline. It is not surprising, then, that Tsachopeñ's main pursuit during those critical years was praying to the stone gods of Palmaso for vitality and abundance. According to Pedro, his grandfather,

> prayed in the early morning and before dusk. He asked Our Father for health, strength and courage for his followers, so that they would not grow old and die too soon. He prayed so that his followers would not fall ill and would not be affected by sorcerous attacks. He also prayed so that cultivated plants would grow strong and gardens would produce abundantly; so that there would be enough manioc, plantains, and all kinds of foodstuffs to eat. And he prayed so that game animals would be abundant and people would have enough game meat.

These prayers (*ma'yocheñets*) were a central aspect of the ceremonies held at the house of worship. Tsachopeñ summoned his followers regularly to gather in the ceremonial center to celebrate and worship the divinities.

According to Pedro, Tsachopeñ's followers "came to listen to what the cornesha' had to say and to learn how they should pray to the divinities."

Also central to temple ceremonies were offerings of manioc beer to Yompor Yompere. This was a very thick special brew prepared by the women who attended the ceremonies. It was called *yompor po'rrartsor* (Our Father's food). Pedro recalled that

> at dawn, they offered Our Father food and manioc beer. They put it in a small seat made of balsa wood. There they worshipped Our Father, so that he would grant us his blessing and would guarantee the abundance of all that which we need to eat and live. When the cornesha' finished praying, he took the manioc beer from the balsa wood seat and handed it over to his followers to distribute among those present.

Worship of the divinities through prayers and offerings is known by the term *čhoreta'teñets*, the root of which, *a'čhor-*, means "to blow." This refers to the act by which the cornesha' blows his breath and prayers into the offered manioc beer. Smith (1976a, 245) asserts that the ritual blowing of the consecrated manioc beer "imitates the primordial blowing by which Yompor Ror is said to share his life force and his fertilizing breath with the Amuesha, game animals, and food plants."[6] He adds that "through this rite, the Amuesha return to Yompor a portion of that which he originally shared with them." Pedro told me that in exchange for the offerings of prayers and manioc beer, Yompor Yompere infused the brew with his *po'rrerrña* (breath), *po'huamenc* (strength), and *pa'nateña* (protection), an act known as *a'ĩoreñets* (to bless through blowing). Through this reciprocal, though asymmetrical, exchange with the stone god Yanesha, people sought to increase their stock of vitality that was depleted by the invading whites.

Pedro also said that the ceremonies held by Tsachopeñ and his followers at Palmaso "were meant to celebrate (*coshame'teñets*) and show their love (*morrenteñets*) for the divinities."[7] The idiom *coshame'teñets* refers to the act of rejoicing in celebration of the divinities through the dancing and singing of special kinds of songs known as *coshamñats*, which are sung a cappella or with the accompaniment of panpipes or drums. Coshamñats songs are said to have been created by the divinities and to have been made known only to those who engaged in a quest for a divine revelation through prolonged fasting, vigils, and sometimes the ingestion of hallucinogens. Yanesha people consider coshamñats music as "a powerful force in itself, capable of producing the profoundest of transformations in the order of things" (Smith 1976a, 167–68). Evidence of this is the power attributed to certain coshamñats songs to increase a variety of plants and animals. In more general terms, however, the power of cosham̃ñats music, songs, and dances lies in the fact that when performed by large groups of people, they make the divinities rejoice in exchange for which they bestow their blessings on the performers under the form of vitality and generative force.

Once introduced into the human world, cosham̃ñats songs are passed from one custodian to another as valued items of mystical knowledge (a brief sample of a cosham̃ñats song in the panpipe style can be heard at Sancahuarero (canción yanesha), http://corinto.pucp.edu.pe/sen/node/123.html). Smith (1976a, 181) has suggested that "the Amuesha treat the knowledge of songs as a form of wealth. Song knowledge, like knowledge of curing rites, magic plants, rituals for hunting success, and so on is one of the few items within the culture that is actively accumulated and whose accumulation bestows a degree of power and prestige." It should be noted, however, that in order to become items of wealth, cosham̃ñats songs have to be shared with everybody in periodic collective ceremonies. It is not the knowledge but the public performance of cosham̃ñats songs that transforms them from items of personal property into items of public wealth. Pedro told me that Tsachopeñ was renowned not only for the large number of cosham̃ñats songs he knew and sung but also for having received many divine revelations in the form of cosham̃ñats songs, one of which bears his name: Tsachope'narečh (Smith 1976a, 282).

The temple of Palmaso was also famous for its sacred fire, which was always kept burning. Known as *cantell* or *yompor poyoročhen*, (Our Father's portent), these fires were said to have appeared in the forest without human intervention. They were regarded as a manifestation of the strength and power of Yompor Ror, the sun god, but also of other divinities. They were thought to be portents of the imminent end of the world, which were revealed to priests in search of a divine message. Such priests kept the god-sent fire in their own houses of worship, but sometimes they shared it with other cornesha'. This, according to Pedro, was the origin of the fire worshipped in Palmaso, which was a manifestation of Yompor Camañter, the solar divinity that illuminates the earth when Yompor Ror is tired.

Prayers, offerings, coshamñats songs, and sacred fires were the main components of priestly forms of public wealth. Although particular individuals could claim to be the owners or temporary custodians of some of these items, insofar as they had made them appear or caused them to be through the entreating of yompor divinities and mellañoteñ spirits, these were considered to belong to the collectivity of followers because they were thought to have been created for their common benefit, and they acquired their maximum generative power when shared in contexts of convivial rejoicing between the Yanesha and the creator gods.

Shamanic Forms of Public Wealth: Valerio Ambrosio

Pa'llerr (tobacco shamans) are considered to be the most powerful of the Yanesha traditional healers. Few, however, are considered to be *pa'llerr etso'ter* (shaman with supreme mastery). Valerio Ambrosio was one such masterful shaman. He did not only dominate the techniques of tobacco shamanism but was also a reputed *apartañ* (herbalist) and *achyo'tañ* (diviner), a combination that Yanesha people consider to be the most effective in curing diseases. In addition, it was said that he possessed six jaguar familiars. I never met Valerio, since by 1977 he had been dead for several years. But two of his sons, Julián and Marín, were kind enough to share with me their recollections of their father. Julián, who was trained by his father but had quit before becoming a fully fledged shaman, was particularly helpful. He provided me with rich and vivid descriptions of his father's shamanic practices.

Valerio Ambrosio was head of one of the four families that founded the settlement of Alto Yurinaki in the early 1950s. He was born in Pucharini, a settlement on the shores of the Upper Perene River, but he moved to Alto Yurinaki to escape from Andean colonist pressures. There, according to Julián, his father became so renowned that he not only cured the people of Alto Yurinaki but was often invited to go to far-away settlements to cure patients in exchange for small in-kind payments, such as smoked fished, game meat, chamairo sticks, and cotton bags. After determining, through the divination of coca leaves, whether the cause of the disease was a water spirit, the spirit of a stone, an evil insect, or a human sorcerer, he prepared himself to fight the evil agent. He first sucked from the patient's body the disease-inducing sorcerous objects that were harming him or her. Then he kept vigil all night long while he chewed coca, drank tobacco juice, and "fought" hard against the evil agent that caused the illness until he defeated it. The art of healing, described by the term *a'crrateñets*, is understood by the Yanesha as the act of giving life, either by curing or feeding a person. By fighting off the human and nonhuman sorcerous beings that prey upon Yanesha people, curing shamans seek to restore a certain balance in the circulation of vitality in which all living beings are involved.

Although a central aspect of Valerio's shamanic practices, healing was not, however, the only ritual activity that he performed on behalf of the collectivity. Equally important was the ritual protection against evil beings that he extended over the entire settlement. The term *cohuampeñets*, used to describe this action, also designates the ritual protection granted by parents and master shamans to confined girls during puberty rituals or shamanic apprentices during their training, both times when they are particularly vulnerable to supernatural attacks. According to Julián, his father used to say that dusk was a dangerous time when a host of malevolent beings lurk around human settlements in search of food, that is, people's vitalities. For this reason, he recommended staying awake late and getting up several times during the night so as to avoid being vulnerable to the attacks of evil beings. He himself slept very little. Julian said,

> at night my father used to go to the small men's house and sit next to the fire to chew coca. Sometimes he spent whole nights keeping vigil. On such occasions, he divined with coca to discover whatever evils threatened the village. Our house was located on top of a hill overlooking the settlement. He used to extend his arm pointing at the village and asked coca if there were any imminent dangers. He took a bunch of coca leaves, put it in between his hands and blew on them, praying to Our Father. Then he chewed the coca leaves and read in the coca whether the village was threatened by some evil. Coca talked to him and told him whether someone would fall ill or die, or whether some evil or enemy was about to arrive in the village.

Yanesha say that the two most common categories of malevolent beings are downriver jaguar spirits and demonic spirits of the oneñet̃ category.

Jaguar spirits are said to live deep in the mountains. There are several different species, some which live *topo* (downriver) and others *teno* (upriver). Yanesha people say that upriver jaguars are benevolent and protective, whereas downriver jaguars are always evil. However, since this opposition is relative, insofar as it depends on the speaker's location, what the system really implies is that local jaguars are good, whereas nonlocal, alien jaguars are bad. These latter jaguars are generally of the type known as *onnoma'yarr* (bee jaguars). They have reddish fur with black spots and are said to visit upriver areas in order to catch and eat people. Since the time that Patonell, the mother of jaguars, killed the human mother of the sun god, and in revenge, the latter almost exterminated jaguars, Yanesha have considered jaguars as enemies of the human race. According to Julián, whenever his father Valerio divined that a downriver jaguar was approaching the village, he sent his jaguar familiars to fight against it.

> My father's jaguar spirits summoned all the flesh-eating animals of the region, and since jaguars are the "fathers" of all animals, they obeyed their orders. Jaguars know all the animals well, and if one of them failed

to answer their call, they punished him with death. My father had two jaguar familiars in his bag under the guise of stones with the shape of a jaguar paw. When he needed them he made the stones turn into actual jaguars to reject the intruders.

According to Marín, Julián's brother, downriver jaguars used to travel to upriver areas in November at the beginning of the rainy season when the Yanesha would be fat after several months of dry-season abundance of fish, game, and food crops. They would come out of their mountain dwellings and go upriver to hunt Yanesha. Valerio, his father, made sure that that the downriver jaguars would not succeed in killing any of his followers.

The spirits commanded by Oneñet̃—oneñet̃, pante, and jo'—are equally hostile to human beings. They produce diseases known as *e'lle'cheñets*. Oneñet̃ is said to be a follower of Yosoper, brother of the creator god and ruler of the underworld. He lives on this earth, and Yosoper can send him to do whatever he wishes, including acts of aggression against human beings, who were the main creation of his brother, Yato' Yos, and whom Yosoper hates. But Oneñet̃ can also act out of his own will to harm human beings and reduce their numbers. According to Marín, Oneñet̃ enjoys killing people by sending them Morpho butterflies, moths, locusts, fireflies, or other evil insects, which enter into their bodies and eat their vitalities. Waiting to catch human beings, Oneñet̃'s associates, in turn, are said to lie in ambush along forest trails, rivers, and streams. Yanesha people know that someone has died as the result of an encounter with these kinds of spirits, because the body of the deceased shows black handprints where the spirit touched him or her. Once a year these malevolent spirits visit Yanesha settlements en masse in search for food. They wander around in groups invisible to human eyes and look for traces of human presence as hunters do when looking for animal tracks or listening to the noises made by game animals. Whenever they hear the sounds of humans singing and dancing, they approach the place at dawn when the party has finished, and everybody is resting. Then, when a woman goes to the river to fetch water or when a man goes into the forest to relieve himself, one of the evil spirits appears to them under the guise of their lover. If the person speaks to the evil spirit, when they go back home they fall ill and, almost immediately, die.

Valerio Ambrosio was renowned for his ability to fend off evil spirits and downriver jaguars. Although the Yanesha would agree that Valerio's knowledge of healing and ritual protection techniques belonged to him, insofar as he had obtained it from a number of plant and animal spirits through an arduous period of training, they would also affirm that such knowledge was an important component of their public wealth; for it acquired its full value when used on their behalf, that is, allohuenacop.

Chiefly Forms of Public Wealth: Berna Pascual Coronel

Founder and long-time headman of Alto Yurinaki, Berna Pascual Coronel, remembered by most simply as Coronel, was one of the first Yanesha leaders to obtain land titles for his settlement. In 1977, when I met him, he continued to be highly respected not only in his community but throughout Yanesha territory. He claimed to have traveled to Lima, Peru's capital, ninety-three times and was reputed to have a deep knowledge of "the ways of the whites." Most of the information in this section comes from talks I had with him, as well as from historical investigations by Frederica Barclay and myself.

In the late 1940s, Coronel, who was by then twenty-two years old, became a disciple of cornesha' Corsoñ-Domingo Cruz Espíritu, who had formed a large *puerahua* (house of worship) in the valley of Eneñaso. When, in 1954, Corsoñ decided to move his temple to Alto Yurinaki in order to escape from increasing colonist pressures, Coronel moved with him. At the time, there were in this area—located on the northern banks of the Upper Perene River—only a few dispersed families that had little interaction with each other. Corsoñ and Coronel, joined shortly after by Berna Dionisio Picón, who had come from Loma Linda, and shaman Valerio Ambrosio (discussed above), from Pucharini, constituted the core around which the settlement of Alto Yurinaki soon coalesced.

The area in which they settled belonged legally to the Peruvian Corporation Company, an organization formed by the British holders of Peruvian debt bonds. In 1889, the corporation received a two-million-hectare land grant in the Selva Central region along both banks of the Perene River (Barclay 1989, 38). It was in this area, which overlapped with large tracts of the Yanesha and Ashaninka traditional territories, that the corporation established the Perene Colony. The government concession stipulated that the Peruvian Corporation had the obligation to colonize the area with European settlers. The company did not comply with this requisite; they established instead seven large plantations for the production of high-quality coffee. These were tended mostly by hired Andean laborers and, to a lesser extent, by local Yanesha and

Ashaninka. By 1946, a high demographic increase at the national level and greater pressure over land had created much discontent over the Perene Colony's monopoly of lands in the Selva Central region. As a result, large numbers of Andean colonists in search for free lands invaded the colony from the west and south.

At the time, when Coronel moved to Alto Yurinaki, the Peruvian Corporation had already started to expand its plantations toward the valley of Yurinaki, whereas colonists of Andean and German origin from the valley of Villa Rica were advancing southward toward the same area (Barclay 1989, 228). The Yanesha, led by cornesha' Corsoñ, who acted as the first settlement leader—am̃cha'tareʔ in Yanesha or *capitán* in local Spanish—asked the company to grant his people a land concession in the valley. The company dismissed his request (Barclay 1989, 228). After Corsoñ's death in 1956, settlement leadership passed to Dionisio Picón, with Coronel acting as deputy chief. At the same time, Coronel replaced Corsoñ as new cornesha'.[8]

That same year large numbers of colonists coming from the valley of Villa Rica invaded the valley of Yurinaki. The local Yanesha informed the company about the invasion and helped its administrator expel the invaders from company lands (Barclay 1989, 229). According to Coronel, it was in this juncture that he and Dionisio Picón started demanding land titles from the company. They had realized that once more white-mestizos sought to exterminate the Yanesha, and that without titles, there would soon come the time when colonists would force them out of their lands. They would then be unable to feed their families. In such circumstances, land, which had previously been abundant, became a scarce resource worth fighting for—very much as was the case among the Ashaninka and Amazonian Kichwa examined by Guzmán-Gallegos and Sarmiento Barletti (chapters 4 and 5, respectively).

The Peruvian Corporation proposed to lease rather than allocate them lands with a clause establishing that they could not cede them to third parties. Coronel and Picón refused to pay for the land and argued that "the Yanesha have always lived here." After enlisting Fernando Núñez Cifuentes, a Perene Colony topographer who had acquired land in the area, as representative of the Yanesha tribe, they asked the Peruvian Corporation to grant them free lands (Barclay 1989, 229). The company agreed to do so, and in 1956, it ceded in perpetuity a lot of 561 hectares to the 35 Yanesha families that lived in the area. The obtainment of land titles for the community, which benefitted 150 Yanesha, was regarded as a great deed, only possible thanks to the skills of their community leaders to deal with white people. As a result, Picón's and Coronel's reputations were greatly enhanced.

Mary Ruth Wise, a missionary linguist of the Summer Institute of Linguistics (SIL) who settled in Alto Yurinaki in the late 1950s, left an interesting testimony of the activities of Picón and Coronel as leaders of Alto Yurinaki.

> He [Picón] signs official papers granting the land to the Amuesha and allocating it to the heads of the families in return for their cooperation in such matters as clearing a road and helping in the survey of the land. Those who do not cooperate can expect no intervention from him on their behalf if Whites come to take the land they've cleared and planted in coffee outside the 600 [*sic*] hectares and, of course, cannot expect to share in the 600 hectares. The two deputy heads share in his responsibilities of land allocation and take over when the "Captain" is away. The first deputy [Coronel] is more popular with the people than the "Captain." As a consequence there is considerable strife for power. (Wise 1958, 13)

This conflict culminated in 1958, when Picón was deposed as settlement leader for selling part of his lands—a lot of nineteen hectares—to white-mestizo colonists. This angered his neighbors, who did not want white-mestizos to settle in communal lands. He was succeeded in the position of strong man by Coronel. It is clear from Wise's report and the following events that by then control over allocation of land had become an important component of a leader's power but only insofar as such control was exercised on behalf of his followers.

The first years of Coronel's leadership were very difficult. Colonists continued to pour into the valley, and in 1959 a group settled within the Yanesha concession. In October of that same year the SIL missionary Peter Fast invited Coronel, his wife, and two other members of Alto Yurinaki to attend the First International Pacific Fair held in Lima. Coronel and his companions caused great sensation among the public and were visited by President Manuel Prado Ugarteche. Coronel took advantage of this meeting with the "chief of the whites" to denounce the invasion of Alto Yurinaki by white-mestizo settlers. As a result of his complaints, the Perene Colony agreed to register the Yanesha concession—which until then was a private agreement—in the Lima Registry of Deeds. The registration of the community's title on November 10, 1961, was no small feat, since at the time Alto Yurinaki had become an island surrounded by a solid block of settlers' lands. Coronel came to be regarded as a true leader, one that had the capacities to deal with foreign Others to obtain from them things that are indispensable for the survival of his or her followers (see Guzmán-Gallegos, chapter 4, and Micarelli, chapter 6, for similar conceptions among the Amazonian Kichwa and People of the Center of southeastern Colombia).

The invasions did not stop, however, and in 1962, Coronel had to once more travel to Lima to denounce a new invasion of communal lands in the area of Chimcamaz. An article published in the evening newspaper *El Comercio Gráfico* (November 12, 1962) informed that, after hearing Coronel's requests, the Ministry of Agriculture had urged the Dirección de Tierras de Montaña (Office of Amazonian Lands) to find a prompt solution to the community's problems. The article is accompanied by a picture of Coronel reading a document that seems to be the land title of Alto Yurinaki (figure 3.2). Coronel kept this four-page document among his most precious belongings—a material expression of his acumen to wrest from white people part of their extraordinary powers. In 1968, when he stepped down as settlement leader, he passed it on to his successor, who showed it to me in 1977. Today, the title is regarded as an important item of public wealth, a material object infused with the powers of white people that ensures their rights over their lands. As such, it is carefully kept and passed from incumbent settlement leaders to their successors together with other important community documents (figure 3.3).[9]

Para reclamar la devolución de las tierras que les han despojado, ha llegado a Lima el cacique de los Amueshas, Berna Pascual Coronel.

En sus gestiones en Lima, el cacique ha conseguido que el Ministro de Agricultura ordene la solución del caso a la Dirección de Tierras de Montaña.

El cacique amuesha llegó en compañía de Cuñibo Espiritu, otro indígena selvático y del maestro bilingüe Pedro López Morales. Son asesorados por Clarence E. Church, Sub-Director del Instituto Linguístico de Verano.

Los amueshas, que denunciaron similar invasión de sus tierras en 1959, han vuelto porque hasta ahora no se les ha solucionado su problema. Ellos tienen títulos de propiedad de los terrenos ubicados en Chimcamaz, zona de Rurinaqui (Chanchamayo). Acusan a varios "criollos" de haberse posesionado ilegalmente de 2 mil hectáreas de cultivo. "Pedimos justicia a las autoridades de

FIGURE 3.2. Newspaper clipping showing Berna Pascual Coronel reading a document in Lima, probably the land title of the community of Alto Yurinaki. Source: *El Comercio Gráfico*, December 11, 1962.

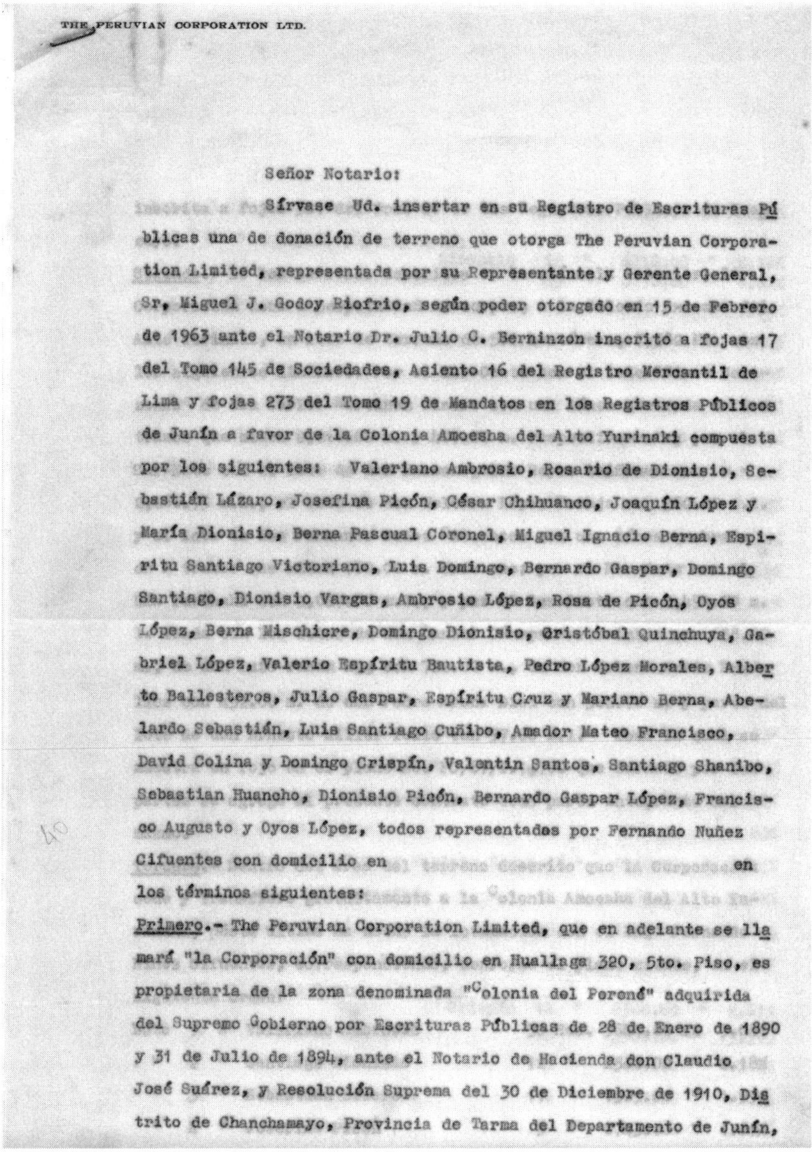

THE PERUVIAN CORPORATION LTD.

Señor Notario:

Sírvase Ud. insertar en su Registro de Escrituras Públicas una de donación de terreno que otorga The Peruvian Corporation Limited, representada por su Representante y Gerente General, Sr. Miguel J. Godoy Riofrio, según poder otorgado en 15 de Febrero de 1963 ante el Notario Dr. Julio C. Berninzon inscrito a fojas 17 del Tomo 145 de Sociedades, Asiento 16 del Registro Mercantil de Lima y fojas 273 del Tomo 19 de Mandatos en los Registros Públicos de Junín a favor de la Colonia Amoesha del Alto Yurinaki compuesta por los siguientes: Valeriano Ambrosio, Rosario de Dionisio, Sebastián Lázaro, Josefina Picón, César Chihuanco, Joaquín López y María Dionisio, Berna Pascual Coronel, Miguel Ignacio Berna, Espiritu Santiago Victoriano, Luis Domingo, Bernardo Gaspar, Domingo Santiago, Dionisio Vargas, Ambrosio López, Rosa de Picón, Oyos López, Berna Mischicre, Domingo Dionisio, Cristóbal Quinchuya, Gabriel López, Valerio Espíritu Bautista, Pedro López Morales, Alberto Ballesteros, Julio Gaspar, Espíritu Cruz y Mariano Berna, Abelardo Sebastián, Luis Santiago Cuñibo, Amador Mateo Francisco, David Colina y Domingo Crispín, Valentin Santos, Santiago Shanibo, Sebastian Huancho, Dionisio Picón, Bernardo Gaspar López, Francisco Augusto y Oyos López, todos representados por Fernando Nuñez Cifuentes con domicilio en en los términos siguientes:

Primero.- The Peruvian Corporation Limited, que en adelante se llamará "la Corporación" con domicilio en Huallaga 320, 5to. Piso, es propietaria de la zona denominada "Colonia del Perené" adquirida del Supremo Gobierno por Escrituras Públicas de 28 de Enero de 1890 y 31 de Julio de 1894, ante el Notario de Hacienda don Claudio José Suárez, y Resolución Suprema del 30 de Diciembre de 1910, Distrito de Chanchamayo, Provincia de Tarma del Departamento de Junín,

FIGURE 3.3. First page of the land title of the community of Alto Yurinaki obtained in 1961 and carefully kept as a key item of the community's public wealth. Source: Peruvian Corporation Archives.

Final Remarks

Generative public wealth differs greatly from the other two forms mentioned above in terms of the producing agents, the nature of its components, its purpose, the agents who own it, and its degree of permanency. Public wealth at the cosmological level is the product of divine creational acts that preceded or, at most, were contemporary with the creation of human beings. It is composed of very tangible, geographical, or environmental elements that provide the means for Yanesha subsistence and perpetuation. Although it was created for the benefit of the Yanesha, and in this limited sense it belongs to them, this kind of public wealth is ultimately the property of the creator god and the higher divinities, who are said to be the *pamo'mte'* (owners) of the land and all its living creatures. It is in this sense that it would be more appropriate to say that the Yanesha belong to the land than that the land belongs to the Yanesha. This kind of wealth may be lost in part through appropriation by other people, or when it is withdrawn by the gods in punishment for Yanesha immoral behavior. Or it might be transformed in positive or negative ways, through, for instance, catastrophes induced by divinities infuriated by the failings of their human creatures. But it is an everlasting divine creation that will never disappear.

At the other extreme, convivial public wealth is a matter of personal achievement. It depends on an individual's capacity to establish harmonious social relationships with as many people as possible by being compassionate, friendly, caring, and generous (Santos-Granero 2000, 270). It is an intangible type of wealth required to ensure conviviality as described by Overing and Passes (2000, 2), insofar as it is aimed at "creating 'good/beautiful' people who can live a tranquil, sociable life together" and at "achieving a comfortable affective life with those with whom they live, work, eat, and raise children." The totality of personal networks of convivial relations in any given settlement may be said to constitute a collective asset, as indirectly signified by the term yamo'tsesha', (the group of people with whom *we* have harmonious social relations). But the ownership of such networks is always a personal matter as indicated by the term *namo'tsesha'*, (the group of people with whom *I* have harmonious social relations). This type of people-produced public wealth is not only the most intangible but also the most evanescent. As I have argued elsewhere, while not an unattainable utopia, indigenous Amazonian conviviality is an ideal that when attained under the guise of a large, beautiful settlement does not last too long, for it contains the seeds of its own destruction (Santos-Granero 2000, 284).

Generative public wealth falls in between the above two and is neither entirely originated in demiurgic acts nor exclusively the product of human individual action. It is a type of wealth obtained from powerful—often supernatural—others through the mediation of human specialists. Comprised of mostly intangible things—knowledge of the correct way to pray and make offerings, knowledge of healing and ritual protection techniques, or knowledge of the ways of the whites—this kind of wealth belongs to the priests, shamans, and strong men who acquired it through their own efforts. Such efforts may entail formal modes of training, like those involved in the formation of shamans and priests; it may involve semiformal modes of apprenticeship, like those required to learn cosham̃ñats sacred songs and music; or it may call for more informal means, such as long periods of living with white people in order to learn more about their lifeways. Whatever the means, in all cases the knowledge obtained constitutes a form of personal property. It belongs to those who have embarked on a quest to obtain it and have suffered in the process. However, since this knowledge can only be fully realized when used for the benefit of the collectivities to which their owners belong, it can also be said to constitute a form of public wealth.

Although in its elementary form, this type of wealth is mostly intangible—made up of specialized forms of knowledge. When put to use, it does assume a material dimension. Through their prayers and offerings, priests obtain divine breath and strength materialized in consecrated manioc beer, cosham̃ñats songs, or sacred fires. Shamans' mastery of curing and ritual protection techniques finds material expression in their jaguar stones, curing songs, the ill-inducing objects they suck from their patients' bodies, and in the cleansed and revitalized bodies of their patients. In turn, a headman's capacity to interact and negotiate with white people is materialized in the things he can obtain from them: land titles, documents, schools, trucks, money, and so forth, as many of the authors in this volume discuss.

The material and immaterial things that compose this type of public wealth are neither eternal as environmental forms of public wealth nor as transient as convivial forms of public wealth. The life-giving knowledge of cornesha', pa'llerr, and am̃cha'taret̃ can be transmitted in a master-apprentice relationship—most often between fathers and sons. But it is always a personal achievement, and as such, it must be recreated by every generation. More importantly, this type of knowledge—in its tangible and intangible expressions—may be lost as a result of the moral failings of those who possess it. It is said that in the past many cornesha' lost contact with the divinities either because of their personal faults or those of their followers, which resulted in the desecration of the *puerahua* and its abandonment by the gods. Master shaman Valerio was said to have been killed while wandering in faraway communities under jaguar guise because he broke the essential shamanic rule of not having more than one wife. And Dionisio Picón, founder and second chief of Alto Yurinaki, was removed from office when he tried to sell communal lands to white-mestizo settlers. When this happens, the collectivities to which the failed specialists belong lose part of their public wealth. They are left unprotected, or as a Yanesha friend put it, "quedan huerfanitos" (they are left like little orphans). They are deprived of parents (leaders) who might support them, of a social network on which to rely for sustenance, and of the ritual means that are crucial to survive and thrive in a context of generalized struggle for vitality. These are the main features of the state of poverty—whether individual or collective—as understood by Yanesha people. And although orphans are attributed important moral attributes and extraordinary powers in mythical narratives, very much as is the case among the People of the Center of southeastern Colombia examined by Micarelli (chapter 6), in real life their fate is always pitied and regarded with horror, insofar as they are often the target of witchcraft accusations (Santos-Granero 2002, 2004).

Generative public wealth is dependent on the morality of its personal owners, and it is contingent on a delicate balance between the Yanesha and all other living beings who, like them, compete to accrue as much vitality as possible. In the three cases analyzed here, the production of generative wealth took place in a context of competition for vitality between the Yanesha and a host of alien others, whether downriver jaguars, soul-eating spirits, illness-inducing insects, enemy Yanesha, or greedy, less-than-human white people. Shamans, priests, and strong men do their best to further the interests of the collectivities they represent or to which they belong by increasing their stock of vitality. They use their knowledge and powers to propitiate the divinities and ensure the increase of game, fish, and garden plants. They defend their collectivities from the attacks of the offended master/owners of animals and plants. They try to prevent killer downriver jaguars and evil spirits from eating the souls/vitalities of their people. And they engage in negotiations with white people who, since colonial times and up to the present, are thought to send epidemics and deprive the Yanesha magically from their means of subsistence (Santos-Granero 1987, 35).

In agreement with Micarelli (chapter 6), however, I contend that generative public wealth does not consist only of the abundance of vitality made possible by shamans, priests, and chiefly leaders but, above all, of the knowledge, ritual techniques, and personal skills that allow these specialists to be at the forefront of the struggle for vitality that pitches the Yanesha against all other living beings. The acquisition of vitality, which is the most important component of a collectivity's well-being, results from having access to such specialized life-giving knowledge in such a way that the specialists themselves become, as it were, items of public wealth (Santos-Granero 1986). Today, some of these specialists—like priestly leaders—have disappeared. But new ones have appeared on the scene. This is the case of those anthropologists, missionaries, and activists who act as advocates for the rights of Yanesha people vis-à-vis the encompassing white-mestizo society. Such specialists also come to be regarded as belonging to the group and as participants in the generalized struggle for vitality in which the group is involved. As in all combats, however, in the struggle for vitality the Yanesha sometimes win and sometimes lose. The accrual of generative forms of public wealth is meant to act as an insurance against the loss of vitality, whereas the intermediation of priests, shamans, and strong men aims at keeping the interspecific competition for vitality from becoming a war of all against all.

Notes

1. Since this is a historical work and most of the people I refer to in the text are long dead, in this chapter I use the actual names of people and places.

2. Yos and Yosoper are names that seem to derive from the Spanish terms Dios (God) and Lucifer, which suggests an important Christian influence in Yanesha mythology. The structure of this myth is, however, typically Amazonian, and with variations, the same myth is found among other native Amazonian peoples.

3. In addition, human beings are said to possess a *choyeshe'mats* (shadow soul).

4. His or her shadow soul may have different destinies in accordance to the moral character of its owner while alive.

5. Yompor Yompere was an older brother of Yompor Ror, the sun god. When Yompor Ror decided to leave this world, Yompor Yompere, his wife Yachor Mamas, and their children took the lead. Furious with them because they did not wait for him, Yompor Ror transformed them into large stones.

6. Amuesha was an exonym used by white-mestizos to designate the Yanesha until the 1990s. Today they prefer to be called Yanesha (we, the people).

7. The italicized terms in parentheses are the ones originally used by Pedro.

8. Coronel closed his puerahua in 1959 due to a shrinking following and, probably, to the attraction he felt for the messianic discourse of the brand of Evangelicalism preached by the Summer Institute of Linguistics missionaries that resided at the time in Alto Yurinaki.

9. Figure 3.3 corresponds to the first page of a copy of the land title of Alto Yurinaki provided to me thanks to the generosity of Frederica Barclay, who found it in the Peruvian Corporation archives of the old Desamparados Central Train Station—now deposited in the Archivo General de la Nación.

References

Barclay, Frederica. 1989. *La Colonia del Perené: Capital inglés y economía cafetalera en la configuración de la región de Chanchamayo*. Iquitos: Centro de Estudios Teológicos de la Amazonía.

Barclay, Frederica, and Fernando Santos. 1980. "La conformación de las comunidades nativas Amuesha: La legalización de un despojo territorial." *Amazonía Peruana* 3(5):43–74.

Duff-Tripp, Martha. 1998. *Diccionario Yanesha' (Amuesha)-Castellano*. Lima: Ministerio de Educación/Instituto Lingüístico de Verano.

Navarro, Manuel. 1967 [1924]. "La tribu Amuesha." In *Oxapampa: Visión histórica y desarrollo de la provincia de Oxapampa, en el departamento de Pasco*, Dionisio Ortiz, Vol. 2:387–95. Lima: Imprenta Editorial "San Antonio."

Orden Franciscana. 1900. "Bosquejo histórico de la misión de San Francisco Solano." In *Anales de la obra de la propagación de la fe en el oriente del Perú*, Vol. 2. Lima: Imprenta y Librería de San Pedro.

Overing, Joanna, and Alan Passes, eds. 2000. *The Anthropology of Love and Anger. The Aesthetics of Conviviality in Native Amazonia*. London: Routledge.

Santos-Granero, Fernando. 1986. "Power, Ideology, and the Ritual of Production in Lowland South America." *Man. Journal of the Royal Anthropological Society* 21(4):657–79.

———. 1987. "Epidemias y sublevaciones en el desarrollo demográfico de las misiones Amuesha del Cerro de la Sal, siglo XVIII." *Histórica* 11(1):25–53. Lima.

———. 1988. "Templos y herrerías: Utopía y re-creación cultural en la Amazonía peruana, siglo XVIII." *Bulletin de l'Institut Français d'Etudes Andines* 17(3–4):1–22. Lima.

———. 1991. *The Power of Love: The Moral Use of Knowledge amongst the Amuesha of Central Peru*. London: Athlone Press.

———. 2000. "The Sisyphus Syndrome or the Struggle for Conviviality in Native Amazonia." In *The Anthropology of Love and Anger. The Aesthetics of Conviviality in Native Amazonia*, edited by Joanna Overing and Alan Passes, 268–87. New York: Routledge.

———. 2002. "St. Christopher in the Amazon: Child Sorcery, Colonialism, and Violence among the Southern Arawak." *Ethnohistory* 49(3):507–43.

———. 2004. "The Enemy Within: Child Sorcery, Revolution, and the Evils of Modernization in Eastern Peru." In *In Darkness and Secrecy: Witchcraft and Sorcery in Native South America*, edited by Neil L. Whitehead and Robin M. Wright, 272–305. Durham: Duke University Press.

———. 2006. "Sensual Vitalities: Non-Corporeal Modes of Sensing and Knowing in Native Amazonia." In In the World and about the World: Amerindian Modes of Knowledge, edited by Fernando Santos-Granero and George Mentore. Special issue in honor of Prof. Joanna Overing. *Tipiti: Journal of the Society for the Anthropology of Lowland South America* 4(1–2):57–80.

Smith, Richard Chase. 1976a. "Deliverance from Chaos for a Song: Preliminary Discussion of Amuesha Music." PhD dissertation, Cornell University.

———. 1976b. "The Amuesha of Central Peru." *Akwesasne Notes* 10(2).

Wise, Mary Ruth. 1958. "Social Structures of the Amuesha: A Sub-system of Peruvian Society." Información de Campo No. 30–6. Lima: Instituto Lingüístico de Verano. (typescript).

PART TWO

Land, Money, and Care

CHAPTER FOUR

Amazonian Kichwa Leadership

The Circulation of Wealth and the Ambiguities of Mediation

MARÍA A. GUZMÁN-GALLEGOS

Early in the morning groups from various Amazonian Kichwa villages made their way to the offices of the Jatun Yaku Association, a member association of the Organization of Indigenous Peoples of Pastaza (OPIP), to celebrate the anniversary of its foundation.[1] Adults and children started working on various tasks.[2] A group of women peeled a bunch of maniocs and cut into pieces of the game meat that the association's feast committee had bought from people living in the interior of Ecuador's Pastaza Province. At about noon, people gathered into small groups and commented on the delay of the OPIP leaders. A bit incensed, Walter, a Kichwa man, said to me that OPIP leaders often did not come if they thought they would have to work. Nodding in agreement, an elderly woman added that once she had participated in one of OPIP's projects with her tilapia pond. No leader had come to visit or help her while the fish were small, but once the fish were big, leaders came, driving fast in the project car. They came "just to eat," the woman said, like the missionaries used to do in past times (*mikungapaklla shamurcanun pagri salla*). She was sure, she added, that this time the OPIP leaders would arrive just in time to eat the game meat and drink the manioc brew provided by members of the association.

Comments that leaders failed to give adequate support to their followers, engaged in illegitimate consumption of the latter's products, or appropriated the work of others were quite common. In this chapter, I explore Amazonian Kichwa notions and practices regarding leadership and suggest that they must be understood together with indigenous notions of public wealth and well-being. I argue that the Amazonian Kichwa relate notions of public wealth and well-being to access and control of resources that originate in the multiple worlds, which in their view make up the cosmos. I contend that public wealth and well-being are crucially related to the production of Kichwa men and women as persons and as a people.

Notions of sameness and Otherness, of personhood and ownership, and the ontological assumption that the cosmos is composed of different worlds are central to Amazonian Kichwa economic and cosmological perceptions regarding access to resources deemed vital for the production and reproduction of people. A notion of particular relevance in this regard is that of *amu*. Amu comes from the Spanish word *amo* and means "owner" and "boss." A person also uses *amu* to indicate that she is someone endowed with productive and transformative capacities received from her kin, who are considered to be the same, and from people defined as Others. These abilities enable her to be the owner of what she creates and to enter into new kinship relations. As a concept, amu reflects common native Amazonian ideas about personhood and ownership (Fausto 2008; Santos-Granero 2009). It also relates to the larger political and economic forces that have shaped the history of the Amazonian Kichwa.

For the Amazonian Kichwa, leadership always entails mediation. Mediation allows for access to vital resources originating in the human and spirit worlds and their transference into the world of the Kichwa. In addition, mediation relates to the transference of life-giving substances and productive capacities from genitors, kin, and other relevant beings into a person's gendered body. Although leadership in contemporary Amazonian Kichwa contexts is diverse, leaders are generally considered to be mediators par excellence who negotiate with powerful human actors on behalf of their people and between human society and the spirit world. As has been widely documented in other native Amazonian societies (Brown 1993; Cepek 2008; Fausto 2007; Vilaça 2005), mediation and the positions of leaders as mediators are ambiguous and contested.

Kichwa notions of wealth and well-being, the notion of amu and common understandings of leadership, and people's expectations regarding their leaders have been deeply influenced by processes of colonization and oil extraction. And access to better public services, such as education and health, comes with the condition that Amazonian Kichwas accept the establishment of oil fields in their lands and, hence, the loss of territorial control. As we shall see, the Amazonian Kichwa consider that access to such services is vital for their reproduction as a people. Indigenous leaders must often find a balance between their supporters' and constituencies' expectations, needs, and desires and contemporary state policies that reduce and limit the Amazonian Kichwa's access to forests and lands.

By focusing on Kichwa notions of public wealth and well-being and addressing the dynamics of sameness and Otherness, as well as notions of personhood and ownership, I seek to overcome the "implicit disciplinary divide" (Cepek 2008, 336) between those works that study ethnopolitical mobilization, new forms of leadership, and contemporary oppression, isolated from daily practices and ontological notions, and those that look at social organization and indigenous cosmologies without reference to recent forms of indigenous leadership.

This chapter is organized into three sections. In the first section I discuss the present-day situation of the Amazonian Kichwa, as well as their notions of public wealth and well-being, in a context of heavy colonization and expansion of the oil frontier. In the second section I describe how wealth and well-being are closely related to the production of strong, gendered persons who can render resources productive, thus creating kinship relations and reproducing Amazonian Kichwa ways of life. In the third section I discuss contemporary Amazonian Kichwa forms of leadership and how leaders as mediators play key roles in the transference of valuable resources that people consider necessary to achieve wealth and well-being.

Amazonian Kichwa Lives: Scarcity, Wealth, and Well-Being

The Amazonian Kichwa, or Amazonian Runa, as they call themselves, number around seventy-five thousand persons. Approximately twelve thousand live in the Pastaza Province (Instituto Nacional de Estadísticas y Censo 2010). In the anthropological literature, the Runa living in the Upper Napo River region and up toward the small town of Baeza are known as Quijos Quichua, or in recent works as Napo Runa. The Runa living in the Pastaza and Bobonaza basins have been called Canelos Quichua. The distinction between Quijos and Canelos refers to the origins of these populations and to different ethnogenetic processes. The Quijos Quichua are considered to be descendants of a pre-Hispanic people whose language is unknown and who inhabited the Upper Napo and the valleys extending west to the Andes (Kohn 2002; Oberem 1980). The Canelos Quichua, by contrast, show strong influence from Zaparoan, Shuar, and Achuar groups (Whitten 1976). In Spanish, the term *runa* is not used. The Runa themselves use neither Quijos nor Canelos Quichua as self-designations. When speaking Kichwa, they use the word Runa to refer to themselves and to distinguish their way of life from that of other indigenous groups and the nonindigenous population. Moreover, they always use the name of the place where a group of people lives preceding the word Runa, such as Copataza Runa, Villano Runa, or Sarayacu Runa. Although they do not use a common ethnic denomination, the Runa from the Pastaza and Bobonaza basins consider themselves similar but distinct from the Runa of the Napo basin. Acknowledging important cultural and social similarities among their various groups, the Runa from Pastaza, the Bobonaza basins, and from Napo refer to themselves in Spanish as Kichwa Amazónicos. In this chapter I use the name Amazonian Runa in those contexts in which the cultural and social distinctions between the Runa people from the Upper Napo River and those from the Pastaza and Bobonaza basins are not relevant. When they are, I specify the spatial origins and belongings. This chapter refers mainly to the Amazonian Runa communities located in the Pastaza Province, particularly those along the Bobonaza and Villano rivers and those located along the borders between the Pastaza and Napo provinces. The latter trace their origins to Tena and Archidona, towns located in the Napo Province, and in some contexts they designate themselves as Napo Runa.

Within the Pastaza Province, important differences exist between the communities located along roads in the colonization zone and those located in the more isolated interior. Some Runa settlements in the colonization zone are surrounded by nonindigenous *colonias* (colonies), while others form part of ethnically mixed colonias. Colonias are divided into privately owned lots. Several of the Runa settlements are also part of *comunas*, areas where land is officially recognized as collective property. Due to migration from the Andean Highlands and to increasing population pressures on land and forests, game and fish are scarce in most of these villages. Virtually no family can subsist on hunting and gardening anymore. People in these settlements depend on earning enough money to buy food and to access education and health care. They work as cattle herders at local haciendas, as maids in nonindigenous households, as teachers, or as employees in the many development projects carried out by private and public institutions. Many move temporarily to Amazonian cities or even farther away to Quito, Esmeraldas, or Guayaquil.

In contrast, the interior zone contains few colonias. Reflecting the colonial past and current relationships to the state, most Runa settlements are located along major rivers, usually close to missions, military posts, or oil camps. These settlements still control vast forested areas. As a result of the pressures from OPIP, in close coordination with the regional and national indigenous organizations CONFENIAE and CONAIE, in the early 1990s the state granted the local Kichwa the property titles for over one million hectares of land.[3] Indigenous demands and the state's response were closely connected to oil concessions in the Pastaza Province (Guzmán-Gallegos 2010, 2012; Sawyer 2004). Today only one oil field operates in the province, though several oil concessions overlap with Kichwa titled settlements. In this zone, people can still subsist on hunting and gardening, though in larger villages there is a shortage of game and fish due to increased population pressure and the various impacts of oil exploitation. Like the Runa living in the colonization zone, the interior Runa consider access to health services and education for their children very important. Although job possibilities are more limited, people work in public nurseries, schools, ecotourism enterprises, or for the oil company.

The Amazonian Runa living in these two zones perceive the titling of lands, as well as the establishment of colonias, comunas, and oil fields as part of ongoing processes that restrict their access to crucial resources and limit their control of the space they inhabit. When talking about their current possibilities and expectations for achieving a good and valuable life, people invariably make comparisons between past and present-day settlements. In these narratives, they usually stress the beauty of their family places and recount how their grandparents cleared a certain part of the forest in order to build a house and plant *chakras* (gardens) with plantains, manioc, and maize. They characterize those days as times of plenty and wealth when their families had abundant food. Household gardens and orchards attracted wild animals, which came to eat fallen fruit. It was easy for men to capture game when they went out hunting. Through collective fishing expeditions, everybody obtained plenty of fish. Those were good times for their *muntun* or *ayllus* (extended families) to grow, or, literally, to "fill up" (*jundarina*). With large houses, well-tended chakras, and good possibilities for hunting and fishing, families lived well and ate properly. They managed to hold weddings and baptism parties. The abundance of food meant that they could give suitable gifts, such as game meat and fish, to the parents of a girl they wanted their son to marry or to the couple they wanted as godparents for their child.

Whenever the Amazonian Runa talk about times of plenty and wealth they equate the availability of nonoccupied lands, the transformation of forests into fertile chakras, and easy access to game and fish with the growth of their families through birth, marriage, and the establishment of ties of ritual parenthood with kin, as well as nonkin. Hence, the Amazonian Runa establish a close connection among access to land, forest, and rivers, their ability to transform the products these provide into proper food, the production of kinship relations, and thereby of people and the possibility of achieving wealth and well-being. This connection forces us to reexamine a common understanding in studies of native Amazonian societies that suggests that the production of people is central to their political economies and cosmologies. In the literature, what the word *people* conotes varies. Rivière (1984) and Fausto (2001) relate it to labor, which they argue is the scarcest resource in native Amazonian societies. Santos-Granero (2009) relates the production of people to vitality, or life itself, and suggests that vitality is the scarcest resource. Thus, according to these authors, wealth and the power to obtain it depends either on the number of people whose labor one can mobilize and control or on the life substances, life forces, or vitality that a person may obtain or conquer in a cosmological competition that includes nonhumans (see also Conklin 2001). Significantly, these explanations do not regard land or natural resources as scarce resources.

As I discuss in the next section, for the Amazonian Runa the production of people, or of persons, is mainly related to the transmission of productive capacities and to the acquisition and maintenance of life forces (see Guzmán-Gallegos 1997, 2009, 2010; Kohn 2002; Uzendoski 2005). Moreover, the Amazonian Runa believe that people are always in danger of losing their productive capacities and life forces; hence, a person's productive capacities and vitality are closely interlinked (see Conklin, chapter 2). From an Amazonian Runa point of view, however, land, forests, and rivers as the habitats or domains of plants, game, and fish are just as scarce as vitality and life and are therefore also central to economic and cosmological concerns. In other words, their wealth and well-being depend as much on access to land and forests as on control and maintenance of their own productive capacities and life forces. The equal emphasis that the Amazonian Kichwa place on the scarcity of land and forest resources and the scarcity of people (productive capacities and vitality) may have to do with, I suggest, their colonial history and the processes of colonization.

Runa access to vital resources, such as land and forests, has been closely related to and limited by the presence of nonindigenous actors. The Amazonian Runa define these actors as powerful Others, whom they conceive as beings that are radically different from themselves. In the past, these Others comprised landlords, missionaries, and merchants. Nowadays, this category also includes civil servants, nongovernmental organization (NGO) employees, and oil company representatives. The Runa see these actors as human beings of a different *laya* (type or sort) or *rancia* (of another substance or material). The Others are considered *chikan* (different, apart) and as *tunu* (another way of being, other habits and thoughts). The Runa consider the Others to be dangerous and threatening but also necessary.

The control that these powerful Others have exercised over land and forest resources has varied throughout time and space. Runa families could not settle within the haciendas or the lands of missions or military posts. Runa families tended, however, to create new family places close to these nonindigenous spaces. This preference resulted from their desire to have access to these powerful actors' wealth, which has taken the form of a variety of valued goods and services that the Runa strive to obtain for their kinfolk.

From the 1930s onward, the processes of colonization changed in character. Waves of mestizo and indigenous peasants from the Andean Highlands led to new processes of colonization based more on control of land and forest resources than on indigenous labor. For the Runa these changes entailed the gradual dissolution of debt-peonage bonds common in the region during the nineteenth and twentieth centuries and the loss of the forests and lands where they had lived in the past. Runa families responded to this process by trying to secure as much land as possible. They did so either by becoming part of the emerging colonias or by making use of national legislation, according to which they, as natives, could obtain collectively owned lands or comunas.

Oil exploration and extraction activities in the Pastaza Province started in the late 1980s, a decade later than in the northern Amazonian provinces. As a result of the liberalization and privatization of the oil sector, several oil fields were given in concession to transnational corporations in the colonization and interior zones. Exploration activities were conducted in several of these fields. Since the early 1990s and up to 2014, one oil field has been in operation: Oil Field 10 located in the interior of the Pastaza Province. The establishment of this oil field led to various indigenous responses and to new processes of relocation. Leadership from OPIP and the majority of its constituency were opposed to exploration and extraction activities; however, several villages and organizations were willing to establish relations with these new powerful Others. The oil company, who sought to obtain social acceptance through multiple favors, undoubtedly established unruly alliances with families and leaders (Sawyer 2004; Guzmán-Gallegos 2010). There were also other important factors that motivated the Runa within the oil field to allow its presence. Due to contractual obligations, the oil company was obliged to provide the affected villages with education and social services. Several Runa family groups considered access to these services of vital importance and moved closer to the wells, that is, to the areas where the company had larger social investments. This led to the demographic growth of existing villages and the emergence of new ones (Fontaine 2004; Guzmán-Gallegos 2012). The Amazonian Runa believe, however, that human access to vital resources is related to more than just the human world. Like other native Amazonian peoples, the Runa conceive the cosmos as comprised of multiple worlds populated by different kinds of beings. In their view, humans depend as much on other humans as on powerful nonhuman Others. Reflecting the historical character of their cosmological beliefs, the Amazonian Runa depict these nonhuman Others, or spirits, as related to different social milieus among which the world of the Runa is situated. They describe the spirit world as consisting of cities, forests, gardens, and rivers.

The Runa refer to the spirits that inhabit these spirit cities as *duiñukuna* or *amukuna* and relate them to particular notions of property and relations of subordination. The words *duiñukuna* and *amukuna* come, respectively, from the Spanish words *dueño* (owner) and *amo* (owner or boss). These duiñukuna or amukuna look like landlords or priests and inhabit several cities, which are organized hierarchically in relation to one another. The largest spirit city, located inside the volcano Sumaco, is thought to be similar to the country's capital, Quito, with houses, streets, and wide roads. Smaller villages are located inside lower mountains and hills. The spirits use cars and even planes, items of wealth to which the Runa usually do not have access. The duiñukuna or amukuna keep their forest animals, which they see as domesticated pets, in enormous farmyards with electric fences. Only the owners can let the animals leave their pens, thereby allowing the animals to become prey for hunters. To persuade animal owners to release their wards, the Runa try to establish relations of symmetrical exchange with these spirits by giving them gifts of food (Kohn 2002).

The Runa also call the spirits that inhabit the spirit jungle world *mamakuna* (mothers) or *supaykuna* (spirits). When talking about the forest spirits in these terms, the Runa refer to relations of kinship, which entail control and care. The Runa describe these beings either as the spirits of powerful animals, such as the anaconda or the jaguar, or as spirits of culturally valued plants, such as manioc or barbasco. In the Bobonaza and Villano areas people also include Nunguli (mother of chakras) in this category, the mother of clay, a spirit jungle called Amazanga, and the water spirits (see also Guzmán-Gallegos 1997; Whitten 1976). These spirits look like the Runa and may be male or female. They live in villages and houses resembling those of the Runa, which are located in the forests, rivers, and chakras—spaces the Runa associate with Runa ways of life. The mamakuna or supaykuna take care of forest animals, fish, and plants, which they regard as their children whom they feed and make to grow and reproduce. They also own special places, such as waterfalls and lakes. From these spirits associated with care and kinship, the Runa receive valuable knowledge and productive capacities, and they obtain access to resources. According to the Napo Runa, people can marry with these spirits, whereas the Runa living along the Bobonaza, Villano, and Curaray rivers believe that intermarriage with such spirits may cause miscarriage and foster anomalies.

Their depiction of the spirit world indicates that Runa notions of public wealth and well-being cannot be understood apart from the mestizo power structures and processes of colonization that, according to the Runa, generate a scarcity of vital resources that affects them as a collectivity. The Runa often contrast past times of plenty, wealth, and well-being with present conditions. As my friend Sabina put it, almost no free forest remains in the colonization zone. Instead, humans—Runa and other kinds of people—live everywhere. Since the Runa can no longer rotate their chakras by leaving some areas fallow, the land has become tired. Due to continuous human presence, the particular smell of cattle, and uncontrolled logging, wild animals and birds have abandoned the area. In Sabina's view, the amukuna resent this and have locked the game within the volcano Sumaco. Fish have also left in response to the trash and oil thrown into the river; the anaconda, the mother of the fish, has taken them to other places. Under these conditions, according to Sabina, it is difficult for the Runa to achieve a good life.

Wealth and well-being are also related to the production of people. A person's productive capacities and ownership over what one creates are central to this process. The designation of those spirit beings, different from and similar to the Runa as amukuna/duiñukuna/mamakuna, underlines in my view the importance that the Runa place on establishing relations with beings defined as Other and on the ability to transform resources into products deemed indispensable for the production of social relations and the achievement of a good life. Like the Ashaninka in Peru and the People of the Center of southeastern Colombia (Sarmiento, chapter 5, and Micarelli, chapters 6, respectively), the Runa establish a close connection between, on the one hand, a person's abilities to produce valuable products and create kinship relations, and on the other, their possibilities for achieving wealth and well-being as a collectivity.

Producing People: Productive Capacities and Ownership

The Amazonian Runa relate notions of public wealth and well-being to the production of themselves as persons and as a people (see Conklin, chapter 2, for similar connections between health and well-being among the Wari'). The production of persons entails the transmission of productive capacities, the acquisition and maintenance of life forces, and the creation of kinship relations. Persons are endowed with certain capacities and life forces through the actions and efforts of their parents and close kin. As such, persons are manifestations of kinship relations. A person who does not have parents or close kin on whom she can count is said to be *wakcha*. Wakcha means not only "orphan," but also "poor." Those regarded as poor are often considered to lack appropriate productive capacities and thus unable to produce valued objects or to create and maintain significant social relations. Those who are wakcha are, in other words, the opposite of those who act as amu (Guzmán-Gallegos 1997).

A person becomes strong and resilient and therefore potentially amu as a result of one's parents' many daily acts of care. Parents are expected to feed their children appropriately and teach them ways to make their bodies strong, such as walking long distances or bathing early in the morning. Physical strengthening is closely entwined with spiritual strengthening. A person's body contains *samai*, which can be translated as "breath," "vital force," and/or "will." A person's samai, like the body, should be strengthened during the course of a person's life. A person receives samai from parents, from other kin, or from shamans who may be acquainted with the person or her/his relatives. As a result of receiving another person's vital force, a person's own samai becomes stronger. Thus, the strength of a person is related to the strength of the body, with the *aicha* (flesh) and the samai in close interaction (Guzmán-Gallegos 2009; Kohn 2002; Uzendoski 2005; Whitten 1976).

The strengthening of a person's body and will is also related to gendering processes. In the Runa communities located in the Napo and the Pastaza provinces, girls obtain knowledge and skills from their female kin, including grandmothers, mothers, aunts, and sometimes, mothers-in-law. Knowledge and skills about manioc cultivation are essential to having *paju* (gendered productive and life-giving abilities [see figure 4.1]). A woman who is *pajuyuk*, a possessor of paju, can make manioc grow abundantly, have beautiful chakras, and in the Pastaza and Bobonaza areas, make beautiful ceramics. According to Runa perceptions, this female paju is literally embodied. It sits in the fingers of a woman's hands. Boys obtain the knowledge and skills to become good hunters from their grandfathers, fathers, and uncles, and in some cases from affinal male relatives. These relatives show young boys how to walk in the forest, use a rifle, and listen to and interpret the movements of animals (Guzmán-Gallegos 1997; Uzendoski 2005).

In addition to the possession of various pajus, Runa people include formal education as a way to develop a person's productive capacities. Since attending public school usually requires paying fees for uniforms and school supplies, parents and close kin make great efforts to send their children at least to elementary school. Runa people consider formal education crucial for obtaining a good job or acquiring a wide range of de-

FIGURE 4.1. Olimpia, Canelos *sinchi warmi*, peeling manioc, 1993. Photo by María A. Guzmán-Gallegos.

sired objects, such as corrugated iron, kitchen utensils, radios, or pretty clothes.

Hence, for the Runa, a person is the result of the many acts of care and love by close male and female kin. Persons become physically and spiritually strong because they have relatives to help them become so. In this sense, all persons are constituted by kinship relations, or relations of sameness, with male and female relatives. In addition, the Runa explicitly relate the gendering of a person to female relations in the case of a woman and male relations in the case of a man (Guzmán-Gallegos 1997). Finally, the Runa assert that strengthening a person also requires the incorporation of alien substances, vitalities, or identities, what Santos-Granero (2009) calls *potentialities of life*. These potentialities of life are often thought to belong to dangerous Others. Formal education may be seen, I suggest, as a potentiality of life that the Runa consider to belong to the mestizo world and that they deem indispensable for attaining a good life.

Bodily and spiritual strength, manifested in a person's productive capacities, enables a person to enter into new kinship relations, whether as a spouse or as a parent, as well as to maintain existing relations. A person achieves these ends by producing enough food and sharing it with others, by helping close kin through participation in collective work, or by helping kin in need of money. In other words, a person creates and re-creates relations by caring for one's children and one's spouse and by entering into relations of symmetrical reciprocity with kinfolk. These productive capacities enable a person to create other persons and relations, as well as to transform the forest into well-tended gardens and family places. They also enable a person to claim ownership over the persons, objects, and places one has helped to create. Such capacities constitute a person as an amu, that is, a person who has control over that which she has produced, and who can make her family achieve a good and wealthy life.

As it is common in other native Amazonian contexts (see Conklin, chapter 2), the view that a person's gendered body, vital force, and will are gradually constructed as the result of various relations also implies that a person is a fragile, unstable being who can be deprived of strength, will, and agency. This happens when a person's body and samai become weakened either as a consequence of attacks by spirits who consider the person to have violated their space (by settling, for instance, near waterfalls and lakes) or of a shaman who wants to harm a person or has been paid to do so. Shamanic attacks lead to illness and the weakening of a person's vital energy and will, as well as to the loss of paju and other potentialities of life, such as highly valued goods and the mental abilities regarded as necessary to acquire knowledge associated with the mestizo world.

A person's productive capacities and one's possibilities to achieve well-being for one's family may thus be seriously jeopardized by acts that induce the deconstitution of the body and the appropriation of the products of one's work. Shamanic attacks may be seen as a way of exercising control over or appropriating a person's or a family's productive capacities by destroying them. Deconstitution, which can also be caused by illnesses, such as flue and cancer, causes a person or family's ownership of vital resources, such as land and forests, to "fade away." Other people, usually close relatives with whom a person does not have good relations, can start planting in untended gardens, and by doing so, claim ownership over them. The deconstitution or disintegration of a person by the acts of others also transforms the relationship between this person and those who want to harm her. Persons once considered close relatives can turn into strangers and even become enemies. So, if the constitution of an individual requires and confirms relations of sameness, the process of deconstitution may entail the creation of Otherness.

The appropriation of Others' productive capacities and the products of their work can have far-reaching consequences for those affected. This is especially true in the colonization zone where, due to scarcity of land and forest, such appropriation may force the affected families or their children to move to other settlements or even to the city. People fear that those who move out will lose contact with their parents and siblings and, by living permanently in the cities, turn into mestizos and forget Runa ways of life. As seen in the next section, notions of personhood and ownership and of sameness and Otherness also have a bearing on common understandings of leadership.

Leadership: Between Sameness and Otherness or the Ambiguities of Mediation

Contemporary Amazonian Runa leadership in the Pastaza Province is heterogeneous. There are, however, certain features common to all kinds of leadership, such as the role of leaders as mediators in securing their followers' life conditions and the need to balance relations of sameness and Otherness throughout this process.

The Amazonian Kichwa consider the founders of family places to be leaders. These are often, but not always, shamans. Family places usually form a part of larger villages, whose elected authorities are also considered to be leaders. Villages may, in turn, be part of comunas. Comunas have their own elected authorities known as the *cabildo* and the *varayuc*. In addition, supralocal organizations, such as OPIP, along with the thirteen associations that belong to it, all have elected leaders. Four other organizations also have leaders, including FENAKIPA, an organization that broke out of OPIP; AIEPRA, which represents the Kichwa who have converted to Protestantism; and ASODIRA and the Organization of the Villages of the Curaray-Liquino's headwaters, which represent the villages situated within Oil Field No. 10.[4]

Although leaders of supralocal organizations contest each other's legitimacy, and their supporters may not recognize the representativeness of other organizations, the Amazonian Runa do not question the heterogeneity of contemporary leadership in itself. Hence, they do not consider some types of leadership as imposed or as less legitimate than others. Rather, in their view, different leaders fulfill different functions within distinct sets of relations. When people talk about how they perceive and evaluate leaders and their actions, and what constitutes their leaders' power, they also refer to the quality of the relations leaders should ideally have with their supporters and highlight the abilities and knowledge that leaders should possess, as well as the limits and reaches of their authority.

According to the Runa, leaders' abilities and knowledge enable them to establish relations with powerful alien actors. Like Runa leaders, these powerful actors are also heterogeneous. In the case of shamans, these actors are spirits: the amukuna, mamakuna, or *supaykuna* mentioned above. In the case of village leaders and leaders of indigenous organizations, these actors are extremely diverse and may include, among others, a variety of Christian missionaries, the municipal, provincial, and national authorities, national and international NGOs, and oil company representatives. The ability to establish relations with these powerful Others empowers leaders in relation to their followers. Such empowerment is expected to benefit those whom the leaders represent and from whom they receive support. Runa leadership and Runa expectations of their leaders have varied historically. In the time of the haciendas, during the first half of the past century, the founders of family places were (and still are) leaders of their kin group, the ayllus, or muntun. Place founders, often shamans, played key roles in establishing relations with local landlords, negotiating group access to resources, and discussing payment conditions or how much their kin had to work for landlords in order to pay their debts. More importantly, thanks to their specialized knowledge, shamans could enter into the spirit world and establish relations with the spirit owners of animals and plants. Through these relations shamans mediated Runa access to previously uninhabited places, as well as the transference of resources from the spirit world to this world. Migrating families could then settle and establish new family places where they could have access to more abundant game and fish without being exposed to the attacks of their spirit owners.

Shamans and muntun/ayllus leaders continued to play an important role in securing as much land as possible for their kin and in the establishment of the first colonias. Often in alliance with missionaries, they helped to found the province's first comunas, such as the Comuna Canelos and the Comuna San Jacinto (Guzmán-Gallegos 1997, 2010; Whitten 1976, 1985). With intensified mestizo migration in the 1950s and 1960s and with greater integration of the Pastaza Runa into the state's administrative structures, literate, bilingual males were often seen as the most appropriate persons to become village leaders and, later on, leaders of supralocal organizations, such as OPIP. Thanks to increasing access to formal education, many of these leaders had completed secondary education, and some had university degrees. The Amazonian Kichwa consider formal education to endow these leaders with the knowledge and abilities they need to be able to negotiate with a variety of nonindigenous actors and to redress enduring ethnical asymmetries.

From the 1980s onward, leaders of supralocal organizations started playing an important role in negotiations with the state regarding the claims and demands of individual settlements and of entire groups, including ethnic or religious groups and groups of communities who collaborated with oil companies. Until 2006, the province's most important organization was OPIP. The main political goal of OPIP has been to secure Runa control over ancestral lands and territories by supporting the creation of comunas, especially in the colonization zone. Since the 1990s their response to the expansion of the oil frontier has been to demand state recognition of a particular territory that belongs to the Kichwa Nation in the Pastaza Province.

From the early 1990s until 2004, OPIP conducted several development projects and helped to administer and distribute public and international funds. Through these projects, OPIP aimed to create sustainable economic alternatives for Runa settlements, especially for those located in the colonization zone. These projects were part of wider political agendas and alliances with national and international environmental organizations. These alliances, which promoted the image of the Amazonian Kichwa as guardians of the forest, have been instrumental in hindering the establishment of new oil fields in the Pastaza Province and in reducing the polluting effects of oil extraction by pressuring the operator of Oil Field No. 10 to implement safer environmental standards (Fontaine 2004; Guzmán-Gallegos 2010, 2012).

As a supralocal, ethnopolitical organization, however, OPIP constitutes a new kind of political structure. It represents and links villages located in different parts of the Pastaza Province in the colonization and interior zones. At the top of OPIP's organizational structure sits the Governing Council, which consists of a president, vice president, secretary, and treasurer, as well as leaders in charge of land, health, and women's issues. As a result of OPIP's supralocal structure, its leaders often represent settlements with whom they have no close relations or that they have never visited. The supralocal representativeness of OPIP depends on the acknowledgement of a shared cultural identity as an ethnic group or Indian nation, the Kichwa Nation. Thus, OPIP represents an imagined community that often downplays the histories, contexts, and differences between particular villages.

The idea promoted by its leadership and generally accepted by its supporters that OPIP represents an indigenous nation, especially in the context of negotiations with the state, coexists, however, with other perceptions of OPIP and its leadership. When OPIP supporters evaluate the organization and judge its leaders, they often stress the importance of kinship relations and allude to particular notions about the constitution of bodies. They explicitly assert that OPIP is the result of the hard work of strong Runa men, who attend countless meetings and embark on taxing trips to faraway settlements, and of Runa women, who make manioc beer to serve at meetings, prepare food for their husbands to carry on their trips, or carry their children long distances while accompanying their spouses to meetings with national authorities. In other words, they regard OPIP as largely the product of the efforts, endeavors, and care of related, gendered people whom they consider to be "the same." The creation of OPIP therefore mirrors the fabrication of persons and kinship relations.

To support OPIP is phrased either as "being OPIP" or as belonging to OPIP's muntun/ayllu, which is in contrast to belonging to another organization's muntun/ayllu. Accordingly, Runa people expect OPIP leaders to behave like parents who take proper care of their children. Being OPIP also implies belonging to the same body. The OPIP "leaders should act as the head and heart of the body and nurture it" (uma shina, shunku shina, yayakuna, mamakuna shina paibak wawakunata kuidasha). People expect these leaders to secure access to lands and forests, channel external flows of goods and valuables, and give unconditional support to the organization's members, that is, to the villages, families, and persons that make up the organization.

Runa people also stress OPIP leaders' Otherness, which makes them different from their followers. The OPIP supporters often qualify their description of OPIP as a muntun/ayllu and as a body. In their view, OPIP is constituted by different muntun/ayllu and different villages—in other words, by different parts. They acknowledge that OPIP leaders belong to a muntun/ayllu other than their own. In their view, since leaders are embedded in kinship relations, they have the duty to maintain those relations by helping their close kin. Thus, OPIP supporters accept and justify, at least to a certain degree, the idea that leaders tend to favor their own kinfolk. Nonetheless, they also expect OPIP leaders to acknowledge and reciprocate the efforts of all those who have created and belong to the organization. They consider OPIP's efforts to title their lands and secure development projects for their villages a form of recognition for the work members have done for the organization.

Being considered the same (whether same body, muntun/ayllu, ethnic group, or nation), as well as Other (nonkin, non-coresident), actualizes a constitutive characteristic of leaders, namely that of being able to establish relations with powerful Others who possess wealth and control its circulation. These relations entail many instances of negotiation and mediation. Mediation has several facets. It implies being able to gain access to different worlds (such as the spirit world) and transfer to the human world the resources and wealth that these powerful Others control. Mediation also involves presenting the views of the Runa in public spheres, especially those linked to the state and to other national and transnational actors.

Mediation is, however, considered an ambiguous enterprise, and the position of leaders as mediators is often contested. It entails the possibility and danger of leaders adopting the position of Other and acting accordingly, gradually becoming Other. The empowerment of leaders always implies their exposure to more powerful actors and the temporary incorporation of their qualities and ways of being. Shamans, for example, can cure and transmit life-giving substances because they are "in a state of identity" with powerful beings (Gow 2001, 150; Guzmán-Gallegos 2009). But shamans must also identify with the patient's humanity. The Runa believe that a shaman who cannot do so has been alienated by the spirit beings who have granted him the power to see and cure; he has thus turned into the Other and may become a killer. Such a shaman may start destroying the bodies and productive capacities of his neighbors and ruin their possibilities to achieve valuable lives and well-being.

The danger of becoming Other is not limited to shamans. As mediators—persons who know the ways of nonindigenous people, have access to their world, and control access to their resources—political leaders also risk turning into these powerful Others. This implies behaving as nonindigenous people, which may eventually lead to an undue accumulation of wealth to the detriment of their followers. The relations that shamans and family leaders established with landlords and missionaries in the past entailed, for instance, becoming key actors in the administration of indigenous labor; in other words, they had to seek a balance between protecting and exploiting their kin. Landlords and local authorities assigned shamans and family leaders the position of *capitanes* (captains). As capitanes, shamans, and family leaders organized the work of their kin in the haciendas, and when the colonias were established, they secured lots for their close kin. However, they often tended to allocate less land to those kin with whom they had strained relations or excluded them altogether. These leaders were often accused of having retained more land for themselves, thereby forcing other families to migrate in search of new lands.

The Runa of the Pastaza Province, including those who support OPIP and those who do not, always acknowledge the role that OPIP has played in achieving state recognition of indigenous lands and in legitimizing, in public discourse, the concept of indigenous territories as existing spatial realities. They recognize the importance of OPIP in denouncing and reducing oil pollution in the communities located within and outside Oil Field No. 10. The Runa often underscore the abilities and knowledge of OPIP leaders, which allow them to establish alliances with key civil servants working for different state institutions, as well as with national and international NGOs. However, those who belong to OPIP's associations and those who support other organizations strongly criticize OPIP leaders for failing to ensure the well-being of the Amazonian Runa as a whole.

Many Runa accuse OPIP leaders of accumulating valued resources for themselves, thereby depriving their supporters of goods and opportunities. They assert that OPIP leaders have tended to favor their own villages and kin to the detriment of others. In their view, the villages of these leaders have received a larger share of the resources controlled by OPIP projects, and leaders' close kin have been given greater access to scholarships and contacts with foreigners who will help them start new development projects. They also point out that the wages earned by those in charge of OPIP projects are much higher than those earned by other employees. Critics argue that these actions demonstrate that leaders and their followers *no somos los mismos* (we are not the same). They further underscore the Otherness of OPIP leaders by comparing them with exploitative nonindigenous actors, as the elderly woman did in the story that begins this chapter when she said that the organization's leaders behave like the missionaries of old times. They do not come to help villagers prepare the association's feast, but "just come to eat."

Always in search of a balance between sameness and Otherness, leaders, from my point of view, constantly need to establish relations of trust with those Runa with whom they do not have kinship relations or are not coresidents with. Relations of trust underline that leaders are "the same" and that they do not engage in undue accumulation (of either land or goods) or in exploitative relations. To establish relations of trust presupposes that OPIP leaders (like the Yanesha specialists discussed by Santos-Granero in chapter 3) ensure the circulation of valued foreign resources and guarantee their followers' access to resources considered vital and scarce, such as land and forest. It also requires leaders to provide their supporters with access to educational and economic opportunities (in this case, scholarships and project resources), which strengthen their productive capacities and abilities, as well as their possibilities to achieve wealth and well-being. In my view, mediators as leaders must secure their followers' possibilities of becoming amu. Not to do so is interpreted as illegitimate accumulation and consumption. In other words, it is the appropriation of what people have created, and it deprives them of the possibilities to achieve a good life.

Concluding Remarks

The Amazonian Runa conceive land, forests, and rivers as public wealth. These are valued resources over which the Runa, as a collectivity, have rights of usufruct and which constitute the base of their well-being. Runa notions of public wealth and well-being cannot be seen apart from ongoing colonization processes and nonindigenous economic structures. These processes and structures have rendered land, forest, and river resources scarce, especially in the colonization zone, and they have led to the establishment of different property regimes. Land and forests have become the property of powerful nonindigenous persons and of the Runa themselves. In order to maintain control over the areas they previously used, the Runa have become proprietors of private lots in the colonias and of collectively owned lands in the comunas.

Private and collective property regimes coexist with Runa notions of ownership. According to Runa perceptions, their collective rights of usufruct depend on the productive and transformative capacities of Runa men and women; these capacities enable them to transform forests into well-tended gardens and family places and to establish hunting and fishing areas. From an Amazonian Runa point of view, the transformation of items of public wealth through labor grants exclusive rights of ownership to those who have transformed them. The Runa consider those endowed with transformative capacities as amu of what they have transformed.

Becoming amu is closely related to the production of strong, gendered persons endowed with life-giving substances and transformative capacities. According to Runa perceptions, a person's physical and spiritual strength results from her/his kin's loving care and entails the incorporation of the vitality of other persons. The Runa regard a person's transformative capacities as part of Runa cultural knowledge and thus as collective assets that are transmitted through kinship relations and through female and male lines. Since the Runa also believe that formal education strengthens a person's capacities, this kind of education has become another nonindigenous collective asset that the Runa strive to acquire. The Runa consider that strong, gendered persons can ensure not only the well-being of their close kin, but also the maintenance of Runa ways of life. Hence, strong persons, as holders of cultural knowledge and as transformers, are the source *and* producers of personal and collective wealth.

As colonization hinders the Runas' possibilities of achieving well-being and wealth, so does the loss of strength that entails the deconstitution of a person's body and social relations. A person's vitality and transformative capacities are always at risk of being lost. Life is, in this sense, fragile and may become scarce. Life's fragility is expressed as the possibility of losing control over one's life forces, one's labor, or the products of one's efforts. These processes of bodily deconstitution invariably lead to illness and even death, and often imply the appropriation of a person's labor and their products by destroying the productive capacities and erasing the traces of their past work. As a result, persons who were once considered kin, and thus "the same," may turn into enemies, or Others. These processes also imply that those affected may become Others themselves by being forced to migrate and by adopting mestizo ways of being.

Runa ideas of public wealth and well-being are closely related to notions and practices of leadership. The main function of leaders is mediation. As mediators, leaders possess knowledge and abilities acquired with great effort that allow them to have access to other worlds and to establish relations with powerful Others. These Others own the resources that Runa people deem vital to producing personal wealth and achieving collective and personal well-being. As mediators, leaders should also ensure the transference of these resources to their followers. Leaders are simultaneously seen as the same and as Other. Hence, they seek to strike a balance between being like their followers and becoming and acting as powerful Others. By becoming Others, leaders may end up wrecking the lives of their followers either by destroying their bodies, appropriating what they have created, accumulating resources that they should have shared, or establishing exploitative relations.

I suggest that for the Amazonian Runa, personal and collective wealth and well-being are related to the abundance of vital resources, to which every Runa should ideally have access. Wealth and well-being are also related to the processes of becoming persons and a people endowed with transformative capacities. Abundance, access to vital resources, and transformative capacities form the base of wealth and well-being. But if they lead to accumulation, they are always thought to endanger and eventually destroy the social fabric. Using the body as a metaphor, one could say that the whole body, as well as each of its parts, should be fed in order to live well and reproduce.

However, feeding the whole body and each of its parts, and thereby achieving what the Amazonian Runa consider wealth and well-being, is still difficult to achieve in the first decade of the twenty-first century. The expansion of extractive activities and the oil frontier implies, once again, the loss of territorial control and the relocation of populations. Even though the state has recognized and titled vast areas of forests as ancestral indigenous lands, in the Pastaza Province in particular, villagers loose access to the places where oil installations are located. Moreover, oil extraction often entails environmental changes affecting the habitats and the resources upon which the Runa depend. Lands, forests, and rivers that, according to the Runa, allow the production of people are consumed by the powerful forces of extractivism.

Ecuador's current government has certainly reversed the liberalization of the oil sector, strengthened the role of the state, and increased public social investments. According to newly approved legislation, resources coming from oil extraction have to be channeled through public institutions, and the affected settlements should receive additional funds (Guzmán-Gallegos 2014). Notwithstanding the importance of these measures, they also mean that in extractive sites, access to education and health services, which the Runa consider to be vital for their reproduction as a people in contemporary contexts, is still a condition of their acceptance of extractive activities. They are thus caught between the impossible choice of maintaining control over their lands and forests and getting access to nonindigenous potentialities of life. So are their leaders. Runa leaders of villages and of supralocal organizations must navigate the tricky waters between channeling resources and securing opportunities for their people, thereby satisfying their needs and desires while contending, to paraphrase Whitehead (2013, 14), the voracious dynamics of extractivism and capitalism.

Notes

1. OPIP stands for Organization of the Indigenous People of the Pastaza Province. In 2002–2003 OPIP's leadership proposed to change its name to TAKIP, Tantanakui Kichwa Pastaza Runacuna. I retain the use of OPIP, as it was the name most used at the time I did my research.
2. Person and place names are fictitious.
3. OPIP is part of the regional organization CONFENIAE (Confederation of Indigenous Nationalities of the Ecuadorian Amazon) and the national group CONAIE (Confederation of Indigenous Nationalities of Ecuador).
4. ASODIRA (Association for Indigenous Development in the Amazonian Region); AIEPRA (Association of Evangelical Indians of Pastaza in the Amazon Region); and FENAKIPA (Federation of the Kichwa Nationality of the Pastaza Province).

References

Brown, Michael. 1993. "Facing the State, Facing the World: Amazonia's Native Leaders and the New Politics of Identity." *L'Homme* 126:307–26.

Cepek, Michael. 2008. "Bold Jaguars and Unsuspecting Monkeys: The Value of Fearlessness in Cofán Politics." *Journal of the Royal Anthropological Institute* 14:334–52.

Conklin, Beth A. 2001. "Women's Blood, Warriors' Blood, and the Conquest of Vitality in Amazonia." In *Gender in Amazonia and Melanesia: An Exploration of the Comparative Method*, edited by Thomas Gregor and Donald Tuzin, 141–74. Berkeley: University of California Press.

Fausto, Carlos. 2001. *Inimigos fiéis: História, guerra e xamanismo na Amazônia*. São Paulo: Editora da Universidad de São Paulo.

———. 2007. "If God Were a Jaguar: Cannibalism and Christianity Among the Guarani (16th–20th Centuries)." In *Time and Memory in Indigenous Amazonia, Anthropological Perspectives*, edited by Carlos Fausto and Michael Heckenberger, 74–105. Gainesville: University Press of Florida.

———. 2008. "Donos demais: Maestria e domínio na Amazônia." *Mana* 14(2): 329–66.

Fontaine, Guillaume. 2004. "Análisis y evaluación de los conflictos en el Bloque 10." Accessed June 2012. http://www.flacso.org.ec/docs/conflictos_b110.pdf.

Gow, Peter. 2001. *An Amazonian Myth and its History*. Oxford: Oxford University Press.

Guzmán-Gallegos, María Antonieta. 1997. *Para que la yuca beba nuestra sangre: Trabajo, género y parentesco en una comunidad quichua de la Amazonia Ecuatoriana*. Quito: Abya Yala.

———. 2009. "Identity Cards, Abducted Footprints, and the Book of San Gonzalo: The Power of Textual Objects in Runa Worldview." In *The Occult Life of Things: Native Amazonian Theories of Materiality and Personhood*, edited by Fernando Santos-Granero, 214–34. Tucson: University of Arizona Press.

———. 2010. "Conflicting Spatialities: Networks, Mediation and Alterity in the Making of Indigenous Territories in Ecuadorian Amazonia." PhD dissertation, University of Oslo.

———. 2012. "The Governing of Extraction, Oil Enclaves, and Indigenous Responses in the Ecuadorian Amazon." In *New Political Spaces in Latin American Natural Resource Governance*, edited by Håvard Haarstad, 155–76. London: Palgrave Macmillan.

———. 2014. "Conflicting Dilemmas: Economic Growth, Natural Resources and Indigenous Populations in South America, October report." Oslo: NOREF

Instituto Nacional de Estadísticas y Censo. 2010. *Censo de población y vivienda. Nacionalidades por provincia*. Quito: INEC.

Kohn, Eduardo. 2002. "Natural Engagements and Ecological Aesthetics Among the Avila Runa of Amazonian Ecuador." PhD dissertation, University of Wisconsin, Madison.

Oberem, Udo. 1980. *Los Quijos: História de la transculturación de un grupo indígena en el Oriente Ecuatoriano*. Otavalo: Instituto Otavaleño de Antropología.

Rivière, Peter. 1984. *Individual and Society in Guiana: A Comparative Study of Amerindian Social Organization*. Cambridge: Cambridge University Press.

Santos-Granero, Fernando. 2009. *Vital Enemies: Slavery, Predation and the Amerindian Political Economy of Life*. Austin: University of Texas Press.

Sawyer, Suzana. 2004. *Crude Chronicles: Indigenous Politics, Multinational Oil, and Neoliberalism in Ecuador*. Durham: Duke University Press.

Uzendoski, Michael. 2005. *The Napo Runa of Amazonian Ecuador*. Urbana: University of Illinois Press.

Vilaça, Aparecida. 2005. "Chronically Unstable Bodies: Reflections on Amazonian Corporalities." *Journal of the Royal Anthropological Institute* 11:445–46.

Whitehead, Neil. 2013. "Hambre divina: La máquina de guerra caníbal." *Mundo Amazónico* 4:7–30.

Whitten, Norman E., Jr. 1976. *Sacha Runa: Ethnicity, and Adaptation of Ecuadorian Jungle Quichua*. Urbana: University of Illinois Press.

———. 1985. *Sicuanga Runa: The Other Side of Development in Amazonian Ecuador*. Urbana: University of Illinois Press.

CHAPTER FIVE

"It Makes Me Sad When They Say We Are Poor. We Are Rich!"

Of Wealth and Public Wealth(s) in Indigenous Amazonia

JUAN PABLO SARMIENTO BARLETTI

Finding out what public wealth is in legal terms in indigenous Peruvian Amazonia is simple. The *Ley de Comunidades Nativas* (Law of Native Communities) states that all *comuneros*, the legal members of a *comunidad*, have collective usufruct rights over the natural resources within the territory they have been granted by the Peruvian state. However, anyone who has visited a comunidad or follows the struggles of the indigenous Amazonian political movement knows that this is not so simple. Defining public wealth in this region is complex. This is because of the culturally constructed quality of wealth and value (Graeber 2001) and indigenous Amazonian notions of ownership (see Santos-Granero, chapter 3, and Guzmán-Gallegos, chapter 4). It is also because of the difficulty to define what is "public" in this setting. Further, concepts of value and wealth must be contextualized by taking into consideration indigenous Amazonian practices of ownership as a moral relationship, as well as local ideas of the connection between moral labor and the acquisition of socially constructive wealth.

This chapter approaches these issues from the perspective of the Ashaninka people of the Bajo Urubamba River in Peruvian Amazonia.[1] I argue that some of the most important assets that Ashaninka people conceptualize as public wealth are the materials that the comunidad receives from contracts with timber companies, involvement in nongovernmental organizations (NGOs) and/or state projects, or compensation from oil/gas companies, as well as the public spaces (e.g., communal house, football pitch, medical center, etc.) built through their dealings with these external agents. All comuneros have usufruct rights over these spaces and materials, and whenever the latter are redistributed, it is done in a completely egalitarian manner. Yet, their rights are deployed through relationships of care toward these assets that resemble those expected between "real" human beings as taught by *kametsa asaiki*, the Ashaninka ethos for "living well."

I make three points in the following discussion of Ashaninka notions of public wealth. The first is to highlight how complicated it is to define the public sphere in the comunidades, as these contain a multiplicity of "communities." As I show later on, these communities are defined by different criteria of belonging (e.g., legal or kin based), which their members can appeal to in different contexts. However, if as pointed out in the introduction to this volume, the public is that which "is open to, may be used by, or may or must be shared by, *all members of the community*" (my emphasis), then on which of these communities should we place our focus? I suggest that we look at Ashaninka notions of public wealth on the basis of the different conceptions of community that coexist at the local level.[2]

Dan Rosengren (2003) has already highlighted the existence of two parallel views of community for the indigenous populations of this region. Following Gilles Deleuze and Félix Guattari (1988), Rosengren argues that indigenous Amazonians may follow two distinct models for the construction of identity. The first is the "taproot" model, an arbitrary system that stresses "origin as unique and culture as identified with ethnicity" (Rosengren 2003, 223). This model uses indigenous self-denominations in ways that agree "with Western geopolitical notions assuming the existence of an organic bond between people, place, and language" (Rosengren 2003, 223). This model can also be applied to the conceptualization of belonging to a *comunidad nativa* as a political entity, for although not all comuneros within a comunidad are related by kinship, they are related by their shared legal rights to the titled territory they live in. The Peruvian state has granted this land to the group based on an ethnic criteria of being an indigenous Amazonian. Their receipt, use, and care of items of public wealth confirm that they are all comuneros within a same comunidad.

Rosengren further argues that self-denominations can also be understood through a rhizomic model of identity that emphasizes "the local, 'unimagined' community where concrete relations are what counts" (Rosengren 2003, 224). So, while the taproot model is based on the notion of belonging to the comunidad as a political space, the rhizomic model is based on the notion of belonging to kin-based units living within that physical space. We can associate the comunidad with the comunero identity assumed by those living within the titled territory. But we can also associate the kin-based units with an *Ashaninkasanori* (real Ashaninka person) identity, which the Ashaninka people assume in everyday interactions.

These are not mutually exclusive categories of group membership, but they should be regarded as two models that an individual may adopt and make use of in different contexts. I have argued elsewhere (Sarmiento Barletti 2011) that by strategically switching between comunero and Ashaninka identities, villagers can confront issues that would have otherwise been too complicated to deal with internally and would have resulted in fissioning in the past.[3] In spite of the porosity of these two models I believe that they are nonetheless helpful as ideal types for the task at hand. This chapter focuses on relations of public wealth at the level of the comunidad but also shows how these assets are used and cared for at the kin-group level.

My second point has to do with ownership as a social relationship in two different senses. Ashaninka comuneros enjoy usufruct rights over public wealth, but as we shall see, ownership is defined and conceived of through social relationships of care. This is most apparent in relation to the *ashitarori* (*dueños*, owners/masters) of animals or plants whose ownership/mastership mirrors the relations of care that human beings establish with their kin (Fausto 2008). The ashitarori of an animal species is responsible for its members, and so they feed them, give them organized living spaces, defend them from overzealous hunters, and allow them to reproduce and thrive. The ashitarori's relations of care with those he/she fabricates into being show that Ashaninka beings are ashitarori of that which they produce and care for through a moral approach that I discuss later on.[4] This highlights a thought-provoking relation, as anthropological texts have usually argued that property is a relation solely between people (e.g., Hann 1998). The Ashaninka experience agrees with this but also hints at a parallel aspect: a relation between people and assets of public wealth. Ownership/mastership is about cultivating or caring for materials, beings, and spaces, and it shows that this relationship is interchangeable with responsibility. This is quite clear in the way comunidad leaders tell comuneros that they should take care of the materials received from the comunidad "as if they were your family" so that these assets become *kametsa* (*lindo*, beautiful) and help them to produce.

The second sense of ownership as a social relationship is related to the fact that comuneros have rights of usufruct over public wealth because they are part of the comunidad. Public wealth is redistributed in order to create and preserve a sense of conviviality within the comunidad, a setting which gathers a variety of groups that are not necessarily linked by ties of kinship. Following Nurit Bird-David (2005, 214), I emphasize that, in the Ashaninka case, it is more important to look at "the property of relations [rather] than relations of property." By publicly receiving an equal amount of, or equal use over, public assets and exercising their usufruct rights over them, members of a comunidad express and regenerate their sense of togetherness and egalitarianism. Thus, we are looking at a performative sense of property rather than a purely concrete legal approach.

My third point is to show, like other contributors to this book, the link between public wealth and well-being. I suggest that public wealth is linked to kametsa asaiki discourses because public assets aid people in their pursuit of this ethos in a practical sense. However, they also create a renewed sense of egalitarianism among comuneros with different degrees of material accumulation. Additionally, these assets need to be cared for in a manner that reflects the social relations among people who put forth this philosophy of living. Kametsa asaiki means "to live well/beautifully/peacefully" in the physical sense of being in one place. This, as we will see, is an important concern in present-day Ashaninka villages. Kametsa asaiki as a communal project is crucial in times of increased social stress; this has been the case when families have moved from dispersed kin-based settlements to crowded villages where they experience material inequality and greater competition for resources. I will not argue that the pursuit of kametsa asaiki is only important at the comunidad level. But I do posit that the emphasis placed on the communal pursuit of kametsa asaiki, which is thus not constrained to a kinship-based group, is a result of Ashaninka experiences during the Peruvian internal war (officially 1980–2000) and the local reconciliation processes that took place in its wake.[5] Any discussion of contemporary Ashaninka groups in Peru must consider the impact of Sendero Luminoso's insurgent war on their lives. Even the groups that did not take active part in the violence caused by Sendero's attempt to topple the Peruvian state received dozens and even hundreds of refugees fleeing from the armed clashes in the Ene and Tambo rivers. The scale of the war (Ashaninka deaths ranged between 6,000 and 8,000) and the circulation of stories about the Maoist insurgents' cruel excesses instilled great fear in Ashaninka groups, who lived in a state of war for many years after the fighting stopped.[6]

Kametsa asaiki is about the creation of the right kind of human being through the teaching of three interconnected sets of knowledge. The first set is the control of antisocial emotions (e.g., anger, jealousy, stinginess, and sadness) and the everyday practice of the socially constructive ones (e.g., love, happiness, and sorrow). The second set is adoption and display of an ethos of hard work. Real people should be socially productive beings who share the product of their work (e.g., expressing generosity and sorrow for others), who are open to receiving the product of the work of others, and who share in the happiness involved in this. The third set, linked to their use of assets of public wealth, is related to the previous one as it is associated with relationships of care (e.g., feeding, bathing, and protecting) between people who relate to each other as Ashaninkasanori. These elements, which link the good life to the construction of strong, productive, and moral human beings and the promotion of convivial social relations, seem to be also present, though to different degrees, among all of the indigenous Amazonian peoples discussed in this volume. An important aspect of these relations is the emphasis on commensality and the enjoyment of socially productive substances (e.g., real food and magical plants) while avoiding the negative ones (e.g., excessive consumption of white people's food and alcohol). This is all about the hard work that goes into the creation of Ashaninka *cuerpos fuertes* and *caras felices* (strong bodies and happy faces). Comuneros are told they must take care of items of public wealth in a similar manner by, for example, feeding motors petrol and oil, keeping them clean, carrying them carefully when transporting them, and keeping them away from the rain. This is obviously not about consubstantiality but about processes of care that make these objects and spaces kametsa and productive. That is why, toward the end of my fieldwork, it did not surprise me that my *compadre* Chato happily claimed, partly in jest, that he took better care of his outboard motor than of Gali, his wife, my *comadre*.

Contextualizing the Ashaninka Publics

There are some key contextual issues that need to be made clear at this point about the Ashaninka people I work with. Firstly, the legislation on the Comunidades Nativas most Ashaninka people live under was "modeled on legislation intended to accommodate existing peasant communities in the [Andean] Highlands, and it presupposed a communal village-type organization of the rural population, a form of social organization foreign to many Amazonian peoples" (Veber 1998, 394). Comuneros—legally everyone living within the comunidad but in practice the male and female heads of each household—have their responsibilities set in an *acta* (charter) approved when the comunidad was founded. Their key responsibilities are to take part in communal work and contribute funds and/or food and manioc beer to the organization of communal events.

Within all comunidades there are several groups of nuclear households that actively relate to each other as Ashaninka in convivial networks of labor, sharing, and commensality. The Ashaninka term for this aggregation of domestic units is *nampitsi*. Traditionally, these were groupings of domestic units or a large single domestic unit/extended family that lived within a territory under the influence of a *pinkatsari* (*jefe*, headman). The population and area occupied by a nampitsi was variable, and the boundaries between different nampitsi were not well defined. Now, while some Ashaninka people translate nampitsi as comunidad, this translation is not common in the Bajo Urubamba. This was a translation offered to help my understanding, as the differences between these units within a comunidad are obvious and were even more so three decades ago in the early days of the comunidades nativas when they were occupied following a dispersed kinship-based settlement organization.

The members of these rhizomic groups are related by kinship ties, which they work hard to create in everyday life. However, they distinguish their *noshaninkajei* (*familia*, my many Ashaninka kin) as those with whom they actively establish relationships of trust and care through commensality and work in contrast to those who they treat *como familia* (as if they were kin). While the same sets of kinship terms are used to refer to members of these two groups, the distinction made between kin and those treated like kin is obvious in acts of sharing. Prized products (e.g., game) only move outside a kinship unit in times of abundance. Other villagers are treated as *vecinos* (neighbors) or simply as comuneros. The distinction between kin and those treated like kin is made explicit due to the scarcity of resources available for sharing in everyday life, especially game and fish. This makes it harder to comply with the responsibility of sharing game with one's kin. But, by redefining who their kin are, this responsibility is less straining on households that already have difficulties in finding food.[7] At this level, and in a context in which there are so few resources and so many bad memories about the Peruvian internal war, kametsa asaiki becomes the most important public asset.

Early comunidades reflected previous Ashaninka settlement patterns, which were characterized by "living apart" in small family groups (Killick 2005). Gerald Weiss (1975) considers these family groups to be the largest stable political units in Ashaninka society. These "small groupings of houses consist of . . . between one and six nuclear families linked by kinship . . . characterized by a high degree of reciprocity and economic cooperation between the different domestic units that make them up"

(Pimenta 2006, 3). This dispersed spatial organization has been explained in terms that range from environmental constraints (Denevan 1974) to the fulfillment of a peaceful life.[8] In fact, much analysis has been aimed at understanding how Ashaninka people could organize into large groups to confront a common enemy when their social organization seemed to be so atomized. We are told that when this occurs, collective action tends to be short lived, and families return to living apart once the threat diminishes. This has led Søren Hvalkof and Hanne Veber (2005, 226) to describe Ashaninka social life as one in which fragmentation and rupture are the norm, and social unity and collective action are only transitory. However, the physical organization of social life for the past decade has been one of villages based on close physical interaction in which families build their houses in lots that are right next to each other.[9] This is due to their desire to defend themselves from Sendero attacks and to take advantage of schools and health posts.

Thus, local settlements went from being family based with less than fifty inhabitants, to villages that average four hundred inhabitants, to some passing the one-thousand mark.[10] These villages include people that took different sides during the internal war and people who lost family or friends to their adversaries. There is also a mix of people from a variety of regions. Some have weak or no kinship links in the refugee areas but still have settled there in search of land or work. At the time I did my fieldwork, Nueva Esperanza's population consisted of people from the Bajo Urubamba, Ucayali, and Tambo rivers. But it also included families from as far away as the Gran Pajonal, Satipo, Rio Negro, and the Ene and Perene rivers.

My informants underscored the potential danger of having large numbers of people living in close proximity and remarked that their ancestors were not able to live in villages because they would have been engaged in constant conflict with each other. Even if Ashaninka people may have conflict prevention mechanisms, as exemplified by their preference for fissioning (see Santos-Granero 2000), they have no successful means of conflict resolution. Yet, fissioning is not viable today, as villagers want to live close to schools and medical posts. Additionally, most houses are built with more expensive and durable materials (e.g., hardwoods and corrugated iron), which are harder to move and too expensive to leave behind. Families also engage in the cultivation of long-term cash crops, such as coffee and cacao, and there is no question about moving these. How are these and other kinds of wealth and value discussed in everyday interactions within this context of heightened jealousy and greater competition for resources? How do they relate to kametsa asaiki?

Lessons from Two Materially Rich Ashaninka Men

Early one morning, like most mornings, Joel (an Ashaninka man in his late forties,) and I sat in his kitchen at breakfast time listening to a popular local radio news show. This show is popular among the inhabitants of the comunidades of the Ucayali and Bajo Urubamba rivers. Indigenous people living in or visiting Atalaya, the district capital, use it to relay messages back to their comunidades. Toward the end of the show its host reminded *nativos*, the Peruvian legal term for indigenous Amazonians, to register for the *Seguro Integral de Salud* ([SIS] Comprehensive Health Insurance), provided by the Peruvian Ministry of Health for those living close or under the poverty line. As the radio host signed off, the host told listeners that as they "live in extreme poverty," the government had decided that the token registration fee for this insurance, one sol (forty cents), would be waived for them.

Joel chuckled as he took another piece of roasted manioc from our collective plate. From a capitalist point of view, and definitely by Atalaya standards, he is far from being poor. Joel is the only indigenous person I know who lives in a comunidad and owns a house made of brick and corrugated iron. He also owns a small hostel in Atalaya, two boats, each with its own outboard motor, a sound system that he hires out for parties, and large coffee and cacao gardens. His economic success is well-known in the area and is only matched by his generosity, which he expressed in very public displays when he was elected as *padrino* (godfather) for local graduating primary and secondary school classes or in the multiple private ways in which he helped people who needed money. Yet, how can we talk about poverty and material possessions among people who do not recognize value solely in terms of capital accumulation? The economic-based logic of *progreso* (progress) put forth by the Peruvian state is a local version of the universalized approaches to well-being that are promoted by global institutions, such as the World Bank and the United Nations. This not only leads to the classification of indigenous people as "poor" but also as "savages" (see Trouillot [1991] on the savage slot), against which the "developed," "modern," and "civilized" claim their normality. For the Peruvian case, the characterization of indigenous people as living in "extreme poverty" and "ignorance" further justifies extractive development projects and the construction of hydroelectric dams in the name of *inclusion social* (social inclusion). These policies and projects directly interfere with indigenous well-being projects in the Amazon and the Andes. As shown below, Joel is not poor, especially when compared to the materially "rich" outsiders in Atalaya because Ashaninka people believe that wealth and labor are only valuable when deployed relationally.

As we left his house and took the trail bordering the village's football pitch, Chato called us for a pre-workday bowl of manioc beer. We sat with Chato for a while and Joel reminded him to sign up for the SIS, as his wife was pregnant at the time. It was then that I decided to ask Joel about the "extreme poverty" characterization. He replied with a statement that provided the title to this paper.

> No Juanito, it makes me sad when they say we are poor. Look at us, look at all my *paisanos* [fellow Ashaninka] with their strong bodies and their beautiful faces. We live in a comunidad with our families, we work together, no one suffers hunger for if you don't have food someone will call you, "come have at least some manioc." And we have coffee, we have cacao. We sell it to buy pots for our wives to make manioc beer, plates so we can eat together, notebooks for our children to study. . . . The comunidad is titled, the comunidad has timber, look! . . . That's how we have built the communal house, bought those cows, the outboard motor . . . everything! We are rich! [referring to the forest] If I am hungry I go to the market. If I am ill, I go to the pharmacy. . . . Look at the people in town. They live sad lives. They don't eat unless they have money. . . . They cut their water if they don't pay. . . . They are stingy. They argue all the time. They don't know how to feel sorrow for others. Here we live beautifully; we know how to live well.

In a way that I am only now starting to understand, Joel listed a series of tangible and intangible items of wealth that are valuable in different ways: life forces (happy humans with strong bodies/beautiful faces), materials (pots, plates, and notebooks), and assets belonging to the comunidad (cows, motors, and communal houses).[11] This is proof of a greater tendency toward accumulation among indigenous Amazonians, who have been for a long time described as intentionally materially poor. But, as noted throughout this volume (e.g., Micarelli, chapter 6, and Guzmán-Gallegos, chapter 4), indigenous Amazonian conceptions of wealth and value have little to do with individual material accumulation.

Joel's material wealth was never referred to in negative terms by other villagers. Instead, I constantly heard people highlight his work ethic, which followed Ashaninka notions of being *trabajador* (hardworking). Joel did not only work long hours with his nuclear family but was also a good *minga* (work party) host. He always provided good food, copious amounts of manioc beer, and kept everyone entertained with his jokes and stories. This kind of happy work is an important aspect of Ashaninka conviviality. It was also pointed out that he never failed to reciprocate when someone else organized a minga. People commented on how Joel's work ethic and his relational approach to labor had allowed him to acquire material assets. Many stressed how generous he was with the outcome of his work, an attitude that demonstrated that he "knew how to feel sorrow for others," as he always shared his possessions and helped others by contributing his labor, giving them loans, hiring them for short-term work, or lending them his tools. Joel even insisted on giving money to all the members of his football team, including myself, to pay for the registration fees at championships. Other people pointed out that he used his money to help his daughters (both single mothers) and to put his son through secondary school in Atalaya. Others still mentioned the fact that his wife was always well dressed and had very large aluminum pots for brewing manioc beer. Generally, people were more interested in emphasizing his qualities as a political leader, and they considered him as someone who knew how to live a peaceful and happy life. The value placed on how Joel acquired his material wealth and how he used it is even more obvious when we compare him to Coto.

The stories about Coto were tales of a man who abused his power as headman of a local comunidad to sign illegal timber contracts with *patrones* (bosses) for his own profit. He had also betrayed the Ashaninka Federation for the Bajo Urubamba, the organization for which he acted as vice president, when he convinced the representatives of the Spanish oil company Repsol to hire him as their local representative even after strongly opposing the company's entry into the Bajo Urubamba. When I first visited his village, I quickly realized why there was so much gossip about him; he did not only possess a metal chalupa boat, but he also owned an expensive Yamaha outboard motor and a rice peeler. He also had an electric generator that he used to run a TV, a DVD player, and a refrigerator from which he sold overpriced beer to local timbermen.

Coto's material wealth was seen in negative terms since he had been able to hoard all of these objects by being lazy, dishonest, and stingy. In fact, from an Ashaninka perspective, Coto is a perfect example of the condition of poverty because he was disconnected from the social relations that Ashaninka people value in everyday life. This approach to social relations as wealth, and to kinship as central to local theories of value, has been highlighted for other indigenous Amazonian contexts (see, among many others, Gow [1989]; McCallum [2001]; Viveiros de Castro [2009]; and Sahlins [2013] on Amazonian understandings of kinship). To illustrate, I was repeatedly told that Coto's lack of desire or will to engage in positive social relations with other Ashaninka people, including his own kin, confirmed that "he does not know how to live well." Even if materially rich by Atalaya standards, his antisocial accumulation of material wealth only proved his poverty in Ashaninka terms. Coto was considered poor because, as opposed to Joel, he had consistently proven his lack of ability to produce and relate to others following kametsa asaiki practices (see Guzmán-Gallegos, chapter 4, and Micarelli, chapter 6, in this volume for similar ideas among Amazonian Kichwa and the People of the Center, respectively). Instead, he had managed to accumulate all those assets in spite of being *flojo* (lazy), as he had not acquired them through hard work but through *engaño* (deceit).[12] Some of his possessions (rice peeler, generator, and outboard motor) were donated by Repsol for all the local comunidades, yet he insisted that they were his. He had paid for the rest of his possessions with the money obtained from working for Repsol or signing illegal timber contracts. His actions were described as stingy, and it was said that Coto *no sabe tener pena* (Coto does not know how to feel sorrow) for his own kin. Thus, he did not love them, as he had not used his material wealth to care for them. People criticized him for dressing well and for staying long periods in Atalaya drinking beer and living in good hostels, while his wife and daughters dressed in old clothes and were very skinny. Even worse, I heard a lot of gossip asserting that he prostituted his daughters to mestizo timbermen.

By being lazy or acquiring assets through deceit, Coto showed the same antisocial tendencies Yine people find in "perverse" children (Gow 1989), who care only for their own desires. Yet, the accumulative approach to well-being is obvious in some villages. Although a degree of material wealth is necessary for kametsa asaiki (e.g., machetes, plates, and pots), the antisocial accumulation of wealth by some comuneros affects the delicate balance of conviviality at the comunidad level. This is most obviously manifested in the increasing concern about theft and witchcraft in the villages I lived in. Theft and witchcraft are said to stem from jealousy directed at people who accrue material wealth antisocially. The rejection of antisocial accumulative practices is also expressed in rounds of gossip positing that some people have acquired their possessions through immoral means, such as stealing or making shady deals with timbermen. This shows that in the Ashaninka case, as with the People of the Center (see Micarelli, chapter 6), wealth becomes antisocial if it is not circulated at least within the rhizomic unit, since the emphasis Ashaninka people place on the relational aspect of wealth is still very influential in defining value. This has to do with a clash between transactions that keep wealth in circulation (cycles of reciprocity) and those that remove it from circulation ([accumulation] Strathern 1999). The jealousy caused by the different degrees of wealth among comuneros is also reflected in the transformation of Ashaninka houses, which were traditionally open but now have walls and a door that can usually be locked. Valuable possessions, once hidden under the roof, are now kept within four walls. This is definitely a change that arises from the more obvious presence of material wealth in villages and the fact that the comunidad does not coincide with the traditional economic unit, that is, the extended family or multifamily household. Mechanisms such as gossip, not being invited to social events, and public shaming in communal assemblies are still relatively successful leveling mechanisms for those who have accumulated wealth through immoral means.[13]

The neoliberal reading of the global market seeks to subordinate everything in the planet to a single standard of value. Joel and Coto show that value does not just derive from labor but from a specific kind of labor that cannot be detached from cultural principles of morality and that make things meaningful and symbolically connected to other aspects of life (Gow 1989; Guzman chapter 4; Micarelli chapter 6; Passes 2000; Uzendoski 2004; and in this volume). In this case, value must be understood in the light of Ashaninka ideas of emotions and through the morality of labor and wealth. These notions are an important aspect of kametsa asaiki, and they play a crucial role in the making of people into Ashaninkasanori. By prioritizing the accumulation of material assets, Coto purposefully disconnected himself from the social relations of care that are a key dimension of kametsa asaiki in everyday life. By doing so, Coto acted like the white and mestizo inhabitants of Atalaya who Ashaninka people criticize for their lack of humanity, which is expressed in their stinginess and their incapacity to "feel sorrow" for the hungry Ashaninka who sit by the port waiting for a boat ride back home. My informants repeatedly pointed out to me that these attitudes prove that the people of Atalaya "do not know how to live well."

So, it is not so much that Joel was able to live well because of the wealth he had been able to accrue, but rather that he had been able to acquire his wealth because he lived well. Thus, like among the Yanesha (see Santos-Granero, chapter 3), wealth depends on an individual's capacity to engage in positive social relationships with others. Coto's antisocial accumulation led him to travel away from the Bajo Urubamba for long periods to avoid the amount of gossip and criticism waged against him. He was regarded as morally poor and unproductive like the people of Atalaya, who do not care for others; a moral judgement that coincides with what Uitoto and Muinane leaders told Giovanna Micarelli (chapter 6), namely, that the real poor are lazy, stingy people, since material wealth has no value if it is not acquired through hard work and if it is not shared with others.[14] Now that we have a better idea of how Ashaninka people experience wealth, value, and ownership, let us complicate this further by seeing how it is put into play in the comunidad and how the public deploys it.

The Entitlement to Public Wealth and the Creation of Community

I opened this chapter by saying that, in legal terms, public wealth in a comunidad is constituted by the natural resources that exist within its boundaries and over which comuneros have usufruct rights. Nueva Esperanza villagers asserted that natural resources were owned by the comunidad as a political institution. Comuneros do not have the right to sell timber without the consent of the headperson, who is the legal representative of the comunidad.[15] The communidad owns timber and thus the money or material goods achieved from selling it. It also owns the assets bought or built with such income, the material donations received from the Regional Government of Ucayali and NGOs, and materials received as compensation from oil/gas companies operating in their territories.[16] Comuneros are entitled to use these assets because they are members of the comunidad as a legal entity. Thus, these goods are what economists term *club goods*.

Public wealth can therefore be understood as the materials and spaces owned by the comunidad. As has been stated, comuneros enjoy usufruct rights over this wealth—rights that are mediated by Ashaninka people's understandings of ownership and value. The comunidad, represented by the headperson, redistributes these assets at public events that are specifically organized for this purpose. These are usually held in the communal house and are accompanied by the consumption of manioc beer and a series of public speeches by the headperson and other communal authorities. Assets received from community deals (e.g., corrugated iron sheets or motors) are distributed equally among the households.

Sometimes the comunidad invests in purchasing more assets (e.g., cows, a larger communal house, boats, and outboard motors), which become available for comuneros to use. Although this may be public wealth over which community members have usufruct rights, the use of these spaces and materials is understood through the relationships of care and responsibility characteristic of the ashitarori relationship.[17] Community leaders repeatedly and publicly advise comuneros that the comunidad's outboard motors or electric generators must be taken care of "como si fuera tu hijo" (as if it were your child) and thus must be fed with petrol and oil and be transported with care. Communal work groups in charge of cutting the grass around the school, clearing community trails, or cleaning the communal house and school are organized "para que la comunidad este linda" (so that the community looks beautiful) and "para poder usarle bien" (so that we can use it well). Comuneros maintained that only by caring for their communal assets would these be able to function properly and look beautiful. This is an explicit reference to the human bodies they care for and help produce in everyday life.

How does the distribution of goods and use of spaces under the taproot model differ from the distribution of items of wealth or game in the rhizomic model? In Nueva Esperanza people only receive comunidad assets or are allowed to use them because they are comuneros. They do not obtain these rights because of any kinship relations with the headman, who acts as the distributor of the assets or who is usually in charge of safekeeping key assets, such as electric generators or outboard motors. Comuneros are entitled to use these assets only insofar as they live within the comunidad. I witnessed a case in which a family that moved out of Nueva Esperanza had to leave behind the corrugated iron sheets that they had received as part of a deal between the comunidad and a petrol company.[18] The comunidad is a community of people that are not related by kinship links but by their rights and responsibilities within a political space. Thus, a group like this cannot exist without the maintenance of the people who comprise it and who have rights and responsibilities that differ greatly from kinship obligations. The distribution of motors, money, corrugated iron sheets, and so on are public acknowledgments of the links and equality between comuneros. This equality is acted out and publicly demonstrated to oppose any possible inequalities in other aspects of the everyday, such as different degrees of material wealth.

Public wealth allows comuneros to become related to each other within the comunidad. This doesn't happen through processes of kinship fabrication but through claiming and confirming membership in a comunidad as equals. This is not to say that there is no sense of connection between Ashaninka people that have no kinship links. Olivier Ordinaire (1988, 91–92) wrote about a greeting that was recited in ritual salutations. "If you are hungry, I will share with you what I hunt and fish and the fruits of my garden, because you are [Ashaninka], and [Ashaninka] people must love each other with true friendship. . . . If an enemy attacks you, I will risk my life to defend you, because you are [Ashaninka]. . . . If [a demon] kills you, your children will be mine, because you are [Ashaninka]."

Stefano Varese (2002, 34) confirms Ordinaire's report when he quotes an Ashaninka man who claimed that even if his ayompari trading partner may not "[belong] to my family or my kinship system; I might not even know him . . . he speaks my language; he is an Ashaninka. He knows the proper greeting, accepts my food and gifts, and repays them with others." But, in spite of this macrocommonality, contemporary everyday life presents major tensions stemming from conflicts created by the internal war, overpopulated villages, and shortage of resources. Kametsa asaiki discourses are framed by an underlying mistrust, and to a certain extent even fear of their current neighbors, who are thought to have become demons during the war, of those who drink too much, forgetting the many years of violence, and get into fights, or of those who steal or may be involved in witchcraft. The reorganization of life into villages has definitely altered the game of sociality and requires a much stronger attempt to create a community for which the distribution of public goods is crucial.

The differences between sections of the comunidad become even more apparent when we look at them from the perspective of its rhizomic units. The tensions arising from the stresses created by jealousy, participation in different sides of the war, overcrowding, and pressure from the outside lead to a fiercer competition for life forces that are key in the fabrication of human beings and kinship as Santos-Granero (2009) suggests. Ashaninka people are the outcome and the embodiment of social relations created through a knowledgeable process of care and controlled bodily transformation. However, comuneros are the outcome of processes of community making that are based on their mutual occupancy of a titled space and of responsibilities to and benefits derived from this political space. At the same time, the assets derived from this political space are crucial to the creation of Ashaninka people at the rhizomic level: outboard motors are used for fishing and boat trips; corrugated metal sheets are used for building houses; electric generators keep the music at parties going for days; the communal house is used for important events (from meetings to feasts); and the school disseminates the knowledge that Ashaninka people believe is key for surviving in contemporary Peru. As such, public wealth does not only contribute to achieving the condition of living well in the practical sense, but it creates a sense of material equality that helps deter jealousy and the anger and violence that may derive from it. Comuneros become manifestations of the egalitarian circulation of public goods through which they construct their social identities. Things, when distributed in such a way, are definitely invested with the properties of social relations (Appadurai 1986).

This stronger and more explicit attempt at conviviality is exemplified in the egalitarian distribution of items of public wealth, and it is clear in the proposition of kametsa asaiki as a communal moral project. This is obvious in the sessions of advice given by comunidad leaders before communal feasts, at communal meetings, and during the imposition of *sanciones* (sanctions).[19] It is also evident in other less formal occasions, such as house visits or manioc beer parties when a communal authority reminds comuneros to live well, and when comuneros remind others that they should teach their children not to steal and how to work like an Ashaninkasanori should.

The literature on Ashaninka and other Arawakan societies highlights the primacy of the individual above the collective, even in the context of the comunidad (Killick 2005; Rosengren 2003). However, I learned during my fieldwork that today, when it comes to the comunidad, sometimes collective well-being takes priority over that of the individual because there is an underlying understanding that the well-being of the individual cannot exist without the well-being of the comunidad. This is important if we consider that never in recent history have so many free Ashaninka people lived in such close proximity. The Ashaninka have now come to believe that the communidad is the ideal spatial organization. They say that when people lived apart from each other "they lived badly, they would make war for anything. . . . It was very sad." Instead, being a comunero is to "live peacefully, free to work on my garden, to fish, [and] to hunt." I was told comuneros can now live peacefully since there are no more wars between Ashaninka people, and "problems are solved with the [headperson] who speaks and decides on the gravity [of the fault] and the sanction." The pursuit of kametsa asaiki at this level is understood as a communal endeavor that deals with all the contextual issues I have mentioned earlier; but it is also a mechanism to deal with external impositions and a means of reinforcing a sense of group identity. The use of and care over items of public wealth exemplify the notions of comunidad and living well.

Conclusion: Wealth, Public Wealth(s), and Well-Being in Peruvian Amazonia

I once asked my *compadre*, Gerardo, to tell me the story of how he had met my comadre, Adelina, and how they got married. He told me, "when I first met your comadre, and we wanted to get together, I had to show to my father-in-law that I was a good hunter [and] hardworking. Now young men have to show that they can make money; now you need money for pots, for plates, for soap, [and] for clothes." Although statements like Gerardo's are now common throughout indigenous Amazonia, the contributions to this volume show that in these societies there is still an important moral component in the process of making and accumulating material wealth that is concerned with how these objects are acquired and then deployed in everyday life.

I have portrayed how the different levels of community within the comunidad nativa complicate the "public" in the notion of public wealth. The conception of community discussed here is not the only one that can be taken into consideration. We could also find a sense of community in the narratives of a homogeneous Ashaninka ethnic group put forth by Ashaninka ethno-political organizations. The notion of community can also be extended to those belonging to a specific Ashaninka territory, like the Enesati, who live by the Ene River, or the Tamposati, who live along the Tambo River. As other contributors to this volume, I have considered public wealth as a precondition for living well, but this kind of wealth can only be understood within the relations of care encompassed by the notion of kametsa asaiki. Access to public wealth in the comunidad creates an identity as comuneros with equal rights and responsibilities, whereas the use and care of items of public wealth is intrinsic to the process of creating an Ashaninkasanori identity. This highlights the role of public wealth in the construction of persons and the reproduction of local collectivities, a central theme to this volume.

What we see in the Ashaninka case is not a purely legal system but one that is also influenced by the way Ashaninka people understand ownership as a social relationship. It is a hybrid that should be viewed as a response to larger systems of power (Fisher 2000). I suggest that the use of items of public wealth is a political statement; the acceptance and use of such items constitutes an explicit message of egalitarian belonging to the comunidad and of social interaction as comuneros. The acquisition and consumption of these public goods as a collective are in stark contrast to the attempts by the Peruvian state to redefine existing relationships and emphasize individual ownership as an ideological principle.[20] This is especially obvious in recent proposals to divide communal territories into individually owned plots.

The introduction to this volume postulates that the study of public wealth is a unique point from which to understand indigenous notions of well-being. What can interdisciplinary debates on well-being learn from Ashaninka concepts of value, wealth, and public wealth? The Ashaninka experience gives us a tool with which to critically interrogate current definitions of well-being. With the rise of personal well-being as a notion of virtue that is in high demand (Furedi 2004), most well-being research focuses on self-knowledge, self-responsibility, and individual agency. Another body of literature defines human well-being in terms of welfare. Dietz, Rosa, and York (2009), for example, define well being as the product of successful nations. Thus, well-being-as-welfare is affected by flows of physical capital (i.e., gross domestic product per capita), natural capital (i.e., a nation's ecological footprint), and human capital (i.e., levels of education).

These studies pay little attention to non-Euro-American notions of well-being, especially as they relate to cultural variations of understanding and usage of the term. I propose that we subject another question to a wider scholarly debate: to what extent do discourses and ideas of well-being reflect ways of thinking about the world? Or what would it mean to take culture seriously when it comes to well-being and indexes of poverty and happiness? How do we understand my friend Joel's frustration with Ashaninka people being labeled as living in "extreme poverty," when from his point of view, they are not? My exploration of Ashaninka notions of value, wealth, and public wealth shows that Joel is rich in what is most important to him: the social relations that matter. If we engage in a qualitative rather than quantitative approach to well-being, one that is sensitive to local articulations of well-being and social capital, and to local logics of social relations (see, for example, Seeger's analysis of music, happiness, and euphoria as wealth in chapter 1), we find that Joel does not live well because of his personal material assets and those he obtains from the comunidad, even if these goods do help. Rather, he has access to these goods because he concentrates on the pursuit of kametsa asaiki. That is why he considers himself to be rich.

Notes

1. Known as Campa until the 1980s, Ashaninka people are speakers of an Arawakan language. Estimates put their population at 100,000 people, and most of them live in the Peruvian Selva Central. Around 2,000 of them live in the Brazilian state of Acre

2. There is another conception of community worth highlighting: Ashaninka as an ethnic category. I cannot expand on this here, but I suggest looking for public wealth in the use of narratives of indigenous knowledge or the use of tropes related to *buen vivir* (good life) that are recognized by the state (see Whitten and Whitten [chapter 7] for the homonymous but clashing uses of the good life by states and indigenous peoples).

3. Communal assemblies, in which there might be a great deal of direct criticism presented by villagers to other villagers, are events in which participants do not relate to each other using kinship terms but instead use their positions within the comunidad (headperson, vice headperson, president of the parents' association, comunero, etc.). Participants return to relating to each other as kin once these assemblies are over.

4. By referring to *beings* rather than *people*, I highlight the accepted possibility that Ashaninka beings are not necessarily human in the biological sense.

5. See Degregori (2011) for a general but insightful account of Sendero Luminoso and the war in the Peruvian Andes and Caruso (2012) and Sarmiento Barletti (2011) for the conflict in Ashaninka territory.

6. In fact, Ashaninka groups in areas of intense colonization and extractive operations still live in a state of war. Sendero Luminoso columns are still active in the Apurimac and Ene valleys and parts of the Bajo Urubamba. But people in these areas also believe that Alan Garcia, who was president 1985–1990 and 2006–2011, wanted to kill them because he sent Sendero Luminoso in the 1980s and petrol companies in his second government (see Santos-Granero and Barclay [2011] on the appearance of white supernatural beings as a response to

neoliberal policies in Peruvian Amazonia). Many of my informants referred to Garcia as *ashitarori kityoncari/compania* (the owner/master of the reds/the companies).

7. The sharing of game is widespread in areas with greater game availability, such as the Ene River.

8. Killick dedicates his doctoral thesis (2005) to the analysis of the social mechanisms that allow Ashaninka people to interact as a group despite the long distances between their settlements.

9. Like their Yine neighbors, Ashaninka villagers speak of the domesticated, ordered space of the comunidad as aesthetically pleasing and as a marker distinguishing those living in a civilized manner and wild forest Indians (Gow 1991, 28).

10. Nueva Esperanza had seventy inhabitants separated into three dispersed settlements in the early 1980s. They ballooned to almost five hundred inhabitants in a village of seventy-four houses in 2007.

11. If we consider Joel's work in indigenous federations, his use of tropes of the forest as a pharmacy or market becomes more than a simple metaphor and can be understood as part of the environmental discourses put forth by the indigenous movement of natural resources as public wealth at a supracommunal level.

12. Nonagricultural, nonforest work can also be hard work. Hard work has to do with morality and involves honesty and care. Leaders who achieve gains for their constituents are seen as hardworking while those who are idle or are thought to appropriate the work of others are not.

13. These leveling mechanisms may lead villagers reproached as antisocial to move to Atalaya. Coto snubbed the gossip in his village, as he had a tight control over it (many people likened him to a patron). But he did encounter problems when he arrived at other villages as a Repsol representative.

14. The value placed in social relations is obvious in ayompari trade. Even if in practice this was the exchange of scarce items (metal tools or salt) and luxury goods (ornaments) by men with different access to them, its purpose was the accumulation of social relations. Hence, objects were valuable because they could become social relations. Ayompari also acted as a redistribution mechanism that created material homogeneity by dispersing goods throughout the group.

15. Projects are discussed in communal assemblies and approved by comuneros, but headpersons still have a great deal of control over timber because they must sign any timber-related contracts. This allows some, like Coto, to abuse their position. This also brings up an interesting question that I cannot answer here: Is the control over wealth more important than its possession?

16. The oil/gas companies in the area (PlusPetrol and Repsol) have stopped paying compensations in cash and instead pay them in material goods that each comunidad selects from a list. This arrangement is also common in large-scale timber contracts.

17. Amahuaca people of the Inuya River share a similar concept (Christopher Hewlett, pers. comm.).

18. I was told that the corrugated iron sheets would then be passed on to future families.

19. Ashaninka people have introduced sanciones, public acts of conflict resolution through rehumanization, to deal with the antisocial actions of some comuneros. Sanciones are a means to reestablish their moral community. They are ritual acts that put antisocial comuneros through a series of physical tests intended to publicly shame them.

20. See Sarmiento Barletti (2012) for an analysis of kametsa asaiki practices as indigenous politics and as a form of resistance to imposition from the Peruvian state and other powerful outsiders.

References

Appadurai, Arjun. 1986. "Introduction: Commodities and the Politics of Value." In *The Social Life of Things: Commodities in Cultural Perspective*, edited by Arjun Appadurai, 3–63. Cambridge: Cambridge University Press.

Bird-David, Nurit. 2005. "The Property of Sharing: Western Analytical Notions, Nayaka Contexts." In *Property and Equality: Ritualisation, Sharing, Egalitarianism*, edited by Thomas Widlock and Wolde Gossa Tadesse, 201–16. New York: Berghahn Books.

Caruso, Emily. 2012. "Being at the Centre: Self and Empire among Ene Ashaninka People in Peruvian Amazonia." PhD dissertation, University of Kent.

Degregori, Carlos Ivan. 2011. *Qué difícil es ser Dios. El Partido Comunista del Perú-Sendero Luminoso y el conflicto armado*. Lima: Instituto de Estudios Peruanos.

Deleuze, Gilles and Félix Guattari. 1988. *A Thousand Plateaus*. Minneapolis: University of Minnesota Press.

Denevan, William. 1974. "Campa Subsistence in the Gran Pajonal, Eastern Peru." *Geographical Review* 61:496–518.

Dietz, Thomas, Eugene Rosa, and Richard York. 2009. "Environmentally Efficient Well-being: Rethinking Sustainability as the Relationship between Human Well-being and Environmental Impacts." *Human Ecology Review* 16:114–23.

Fausto, Carlos. 2008. "Donos demais: Maestria e domínio na Amazônia." *Mana* 14(2):329–66.

Fisher, William. 2000. *Rainforest Exchanges: Industry and Community on an Amazonian Frontier*. Washington, DC: Smithsonian Institute.

Furedi, Frank. 2004. *Therapy Culture*. London: Routledge.

Gow, Peter. 1991. *Of Mixed Blood: Kinship and History in Peruvian Amazonia*. Oxford: Clarendon Press.

———. 1989. "The Perverse Child: Desire in a Native Amazonian Subsistence Economy." *Man* 24(4):567–82.

Graeber, David. 2001. *Toward an Anthropological Theory of Value: The False Coin of Our Own Dreams*. New York: Palgrave.

Hann, Chris. 1998. "Introduction: The Embeddedness of Property." In *Property Relations: Renewing the Anthropological Tradition*, edited by Chris Hann, 1–47. Cambridge: Cambridge University Press.

Hvalkof, Søren, and Hanne Veber. 2005. "Los Ashéninka del Gran Pajonal." In *Guía etnográfica de la alta amazonía. Volumen V: Campa Ribereños/Ashéninka*, edited by Fernando Santos and Frederica Barclay, 75–279. Lima: Smithsonian Tropical Research Institute/Instituto Francés de Estudios Andinos.

Killick, Evan. 2005. "Living Apart: Separation and Sociality Amongst the Ashen-inka of Peruvian Amazonia." PhD dissertation, London School of Economics.

McCallum, Cecilia. 2001. *Gender and Sociality in Amazonia: How Real People are Made*. Oxford: Berg.

Ordinaire, Olivier. 1988. *Del Pacífico al Atlántico y otros escritos*. Lima: Instituto Francés de Estudios Andinos.

Passes, Alan. 2000. "The Value of Working and Speaking Together: A Facet of Pa'ikwené (Palikur) Conviviality." In *The Anthropology of Love and Anger: The Aesthetics of Conviviality in Native Amazonia*, edited by Joanna Overing and Alan Passes, 97–113. London: Routledge.

Pimenta, Jose. 2006. *Reciprocidade, mercado e desigualdade social entre os Ashaninka do Rio Amonia*. Brasilia: Serie Antropologica.

Rosengren, Dan. 2003. "The Collective Self and the Ethnopolitical Movement: "Rhizomes" and "Taproots" in the Amazon." *Identities* 10(2):221–40.

Sahlins, Marshall. 2013. *What Kinship Is—and Is Not*. Chicago: University of Chicago Press.

Santos-Granero, Fernando. 2000. "The Sisyphus Syndrome or the Struggle for Conviviality in Native Amazonia." In *The Anthropology of Love and Anger: The Aesthetics of Conviviality in Native Amazonia*, edited by Joanna Overing and Alan Passes. 268–87. London: Routledge.

———. 2009. *Vital Enemies: Slavery, Predation, and the Amerindian Political Economy of Life*. Austin: University of Texas Press.

Santos-Granero, Fernando and Frederica Barclay. 2011. "Bundles, Stampers, and Flying Gringos: Amazonian Perceptions of Capitalist Violence." *Journal of Latin American and Caribbean Anthropology* 16(1):143–67.

Sarmiento Barletti, Juan Pablo. 2012. "Les enjeux politiques du "bien-vivre" en Amazonie autochtone." *Recherches Amérindiennes au Québec* 42(2–3):49–61.

———. 2011. "Kametsa Asaiki: The Pursuit of the "Good Life" in an Ashaninka Village (Peruvian Amazonia)." PhD dissertation, University of St. Andrews.

Strathern, Marilyn. 1999. *Property, Substance, and Effect: Anthropological Essays on Persons and Things*. London: The Athlone Press.

Trouillot, Michel-Rolph. 1991. "Anthropology and the Savage Slot: The Poetics and Politics of Otherness." In *Recapturing Anthropology: Working in the Present*, edited by Richard G. Fox, 17–44. Santa Fe: School of American Research Press.

Uzendoski, Michael. 2004. "Manioc Beer and Meat: Value, Reproduction, and Cosmic Substance among the Napo Runa of the Ecuadorian Amazon." *Journal of the Royal Anthropological Institute* 10(4):883–902.

Varese, Stefano. 2002. *Salt of the Mountain: Campa Ashaninka History and Resistance in the Peruvian Jungle*. Norman: University of Oklahoma Press.

Veber, Hanne. 1998. "The Salt of the Montana: Interpreting Indigenous Activism in the Rain. Forest." *Cultural Anthropology* 13(3):382–413.

Viveiros de Castro, Eduardo. 2009. "The Gift and the Given: Three Nano-Essays on Kinship and Magic." In *Kinship and Beyond: The Genealogical Model Reconsidered*, edited by Sandra Bamford and James Leach, 237–68. New York: Berghahn.

Weiss, Gerald. 1975. *Campa Cosmology: The World of a Forest Tribe in South America*. New York: American Museum of Natural History.

CHAPTER SIX

Divine Banknote

The Translation of Project Money into Public Wealth

GIOVANNA MICARELLI

All margins are dangerous. If they are pulled this way or that, the shape of fundamental experience is altered. Any structure of ideas is vulnerable at its margins.

—*Mary Douglas,* Purity and Danger

Cuando hay, póngase triste, porque se va acabar; y cuando no hay, póngase contento, porque va a llegar. (When you have it, be sad, because it will end; and when you don't have it, be happy, because it will come.)

—*Uitoto elder*

The identification of development with money and Western goods is a topic discussed by anthropologists working in the global economic periphery (Pigg 1992; Taussig 1980). In Amazonia, the budgeting, disbursement, and expenditure of money, controlled by a powerful but unruly technical and bureaucratic apparatus, have also become the mark of development for its "beneficiaries." This is surely revealing of development's "unintended consequences," which Ferguson (1994) aptly characterizes as the expansion of bureaucratic state power. Moreover, such interpretations constitute the pivotal point of different regimes of value, and they offer a window on the processes through which modernity is understood and appropriated by people living at its margins. The unintended consequences of development, then, may also involve the strengthening of cultural forms that run counter to the implicit telos of development. And although we have informative studies of development as a process linked to Western modernity and historicity (Ferguson 1994; Escobar 1995; Edelman and Haugerud 2005), we know little about how development plays out in the emergence of interethnic identity politics or what cultural meanings are harnessed in political processes that challenge the implicit beliefs of development and its practical workings. This chapter is partly intended to correct that lack through a consideration of native notions of wealth, leadership, and well-being that came into view during a specific development encounter: a project funded by the United States Agency of International Development (USAID), a bilateral agency working with the People of the Center of southeastern Colombia.[1] In particular, I take as the point of entry to such notions the symbols and performances that people deployed in dealing with project money. My suggestion here is that money is the linchpin where the external world of radical alterity (*lo de afuera*) and internal world of shared substances (*lo de adentro*) swing into each other. Sahlins (1999, xvi) made the point that engagement with world capitalist domination was not enough to undo indigenous cultures. He showed how foreign money is assimilated "in the logics of the familiar" through processes of "indigenization of modernity" and inserted in existing exchange obligations. Similarly, Parry and Bloch (1989, 19) emphasized that money does not give rise to a particular cosmology, but that "an existing world view gives rise to particular ways of representing money." Writing about the Tukanoan people, Hugh-Jones (1992, 58) showed that indigenous demands for foreign goods are not merely a response to external pressures, and that "to possess [manufactured goods] is to share in the world from which they derive and to appropriate some of the transformational power that is used to make them."

For Silvia Rivera Cusicanqui (2010), historical modernity, introduced in the Andean world through progressive processes of colonization, was an arena for the development of what she calls *indigenous modernities*, which were structured from long memory of internal mercantile circulation in which women played a fundamental role. According to Rivera, women had the knowledge of exchange routes, and they traveled and exchanged products; but, more importantly, they were also in charge of the rituality of the margins and the domestication of the external elements that threatened humanity. In the colonial world they took on the responsibility of domesticating the new savage world of money and accumulation through redistributive practices shaped around the logics of reciprocity.

During my fieldwork in Peruvian and Colombian Amazonia, I came to appreciate the indigenous knack for reinterpreting modern things, from money to trash. These incorporations, which show the vitality of indigenous cultures, often extend to support indigenous political claims. For example, Global Positioning Systems (GPS) are used to map sacred landscapes and claim territorial rights; money can buy ritual substances, such as tobacco, that are essential to cultural and social reproduction; and cameras record cultural and political events. With a stroke of luck, they can even capture a spirit's image, which can then be used as proof of the veracity of indigenous cosmological visions, as I personally witnessed in Leticia. A Uitoto leader's claim that "in the indigenous tradition we have video screens, radars, and telecommunications" to publicly defend indigenous education against state education suggests that modern stuff is not all that foreign in indigenous perceptions.

However, I also came to understand that these appropriations aren't unproblematic; in spite of a seemingly indigenous fascination with the margins, margins are dangerous. The People of the Center, for example, consider money to be "hot" and potentially pathogenic. They include development in their etiology as one of the "illnesses of the white man's trail." To take indigenous peoples' own understandings seriously, then, is not just to ask how they incorporate modern money creatively into their social practices but also to ask how they deal with these dangerous margins and what may be the place of such endeavors in their cosmological views. The former question, which focuses on the product—money's switch of meaning as it goes from A to B—rather than the process, may work to counter suspicious ideas of authenticity implicit in the view of money as incompatible with indigenous communities. But its drawback is that it treats margins as if they were not constitutive of human experience, implies a static notion of signification, and views cultures as bounded and self-contained wholes.

These implications are thorny in general, but they are even more so in Amazonia where humanity and sociality are conceived as projects in the making and by no means as finished products (Viveiros de Castro 2001). Actually, once one assumes a native Amazonian perspective, margins prove to be rather central to human experience; humanity and sociality are energized precisely by what plays out at the margins and by how margins are dealt with. Accordingly, my suggestion is that modern stuff is not just recast to fit indigenous cosmological understandings, it serves symbolically and materially to feed and expand such understandings in acts that have more than political significance. Among the People of the Center, for instance, money, is the subject of constant debate. Its meanings are ambiguous, and its uses are controversial. However, all the tinkering with the idea and significance of money seems to be necessary to invigorate personal and collective identities and visions of well-being.

This discussion is based on extensive fieldwork in the Resguardo Indígena Tikuna-Uitoto Km. 6–11, an indigenous territory located on the Colombian Amazon, and, especially, on a two-year consulting experience for the indigenous organization known as "El camino del tabaco, el mambe, la manicuera y el yagé" (the path of tobacco, mambe, manicuera, and yagé).[2] In 2008, a group of indigenous elders I had known since about a decade earlier intensified their search for allies to back the process of cultural reaffirmation and intercultural organization that they were carrying out in the resguardo. Longtime friends of the group, including myself, resumed conversations with the elders and jointly agreed to put together a proposal for a USAID grant. Eventually, funds were granted in 2009 and again in 2010. Before moving on to the discussion of the clashing visions of wealth that emerged in the process of managing the project's budget, I place the elders' project in a broader context of development entanglements and critical accounts that was key in shaping their rationales and practical responses.

Sleeping on Top of Money: Images of Development

The Resguardo Indígena Tikuna-Uitoto, Km. 6–11 is situated just a few miles from the Colombian town of Leticia along the national borders of Colombia, Peru, and Brazil. With about 7,540 hectares, it has a population of approximately 1,600 individuals who represent at least 10 different ethnic groups.[3] This diverse makeup results from the interaction of several processes of migration, displacement, and reterritorialization mostly related to rubber extraction (1880–1945). It also results from millenarian movements in the case of the Tikuna (1950s), state-level expansion, and more recently the armed conflict between the Revolutionary Armed Forces of Colombia, paramilitary groups, and the State. In response to the provision of centralized state health, education, and housing services by the 1970s, indigenous communities began to form along the planned road between Leticia and Tarapacá. These *comunidades indígenas* were crucial to harnessing dispersed indigenous people to the state apparatus, and so they became the natural terrain of development for state institutions and nongovernmental organizations (NGOs). Likewise, the discourse of empowerment and sustainability converged on the idea of community and communal participation.

This imposed but fragile form of organization generated, however, more problems than gains. It increased forms of control and dependence and prompted a series of interethnic conflicts mostly about leadership and access to natural and economic assets that frustrated progress toward greater political organization and self-determination. Development is now a lingering presence in community life, and while people strive to acquire development money, they also claim that development "makes them ill." They refer to this schismogenic condition simply as "*la crisis*": a loss of control that becomes pathogenic and affects health on physical, psychological, social, environmental, and cosmological levels. The following excerpt of a conversation between two Uitoto leaders of the Km. 11 community provides clues for exploring the way in which the crisis is culturally construed.

> "We always talk about development, but what did it bring to us? We are complaining. In what did we fail? We have to become aware, wake up the truth that has been obscured. We are not thinking with our principle of origin. We are sleeping on top of money."
>
> "I made an estimate of all the economic and infrastructure projects that have been implemented in the Km. 11 community from 1995 to 1998. 135,000,000 pesos were invested by the national government [65,000 US dollars, when the minimum salary was $115 per month]. . . . Through us a lot of money is arriving. But if we don't put it [money? our principle of origin?] in practice. . . . Because there are two cultures. If we work with both, you can be sure, we will go ahead."
>
> "A positive force is nothing; it needs to join a negative force to produce something. We are unnecessarily wasting energy and we are going crazy. . . . We are fools for trying to pacify the other [Western] criterion."
>
> "Money is the heart of the White man, and for this reason it is difficult for us to manage it. But that's not true, because indigenous people from their ancestral part have managed their money, their resources, their economy."

It is clear from this conversation that the leaders see themselves and their communities as a channel through which "money is arriving." But money has brought no prosperity to the community. Why? On the one hand, people don't put money into practice; they are "sleeping on top of money." On the other hand, the productive interaction between contrasting forces, cultures, and criteria is lacking. To put these ideas together may yield a better sense of the "principle of origin" evoked by the leaders. It suggests a view frequently discussed in Amazonian anthropology, to wit, that the source and driving purpose of life hinge on the dynamic exchange between seemingly contrasting forces. This exchange fertilizes the constant flow and transformation of vital energy. But for energy to flow, people must do their part. If they are lazy, money will be useless, and its accumulated "heat" will start producing all kinds of problems.

Disapproval of laziness and praise of work, are constant themes in indigenous moral evaluations and formalized teaching (Candre and Echeverri 2008 [1993]; Griffiths 2002; Londoño Sulkin 2004). In noticing parallels with the Protestant work ethic, Griffiths (2002, 249) rightly argues that "whereas the Protestant ethic values labour as a path to otherworldly salvation . . . the Uitoto regard perpetual work as a way to maintain good relations with both people and the spirit-beings in daily life." As shown below, work denotes a physical or mental activity, as well as ideas of effective mediation, predation, and transformative action evaluated on the basis of underlying intention and tangible contribution to generalized well-being. For example, community leaders prepare *mambe* and *ambil* before visiting institutional offices in town, which infuses these substances "con un pensamiento" (with intentional, powerful thought).[4] The aim of leaders should be twofold: to catch or "hunt" institutional money and provide for community well-being. Project money, as any exogenous substance resulting from a predatory undertaking, is potentially pathogenic; it is hot. To make it fit for human consumption it must be "cooled" and transformed through work and other social practices. Leaders and community members share responsibility for the failure of development projects when they go after money motivated by personal interests rather than collective well-being, when they idly wait for the arrival of money without committing to work, or when they fail to channel money into the vital circuits of reproduction (see Guzmán-Gallegos, chapter 4, for similar views among the Amazonian Kichwa). In brief, they are not thinking with a "principle of origin," so the "other criterion" takes over. This situation weighs mostly on leaders and prompts fierce debates about their legitimacy.

The Tobacco Trail

A significant issue in the resguardo politics, as elsewhere in Amazonia (Jackson 2002), relates to contrasts between elected community leaders and traditional authorities often associated with *malocas* (large communal houses).[5] The first maloca was built in the 1950s on the shore of the Tacana River thirty-six years before the legal constitution of the Km. 6–11 Resguardo. But as the five communities of the resguardo began to form, malocas were located within or close to the villages, and their construction was carried out mostly with state funds. In 2000, only one out of the seven malocas of the resguardo was considered at least *nearly* traditional (Micarelli 2010), and all previous attempts to consolidate an organization of traditional authorities had failed. In 2002, however, a respected shaman decided to build a huge maloca on the eastern shore of the

Tacana River in the right way by making agreements with the spirit masters of the land, opening and growing *chagras* (horticultural plots), hosting repetitive *mingas* (communal work meetings), making allies, and above all, reactivating the transmission of the Speech of Coca and Tobacco.[6] Three years later, the maloca was inaugurated with the first of a lengthy series of dance rituals and the shaman's own dance ritual "career." Ritual events have been performed cyclically since then. This achievement marked a new trend in the resguardo's politics and prompted a shift from a focus on the road to the river, from communities to a network of malocas and *mambeaderos* emplaced in the territory.[7] The physical and symbolic connections linking these sites together are conceived of as a path used to invite guests to dance rituals; since invitations are handed out together with bundles of ambil, the path is called "the tobacco trail."

In the years following the inauguration of the maloca ([figure 6.1] named Joko Ailloko Rïerue Nabïrï, [the place where humans mature in friendly companionship] in Uitoto), thirteen elders of Uitoto, Muinane, Bora, Ocaina, Yucuna, Macuna, and Inga ethnicity led by the maloca owner resumed conversations addressing how to bring about forms of organization and management of the territory that place culture at the core while respecting cultural differences.[8] The focus on territory, conceived of as an expanding network of socio-environmental relations that

FIGURE 6.1. In Uitoto language, "Joko Ailloko Rïerue Nabïrï maloca" (the place where humans mature in friendly companionship). Photo by Marcela Lucía Rojas.

must be cared for with proper physical and spiritual work, reveals the strategy with which the elders address resguardo issues.

Firstly, they conceive of the production of people and place as a single process, one that restores mythical cosmogony in which the attribution of peoples to places, and places to peoples, simultaneously produced locality, morality, and identity/difference. They pursue this endeavor through the reactivation of the *ley de origen* (law or principle of origin) expressed in the teachings of coca and tobacco, the organization of collective work activities, such as the mingas, and the massive dance rituals mentioned above that are performed with the purpose of "curing the world." The name given to the organization and its council of elders, "El camino del tabaco, el mambe, la manicuera y el yagé," is indicative of these rationales; mambe (coca) and tobacco (either under the form of paste or snuff) are ritually consumed by all members of the council regardless of their ethnic differences. Tobacco, in particular, has a divine connotation. It relates to the breath of life and powerful thought-knowledge of the creator god Grandfather of Tobacco, and as noted, it is offered to invite chanters to rituals, as well as in payment for songs. *Manicuera* is a sweet manioc potage that the wife of the owner of the maloca offers to chanters during dance rituals; its name acknowledges the council's only female member and women's life force in general. Finally, *yagé* (*Banisteriopsis caapi*) is the plant of power of one of the elders, who is of Inga ethnicity. By stressing these symbols, the elders seek to reunite political and ritual leadership, as well as to highlight shared cosmological perceptions that regard well-being as emplaced in, and dependent on, a web of life properly tended by ritual experts. Secondly, the emphasis on the territory allows the elders to address ongoing interlineage and territorial conflicts through the strengthening of forms of administration that ground the organization of diversity in the physical space and link territorial rights to morally evaluated outcomes of social practice. Evidence suggests that before the devastating effects of the rubber boom, malocas were actively interconnected in a regional system of social organization. Each maloca, or more precisely each patrilineage, owned specialized hereditary knowledge and was characterized by a certain degree of expertise and exclusive rights.[9] Representatives from different malocas assembled periodically into regional or subregional councils to plan collective activities, and chieftaincy rotated among malocas. Although areas of knowledge were, and still are, ranked, such rank depended mostly on the task at hand or the skills of a leader (Micarelli 2009). In this regard, the importance that the People of the Center attribute to the "orphan" in moral, mythical, and historical narratives is an instance of their ambivalence toward rank and rights. The orphan is someone who is able to achieve the status of leader not for belonging to a high-rank lineage but through physical and spiritual hardship aimed at materializing the ideal state of generalized well-being and conviviality.[10] These understandings permeate the debates about territorial rights; more than property titles, it is how people effectively manage resources and landscapes that is conducive to legitimacy.

Finally, by placing the territory at the core of their agenda, leaders respond to institutional discourse while harnessing Western environmental ideas to their cause. And they reverse the development discourse's focus on necessities by placing emphasis on peoples' own assets—what they have, rather than what they lack.

The elders describe this process as a life project, one that seeks to benefit present and future generations; it is a proposition that constitutes a sharp detour from the fragmented temporality of development planning. So, the question is why they decided to fetch development money and become entangled in development formalities, standards, and broken temporality. Money is now an important part of indigenous economies and provides substantial goods ranging from foodstuffs to mobile phones. Thus, there's no doubt that among organization members and supporters, it is expected that they obtain additional funds to augment the scant earnings that they receive from temporary jobs and product sales. More importantly, ensuring access to money is one of the ways leaders legitimize their positions and expand their influence over wider networks of people, just like trade goods did in the past (Guzman-Gallegos, chapter 4; Henley and Mattéi-Muller 1978; Helms 1987; Myers 1981; Oberem 1974; Scazzocchio 1978; Whitehead 1994). Therefore, the analysis of money and its seductions should be located in a broad field of indigenous perceptions of power and political control as much as within colonial modes of encroachment that hinge on the distribution of Western manufactured goods—a field of maneuvers where leaders must prove their capacity to negotiate with dangerous Others.

The story of the Muinane chief Makapaamine, recounted by ethnohistorian Pineda Camacho (1985), is illustrative of cultural forms that may still resonate in leaders' present rationales for engaging in development projects. Makapaamine and his group established commercial relations with Brazilian traders and exchanged food, furs, *balata* (*Manikaria* sp.), and *juansoco* (*Couma macrocarpa*) for manufactured goods. News of such commerce traveled upriver and caught the attention of other chiefs, who went to ask Makapaamine for information on the white men, who were known only through myths. In the beginning, relations between indigenous people and traders were good, but soon the whites began to pillage and to abduct and abuse indigenous women. As a result, Makapaamine, without consulting the council of chiefs, decided to force the whites out. He launched attacks on the whites' boats, killed the traders, and hid the trade goods in a cave so that only his people could have them. This feat set off a political crisis throughout the region. The chiefs accused Makapaamine of interrupting commerce with the whites, and together they decided to kill him. But Makapaamine had shamanic powers, which he preserved in a magical quartz stone. He was clairvoyant, he didn't need to sleep, and he subsisted by licking wild ambil (*ambil de monte* used by sorcerers). In fact, although he did not have the rank of *capitán*, he was able to capitanize himself due to his powers (Pineda Camacho 1985, 126). So the attempts to assassinate him failed again and again.

This narrative is indicative of how new systems of ethnic rank may have formed with regard to the distribution of Western manufactures (Whitehead 1994), and it suggests a deep systemic relationship between shamanic power and the control of exogenous goods.[11] In spite of clear differences between money and manufactured goods, this provides reasons for exploring indigenous interpretations of money in connection with the triad of affinity, predation, and exchange so crucial in many Amazonian cosmologies (Viveiros de Castro 1992; Fausto 2001; Vidal and Whitehead 2004; Santos-Granero 2007, 2009b).

To Catch a Project: Traps

> Voy a mirar que animalito cazamos. Pues hablé con mi mamá, y dijo: "Está bien. Hay que armar trampa. Cualquier ratón sirve para hacer illyco." Pues apenas voy a mirar el documento, para nosotros ver y pensar cuál se puede coger. (I'll see what little animal we can hunt. For I talked to my mom, and she said: "Okay. We have to set a trap. Any mouse serves to make illyco" [an Uitoto dish]. Well, I'll just look at the document, so that we can see and think which one we can catch.)
>
> —*Uitoto man*

I mentioned earlier how leaders "hunt" development money with the power of coca and, above all, of tobacco. Seemingly, the world of the white people is like the forest, where exogenous and potentially pathogenic substances that are nonetheless indispensable to human life are controlled by powerful others—alien institutions or the masters of animals—who are construed in analogous terms: tricky, dangerous, but also seducible (Juan Alvaro Echeverri, pers. comm.). People refer to project money using the term *cacería*, meaning "hunting" and "game," such as in "ir de cacería" (to go hunting [a project]), "armar cacería," (organize a hunt), or "repartir cacería" (divide up the game [project money]). Hunting is considered to involve powerful mental vision, as well as technical skills. It is said that a good hunter hunts from his bench where he dreams and entices the prey with the power of his *ambil de cacería* (hunting tobacco), so that eventually the prey will come to his feet. As he sets his invisible trap, he must be careful not to scare the animals by calling them by their real names. Instead, he names them as fruits: black *umarí* (*Poraqueiba sericea*) for peccary, green umarí for tapir, moriche palm fruit (*Mauritia flexuosa*) for deer, and so on. He must also be able to seduce and, at times, to trick the masters of the animals into releasing their wards, which is a difficult task since such spirits are generally mean and won't let them go easily (one of the purposes of dance rituals is precisely to appease and make agreements with these spirits). It is significant in this regard that hunting is not an undifferentiated pursuit. Ideally people don't just go hunting, they go hunting a precise animal, which appeared in the tobacco dream.

This applies to development money, as well as to game, as evidenced in the following text messages sent to our working team by a young Uitoto leader on behalf of the elders while we were putting into final form a project proposal that they had devised.

1. Fue visto con ojo de tabaco,
 el umari cae, pongase fuisioso [*sic*],
 el espiritu mostró bien.
 Hay que amanecer cacería.
 It was seen with tobacco's eye.
 The umarí falls, be sensible.
 The spirit showed well.
 Game must be dawned.
2. Que sea para umarí negro,
 en cacería de tabaco,
 acá se armó para canangucho.
 Let it be for black *umarí*.
 In tobacco hunting.
 It was arranged here for *canangucho* (*Mauritia flexuosa*).
3. ¿Como va la trampa?
 How is the trap going?

As noted earlier, tobacco is considered to be a powerful divine substance. In creation myths the creator god, surrounded by emptiness, looked into his body, and he found a dreamed thread of *izeiki* ([tobacco smoke or cotton wad in Uitoto] Preuss 1994 [1921/1923], 19–21) with which he bound the bottom of emptiness to form life. However, tobacco ambil also denotes a more ambivalent and, somehow darker, field of purpose. In the narratives presented by Preuss, ambil is associated with shamanic trance and transformation (1994, 168), cannibal vengeance (1994, 203, 223, 255), spiritual aid in hunting, curing and fighting (1994,

148,168), with conjuring up the spiritual power of the ancestors (1994, 300), and as noted above, with invitations to dance rituals and payment for songs. One of Preuss's informants commented that it is because of ambil that people have "knowledge of tradition." With the exception of cannibalism, all these usages are still effective today. It is interesting to note that the loanword ambil itself is plausibly linked to the Shiwilu (Jebero) term *ampiri*, meaning "poison," and to the Quechua terms *hampi* (remedy, poison) and *hampiri* ([witch doctor] Laime Ajacopa 2007). Such polysemy acquires clear significance in regard to Wilbert's (1976, 5) apt characterization of tobacco as a means to enter into contractual relations with the spirit world and as a catalyst in the trade of energies that guarantee the existence and maintenance of life. As such, the thread of tobacco not only works to bind reciprocal relations of exchange and interdependence but also to predatorily ensnare such energies. This suggests once more that curing and killing, vengeance and conviviality, and predation and reciprocity can easily transform into each other in native Amazonian thought (Santos-Granero [2007, 2009b] and chapter 3 in this volume). As complementary forces, the outcomes of their dynamic interaction depend more on a question of balance than on fixed dualism. As a Muinane leader put it, "the universe is not in a state of perfection because evil and good are joined. Within the origin of health lies the origin of illness. It starts from creation, because any work produces waste, sweat, fatigue. Then, diseases were also created, and humans with their (faulty) actions pull them out, call them up. Humans are the most dangerous virus; with everything they do, if they don't do it well, evil multiplies." These considerations haunt leaders as they set on their prey through tobacco dreaming; what they call forth is the materialization of their thought, which they will feed to people. A faulty vision or a lack of capacity to fix the prey's exogenous humor can have dreadful, extended consequences. The following interpretation is an instance of how negative outcomes can be foreseen and prevented.

Clashing Interpretations of Tobacco Visions: Leadership at Stake

A Muinane leader and ally of the council was staying with us in Bogotá when we received the text messages quoted above. He offered a critical interpretation of the tobacco dreams and their transformative power.

> Black *umarí* is peccary [*Tayassu* sp.], but on the negative side it is scorpion. *Moriche* [*Mauritia flexuosa*] is the seed of governability: deer. Red moriche is rank. This means that some of the three malocas that have

> legacy, rank, want to take over. Peccary eats the fruit of [the informant's totemic plant]: the spirit that can devour us comes from peccary. Peccary pertains to the "basket of abundance." However, peccary is very fierce, ravening, and poisonous like scorpion. Peccary devours its offspring. . . . If this were an educational program it would be a disaster! One can say: if the project is not managed well, the elders eat the children; the new generations are shut off. Red deer is prostitution. Finally what it may say is that the grandfather is corrupt. *This poison must be sweetened; one must know how to fix it. Ritual events are for this. One must ask, one must inform, because money is not ours.* (emphasis in original)

This reasoning is revealing in many ways. It warns of danger, but it does not necessarily reject the pursuit. It also warns about the need to "fix poison" in the appropriate way, namely, through good planning and administration, performance of ritual ceremonies, and by "asking" and "informing." To ask and to inform define the terms of an agreement made with the divinity as much as with the collectivity, especially when the movement of valuable possessions is involved.[12] To summarize these understandings schematically, although money is controlled by foreign institutions, as game is controlled by the masters of animals, the ultimate lord of all riches is the Grandfather of Tobacco. By asking the creator directly, the leaders bypass the jealous masters of resources, and tobacco dreams will materialize as game, even if the masters are not willing to release the prey.[13] The same informant who provided the above interpretation of tobacco dreams compared tobacco to a banknote—a "divine banknote." At the front there is the creator's knowledge, whose value takes precedence over everything else. At the back there is the world and, more precisely, the resources that one is going to ask for. When leaders ask the owner of all things for resources, they must make their intentions clear. Resources are meant to maintain the life of humans and of the earth and redistribute goods through networks of solidarity and interdependence. After all, money is not theirs. They conjure the power of tobacco as "tobacco of life," which entails committing thought-intention, speech, and work to the generation of abundance for all. In so doing, they appease the energy of what they predatorily got from the outside and feed it to the exchange networks that guarantee the constant circulation of vital energy. In this way "wealth doesn't go bad."

Personal assets, such as knowledge, seeds, and people, can be achieved by individual agents through skillful predatory capture of foreign substances. But such accumulated assets must be multiplied and passed on, or they will turn into a person's "coffin," as my interlocutor bluntly put it. "Un abuelo sí acumula conocimiento, pero eso pesa. El abuelo tiene que enseñar, para aliviar ese peso, para no enfermarse." (A grandfather [knowledgeable person] does accumulate knowledge, but it weighs. The grandfather has to teach, to relieve this burden, to avoid getting sick.) Personal wealth is inherently destructive if it doesn't foster common good, and ungenerous persons are like the stingy masters of resources who become themselves the prey of malevolent spirits. This suggests that wealth in general cannot do without predation and that it cannot do without sustained curing and transformation of the substances obtained through such predatory feats (see Sarmiento Barletti [chapter 5] for similar ideas among the Ashaninka). What's more, it suggests that wealth can only be maintained if it invigorates the exchange of energy that is indispensable to the reproduction of life and generalized abundance. In a way the only enduring wealth is *public* wealth but not in the sense of collective, inalienable property. Public wealth is basically a matter of usufruct; it is entrusted to people by the ultimate owner of all things with the condition that people put it into good use. The rapacious figure of the white cannibal—alternatively called *pishtaco*, *ñaqak*, or flying gringo—is the epitome of capitalist violence in Amerindian perceptions (Santos-Granero and Barclay 2011; Whitehead 2014). The white cannibal, who devours indigenous body organs to keep himself forever young and pillages their environments, appears in this region as the *mochacabeza* (Cure 2005). These persistent threats are revealing of indigenous notions of inequality rooted in the view of life as a scarce resource (Santos-Granero 2009b; Santos-Granero and Barclay 2011).

In the following sections, I rely on the key concept of *work* to argue why public wealth is, above all, a matter of transformative knowledge and capacities needed to materialize the creator's dream in daily life, and why it can be considered as a form of collective, but *alienable*, patrimony.

Managing Project Money

> No se llama proyecto porque proyecto es robo y corrupción. Se llama cacería y después se llama trabajo. Se piensa y se llama para dar trabajo a la gente. (It's not called "project" because project is theft and corruption. It is called "hunting," and then it is called "work." It is thought and summoned [into being] to give people work.)
>
> —*Uitoto man*

At the onset of the USAID project, the council of elders, and especially the council head, faced the thorny task of managing project funds. Soon, they were caught in a crossfire between organization members, each of whom wanted part of the prey, and the funding agency with its strict budget rules. The outcome of the project clearly depended on the possibility of reaching an agreement with both sides, an endeavor that was entangled with difficulties. In the middle ground of budget management, tensions escalated between different regimes of value and between collectivity and individuality. To begin to handle this situation, the leaders looked into project rules for direction and came up with the first conclusion: "aquí no hay recursos para repartir" (here there are no funds to distribute).[14] This conclusion stirred outright discontent among some organization members and supporters. People started suspecting that the council was trying to gain control of the project's funds; if the project was meant to benefit the whole community, why couldn't the money be distributed? However, through a clever maneuver of cultural interpretation, the council arrived at a second conclusion that put an end to the criticism and received the community's general approval: "estos recursos son para trabajar" (these funds are for working). Consequently, the council assigned duties for all the project activities and made sure that they were reasonably distributed among the organization's various mambeaderos and malocas according to their skills, legacy, and trajectory. Even one of the road communities (Km. 11) was strategically included in the plan with the explicit intention of expanding the organization's popular support. So, funds were actually distributed among groups rather than individuals but on the basis of work and its shared cultural meanings and the socially accepted modes of organizing labor. In this manner, the council was able to summon a broad network of people and to strengthen intercultural solidarity (figure 6.2).

As in Rivière's (1984) *Individual and Society in Guiana*, labor relations, and access to labor, were fundamental to leadership. At the same time, the way in which work was construed and organized was clearly concerned with the process of forming social persons, as Turner rightly suggested (2003, 11; see also Griffiths 2002). Additionally, the People of the Center's notion of work extends beyond labor (in Rivière's sense) to a series of less tangible mind-body activities aimed at the transfer and circulation of vital energy, an endeavor that evokes Santos-Granero's (2009b) characterization of native Amazonian economies as *political economies of life*.

Among project activities crucial emphasis was placed on ritual events, mingas, transmission of cultural knowledge, and dialogue sessions in the mambeaderos, which were fundamental for the correct organization of socio-environmental relations.[15] Here the problem was not only how to fit these activities into the rigid agency formats but also how not to corrupt cultural practices with the input of Western money. The elders prided themselves on their commitment to the overall process, and the council head in particular had earned the people's respect by proving that

FIGURE 6.2. The maloquero's wife, her albino daughter, and other helpers wrapping mashed manioc in Caraná palm leaves to be offered to the guests attending the dance ritual. Photo by Marcela Lucía Rojas.

he could build a maloca and organize huge dance rituals with abundant food for all the guests on the basis of work, not money.[16] The incorporation of money into these processes was in itself quite problematic. The answer was to harness money to culturally accepted methods by converting it into something else: first into exchangeable substances and then into work. Thus, money was used, for instance, to buy goods for cultural experts in exchange for teachings, swidden farm products and labor for making food offered in mingas, huge amounts of peanuts to pay back gifts in dance rituals, packed tobacco for making ambil, and labor for the making of salt cakes to pay ritual chanters.

All these expenses were described as exchange materials in budget reports. In this manner, money was absorbed into the circuits of production, reciprocity, and commensality. Incorporated into a gift economy, money lost its abstract value and was transformed into inalienable exchange possessions and services that reaffirmed relationships (Gregory 1997; Weiner 1992). Such incorporation always bore, however, a shade of incompleteness, and money could at any time turn into a controversial issue. Rather than a simple operation of conversion of money into services and inalienable possessions, this situation evokes the indeterminate, endless task of translation, characterized by Benjamin (1997), in nearly shamanic terms, as an immersion into foreign modes of thought that maintain, albeit fragmentarily, the continuing life of the original. As such, the domestication of the "original" is never total. Similarly, indigenous creative reworkings of money do not make its alterity dissolve completely, and my suggestion is that this reflects native Amazonian cultural rationales. Money—as other exogenous items—is a token of a successful incursion into the world of Others, either through predation or through relations of exchange, affinity, and friendship from which value and prestige is derived. Moreover, the alterity retained in translation—the continuing life of the "white-man's heart"—shapes the understanding of one's self-identity. If for native Amazonians "the self is only possible through the incorporation of the other" (Overing 1981; Santos-Granero 2009a, 478), such incorporation is not meant to completely erase alterity but to rework it into the fabric of society like different fibers are interwoven to make a basket (Micarelli 2010). This unrelenting task is not only self-shaping but it is also needed to channel personal and exogenous assets into the creation of conviviality. The reasons for centering the project on the cultural activities mentioned above should become clearer inasmuch as these activities are linked to the notion of work as a cultural endeavor by which persons and society are fabricated.

Culture as Work and the Work of Culture

> El trabajo es para comer, tomar, curar, para dar de comer a la humanidad. Por eso nosotros estamos intentando con trabajo, abundancia, aprovechando el verano para sembrar toda clase de fruta, trabajo para arreglar, que no se logra solamente de documentos: hay que sufrir. . . . Por eso aunque digan que soy perezosa allí esta mi chagra, mi maní, mi manicuera, mi maloca, mis nietos. Esa es mi semilla bien plantada que no es papel; es vida. (Work is for eating, drinking, curing, for feeding humanity. That's why we are striving with work, abundance, taking advantage of the summer to plant all kinds of fruit, work for mending, which cannot be achieved only from documents; one has to suffer. . . . So, even if they say I'm lazy, there is my chagra, my peanut, my manicuera, my maloca, my grandchildren. That's my seed well planted, which is not paper; it is life.)
>
> —*Uitoto woman*

> Lo que se busca es unión de pensamiento para encontrar palabra buena de trabajo, mirando a los niños que están creciendo. ¿Qué va a ser de esta gente a futuro? No sé si lo hago entender. . . . Es nuestra cultura.

> (What we seek is union of thought to find a good word of work, watching the children that are growing. What will happen to these people in the future? I do not know if I make it clear. . . . It is our culture.)
>
> —*Muinane man*

These statements, made by council members during a project meeting, are particularly interesting for the emphasis placed on work as a practice that defines human culture and life. Griffiths' (2002) analysis of Uitoto notions of work provides indispensable elements for illustrating this point. From a Uitoto perspective—one shared by all the People of the Center and by other native Amazonian societies, such as the Yucuna and Macuna—work is the source from which not only the human body, identity, and society but also life and the cosmos are continuously recreated. Work confers identity in collective and individual ways: as relations that define gender, age, and social categories, as well as a special talent that defines a person's creative self. Persistent work effort and the ingestion of proper foods and beverages—themselves the product of people's work—gradually shape gendered bodily forms, habits, and dispositions throughout a person's life. Productive activity is also a way to reinforce benign sentiments among coworkers and create and maintain good relationships with people and the spirit world (Griffiths 2002, 248). These habits are a source of true identity. For instance, a woman who shows unproductive behavior "is suspected of being possessed by [a] spirit mother of forest animals" (Griffiths 2002, 254), and she may even turn into a real animal and be hunted and eaten by humans (Nejedeka Kajutne 2012).

Besides practical effort, work also refers to a series of activities, such as mindfulness imaging, teaching, or curing, which are fundamental to the fabrication of sociable selves and relations. As such, work spans different overlaying planes of reality; some are visible and material, and others are invisible and spiritual. Such planes mutually affect each other; anything that occurs in one plane reverberates through the others.[17] The "dream of abundance" described in Candre and Echeverri (2008 [1993], 58–63) provides a fascinating illustration of these ideas. In the account given by Uitoto elder Hipólito Candre, cultivated plants are first dreamt as "tobacco breath"; but for the dream breath to materialize into real plants, people have to work. A dream of good work progressively shows in good speech—the word of advising—in tranquil, productive work, and ultimately in generalized health and abundance (see Conklin, chapter 2). At the same time, good intent, mood, and effort, are essential to bring tobacco dreaming into existence.

These views resonate with current Amazonianist debates concerning the relation of bodily form and habits with human identity (Rivière 1984; Santos-Granero 2012; Viveiros de Castro 1996, 1998). As evidenced in the quotes above, work shapes ongoing personal and collective identity, but above all it is the means by which people may materialize the creator's knowledge of life and achieve well-being. The frequent claim that ultimately work is shown in the dance is revealing in this regard. It alludes to the abundant food, beverages, and ritual substances shared and consumed during dance rituals, as well as the broad outcomes of ritual performances, which extend after the ritual has concluded (figures 6.3 and 6.4). Besides commensality, a successful dance is characterized by absence of accidents and fights, as well as by good weather, cheerful sentiments, and good health among participants. As noted, the ultimate purpose of dance rituals is to cure the world, appease the spirit masters of the territory, and reestablish a state of generalized abundance, good health, and tranquility; in a nutshell, it is to reaffirm the value of tobacco's divine banknote.

People pride themselves on their capacity to work, which they refer to as "nuestro propio ornamento" (our own adornment), and it is sometimes compared to a feather crown. This suggests that work may be seen as a collective patrimony that is doomed to disappear if people do not work and that is, therefore, alienable. Such perspective leads into the People

FIGURE 6.3. Guests arriving to the Jimoma dance ritual reenacting the mythical rivalry between the Uitoto and the ancient Jimoma people, which was celebrated during the course of the USAID project in 2010. Photo by Marcela Lucía Rojas.

FIGURE 6.4. Piles of cassava bread to be offered to guests attending the dance ritual. Photo by Marcela Lucía Rojas.

of the Center's notion of poverty. In the claims people make about themselves, poverty is regularly associated with the state of being an orphan. However, among the People of the Center the claim of being "as poor as an orphan" is always made by individuals who are not poor—successful farmers or heads of maloca. This reflects the general use of dissimulation in native philosophy, which is based on the principle that power is manifested in deeds and not words, to the extreme of shunning overt praise of individual accomplishments. The orphan personifies the Orphan Grandson of the Center, a key character of creation myths who is described as a holder of knowledge and is endowed with the capacity to materialize a life of abundance. By concealing his true capacities, he is able to fool the evil agents that threaten creation and to attain a "node of power." I add to this the generative power to forge relations from scratch, a sort of degree-zero of creative agency. As Uitoto and Muinane thinkers made clear "the orphan is not poor; he is the richest of all." When asked "who, then, is the poor?" people reply with no hesitation. "A lazy one! *Un perezoso*!" If sociality is seen to be an ongoing creation rather than a given condition, one which depends on people's capacities and dispositions for giving and (often predatorily) taking, then a *chronic* lack of social relations is indicative of some other shortage: a lack of bodily affects and dispositions for nurturing exchange with other humans, nature, and the spirit world. According to Overing and Passes (2000, 98) "society itself [is] being produced at the same time, and performatively so, in and through the process of work." For these reasons, although the People of the Center associate poverty with orphanhood, such association is not conclusive as it is in the case of the Yanesha and Canelos Quichua (see Santos-Granero, chapter 3, and Whitten and Whitten, chapter 7).

Conclusion

> ¿Para que se mambea y se chupa ambil? Para pensar bien, para hablar bien, y para trabajar bien. . . . Y para que esto se convierta en abundancia para todos. (What do we consume mambe and ambil for? For thinking well, speaking well, and working well. . . . And for turning this into abundance for all.)
>
> —*Uitoto leader*

Most contributions to this volume suggest that the abundance of life, vitality, or energy is tightly linked to indigenous notions of public wealth and well-being, a proposition with which I also agree. I don't argue, however, that for the People of the Center public wealth *is* the abundance of life, vitality, or energy. Nor do I contend that public wealth and well-being are the same. The views presented here suggest that although public wealth hinges on "everything that an individual obtains from powerful Others to ensure the life, good health, and reproduction of the members of the collectivity to which he or she belongs" (Santo-Granero, chapter 3), it seems to consist of something different than usable or exchangeable items or vital substances. They suggest that public wealth is, above all, a matter of the transformative knowledge and capacities that make the good life possible—the skills needed to maintain a constant exchange of vital energy and to restore the healthy fabric of abundant life on a permanent basis. "The knowledge of the creator to live on this world . . . this is the real wealth," an informant said. And the materialization of the creator's knowledge rests on people's work. But as the image of the divine banknote makes it clear, such knowledge is embodied in the land, the territory, and the ecological resources that sustain life. Managing the world well is people's responsibility in order to pay back the creator and maintain the life of humans and of the earth. In a way, it could be said that public wealth instantiates this contractual agreement between god and humans.

These faculties have been entrusted to people by the creator but not indistinctly. According to creation myths, each group received its own share of the knowledge of life together with a territory; this entrustment was the source from which identity, difference, and the need to maintain exchange relations with other groups ([in a sort of "ecology of knowledges"] Santos 2009) originated. The difference between the terms *public* and *common* can be helpful to further link public wealth and identity. According to Piangiani (1907, 1:319) *commúnem* refers to something "of which no one has the property but that everybody can use, such as air, sea water, etc." Whereas *públicus* is the domain of one group, and access to it is more limited. From the perspective of the People of the Center, public wealth defines a people's domain through its proven capacity to bring the creator's knowledge into being. This capacity shows how material and immaterial resources, common to all members of the group but property of the creator god, are managed. The way in which knowledge and capacities—a people's wealth—are made visible in forms of resource management establishes a people's entitlement to such resources and shapes a community's self. Although the materialization of the knowledge of life is in the first place a personal, self-shaping responsibility that reflects individual capacities, personal selves exist only through the sociable links they maintain with others.

As I have tried to show, work implies the skillful capturing and reallocation of vital substances in open cycles of energy exchange that are "always asymmetrical even if momentarily balanced" (Santos-Granero 2009b, 209; see also Fausto 2001). The unrelenting job of responsible humans is to affect the dynamic interplay of balance and asymmetry that will allow the constant circulation of life force so important to indigenous perceptions of well-being.

Notes

1. The People of the Center is a linguistically diverse but culturally relatively uniform cluster of ethnic groups that include the Uitoto, Bora, Miraña, Muinane, Andoke, Nonuya, and Ocaina. It comprises approximately seventy-five hundred individuals living on the Caquetá, Putumayo, and Amazon regions of Colombia, and in the northern Amazon region of Peru.

2. All these are important ritual substances. Tobacco may be consumed as tobacco paste or snuff. Mambe is a fine powder obtained from pounded, toasted

coca leaves mixed with the ash of Cecropia leaves, and sieved carefully. Manicuera is a sweet manioc potage. Yagé (*Banisteriopsis caapi*), also known as ayahuasca, is a hallucinogenic vine.

3. Ninety percent of the resguardo's population consists of indigenous individuals from People of the Center and Tikuna; the rest are Cocama, Yagua, Yucuna, and Macuna, among others.

4. Ambil is a tobacco paste, which is often mixed with salt obtained from the ash of a variety of plants.

5. This contrast is not clear-cut, and it does not imply an intrinsic dichotomy. Although community leaders are elected, people take into consideration cultural factors, such as their lineage. However, not all traditional leaders belong to high-ranking lineages, and some may even belong to the category of "orphans."

6. The Speech of Coca and Tobacco, also known as Speech of Life (*rafue* in Uitoto; *fiivojï* in Muinane), refers to ritualized speech performances. According to Candre and Echeverri (2008 [1993], 28) "rafue is the activity by which words transform into things—it is the movement from named to real through time" (my translation).

7. The place where men meet at night to ritually consume mambe and ambil.

8. Even though the meaning of the Uitoto word *nabïrï* is closer to the translation I adopt here, the translation commonly provided locally is "the place where humans sweetly mature." For the People of the Center "sweet" (*naïmekï* in Uitoto) is a polysemic concept that evokes embodied notions of tranquility, harmony, and good health. A short documentary about the process by which the resguardo's elders defined the guiding principles of their organization is available at http://www.youtube.com/watch?v=8MoW7viVMVA.

9. These data confirm Whitehead's (1994, 27) suggestion that ethnicity does "not necessarily coincide with particular economic, political, or linguistic systems but could also be founded on an economic technique or specialization that was part of . . . a wider system of exchange."

10. For the People of the Center the term *orphan* may also refer to captives, slaves, servants (Gasché 1982; Preuss 1994 [1921/1923]), or a man who has chosen to live in his wife's maloca under the protection of his father-in-law (Pineda Camacho 1985, 61).

11. In a myth of integration through trade (Guyot 1979), the masters of trade are powerful spirits that mark the trail of commerce along the Caquetá River and move upstream like the first Brazilian traders.

12. In teaching and learning, for instance, these terms regulate the transmission of knowledge. Without these formalities, knowledge can be seen as stolen.

13. "El sueño amanece como cacería" literally means "the dream dawns as game."

14. USAID rules stated that funds could only be employed for planned activities and could not be divided among beneficiaries.

15. Other activities included GPS mapping and the establishment of an ecoturism program.

16. Craving for money can indicate a pact with wicked spirits; so, in contrast to healers, dark sorcerers charge money for their services to satiate the voracity of their spirit helpers.

17. For instance, during teaching and learning people carefully attend to the material qualities of the body and the senses and deploy regulatory bodily practices. But thinking, as any work, produces filth that has to be physically and spiritually cleansed in order to prevent the inception of debilitating illnesses.

References

Benjamin, Walter. 1997. "The Translator's Task." *Traduction, Terminologie, Rédaction* 2:151–65.

Candre, Hipólito, and Juan Alvaro Echeverri. 2008 (1993). *Tabaco frío, coca dulce: Jírue dïona, rïérue jíïbina*. Leticia: Universidad Nacional de Colombia.

Cure, Salima. 2005. *Cuidado te mochan la cabeza: Circulación y construcción de un rumor en la frontera amazónica de Colombia, Perú y Brasil*. MA thesis, Universidad Nacional de Colombia, Leticia.

Echeverri, Juan Alvaro. 1997. "The People of the Center of the World: A Study in Culture, History, and Orality." PhD dissertation, New School for Social Research.

Edelman, Marc, and Angelique Haugerud, eds. 2005. *The Anthropology of Development and Globalization: From Classical Political Economy to Contemporary Neoliberalism*. Malden, MA: Blackwell.

Escobar, Arturo. 1995. *Encountering Development. The Making and Unmaking of the Third World*. Princeton: Princeton University Press.

Fausto, Carlos. 1999. "Of Enemies and Pets: Warfare and Shamanism in Amazonia." *American Ethnologist* 26(4):933–56.

———. 2001. *Inimigos fiéis: História, guerra e xamanismo na Amazônia*. São Paulo: Edusp.

Ferguson, James. 1994. *The Anti-Politics Machine: "Development," Depoliticization, and Bureaucratic Power in Lesotho*. Minneapolis: University of Minnesota Press.

Gasché, Jürg. 1982. "Las comunidades nativas entre la apariencia y la realidad. El ejemplo de las comunidades Huitoto y Ocaina del río Ampiyacu." *Amazonía Indígena* 3(5):11–31.

Gregory, Chris. 1997. *Savage Money: The Anthropology and Politics of Commodity Exchange*. Amsterdam: Harwood Academic.

Griffiths, Thomas. 2002. "Finding One's Body: Relationships Between Cosmology and Work in North-West Amazonia." In *Beyond the Visible and the Material.*

The Amerindianization of Society in the Work of Peter Rivière, edited by Laura Rival and Neil L. Whitehead, 247–62. Oxford: Oxford University Press.

Guyot, Mireille. 1979. "La história del mar de danta, el Caquetá. Una fase de la evolución cultural en el noroeste amazónico." *Journal de la Société des Américanistes* 46:97–122.

Helms, Mary W. 1987. "Art Styles and Interaction Spheres in Central America and the Caribbean." In *Chiefdoms in the Americas*, edited by Robert D. Drennan and Carlos A. Uribe, 67–84. Lanham, Maryland: University Press of America.

Henley, Paul, and Marie Claude Mattéi-Muller. 1978. "Panare Basketry: Means of Commercial Exchange and Artistic Expression." *Antropológica* 49:29–130.

Hugh-Jones, Stephen. 1992. "Yesterday's Luxuries, Tomorrow's Necessities: Business and Barter in Northwest Amazonia." In *Barter, Exchange and Value: An Anthropological Approach*, edited by Caroline Humphrey and Stephen Hugh-Jones, 42–74. Cambridge: Cambridge University Press.

Jackson, Jean. 2002. "Contested Discourses of Authority in Colombian National Indigenous Politics: The 1996 Summer Takeovers." In *Indigenous Movements, Self-Representation, and the State in Latin America*, edited by Kay B. Warren and Jean Jackson, 81–122. Austin: University of Texas Press.

Laime Ajacopa. 2007. *Diccionario bilingüe. Iskay simipi yuyayk'ancha. Quechua-Castellano, Castellano-Quechua*. La Paz: Proyecto de Educación Intercultural Bilingüe.

Londoño Sulkin, Carlos David. 2004. *Muinane: Un Proyecto Moral a Perpetuidad*. Medellín: Editorial Universidad de Antioquia.

Micarelli, Giovanna. 2009. "'Ordenar el pensamiento': Place-Making and the Moral Management of Resources in a Multi-Ethnic Territory, Amazonas, Colombia." In *Mobility and Migration in Indigenous Amazonia*, edited by Miguel Alexiades, 195–219. New York/Oxford: Berghahn Books.

———. 2010. "Pensar como un enjambre: Redes indígenas en las márgenes de la modernidad." In *Perspectivas antropológicas sobre la Amazonía contemporánea*, edited by Margarita Chaves and Carlos Del Cairo, 489–510. Bogotá: ICANH/Universidad Javeriana.

Myers, Thomas P. 1981. "Aboriginal Trade Networks in Amazonia." In *Networks of the Past: Regional Interaction in Archaeology*, edited by Peter D. Francis, F. J. Kense, and P. G. Duke, 19–30. Calgary: The University of Calgary Archaeological Association.

Nejedeka Kajutne, Aniceto. 2012. *Taagai Búuamïsi jïïbegeejï: La história de los dos hermanos boa*. Bogotá: ICANH.

Oberem, Udo. 1974. "Trade and Trade Goods in the Ecuadorian Montaña." In *Native South Americans. Ethnology of the Least Known Continent*, edited by Patricia Lyon, 346–57. Boston: Little, Brown and Company.

Overing, Joanna. 1981. "Review Article: Amazonian Anthropology." *Journal of Latin American Studies* 13(1):151–64.

Overing, Joanna, and Alan Passes, eds. 2000. *The Anthropology of Love and Anger. The Aesthetics of Conviviality in Native Amazonia*. London: Routledge.
Parry, John, and Maurice Bloch. 1989. *Money and the Morality of the Exchange*. Cambridge: Cambridge University Press.
Piangiani, Ottorino. 1907. *Vocabolario etimologico della lingua italiana*. Roma: Albrighi, Segati e C.
Pigg, Stacy Leigh. 1992. "Inventing Social Categories through Place: Social Representations and Development in Nepal." *Society for Comparative Study of History and Society* 34(3):491–513.
Pineda Camacho, Roberto. 1985. *História oral y proceso esclavista en el Caquetá*. Bogotá: Banco de la República.
Preuss, Konrad Theodor. 1994(1921/1923). *Religión y mitología de los Uitotos*. Bogotá: Editorial Universidad Nacional, 2 vols.
Rivera Cusicanqui, Silvia. 2010. *Ch'ixinakax utxiwa: Una reflexión sobre prácticas y discursos descolonizadores*. Buenos Aires: Tinta Limón.
Rivière, Peter. 1984. *Individual and Society in Guiana: A Comparative Study of Amerindian Social Organization*. Cambridge: Cambridge University Press.
Sahlins, Marshall. 1999. "What is Anthropological Enlightenment? Some Lessons of the Twentieth Century." *Annual Review of Anthropology* 28:i-xxxiii.
Santos, Boaventura de Sousa. 2009. *Una epistemología del sur. La reinvención del conocimiento y la emancipación social*. Buenos Aires: Siglo XXI Editores/CLACSO.
Santos-Granero, Fernando. 2007. "Of Fear and Friendship: Amazonian Sociality Beyond Kinship and Affinity." *Journal of the Royal Anthropological Institute* 13(1):1–18.
———. 2009a. "Hybrid Bodyscapes: A Visual History of Yanesha Patterns of Cultural Change." *Current Anthropology* 50(4):477–512.
———. 2009b. *Vital Enemies: Slavery, Predation, and the Amerindian Political Economy of Life*. Austin: University of Texas Press.
———. 2012. "Beinghood and People-Making in Native Amazonia: A Constructional Approach with a Perspectival Coda." *HAU: Journal of Ethnographic Theory* 2(1):181–211.
Santos-Granero, Fernando, and Frederica Barclay. 2011. "Bundles, Stampers, and Flying Gringos: Amazonian Perceptions of Capitalist Violence." *Journal of Latin American and Caribbean Anthropology* 16(1):143–67.
Scazzocchio, Françoise B. 1978. "Curare Kills, Cures, and Binds. Change and Persistence of Indian Trade in Response to the Contact Situation in the North-Western Montaña." *Cambridge Anthropology* 4(3):30–57.
Taussig, Michael. 1980. *The Devil and Commodity Fetishism in South America*. Chapel Hill: The University of North Carolina Press.
Turner, Terence. 2003. "The Beautiful and the Common: Inequalities of Value and Revolving Hierarchy among the Kayapó." *Tipití: Journal of the Society for the Anthropology of Lowland South America* 1(1):11–26.

Vidal, Silvia, and Whitehead, Neil L. 2004. "Dark Shamans and the Shamanic State: Sorcery and Witchcraft as Political Process in Guyana and the Venezuelan Amazon." In *In Darkness and Secrecy: The Anthropology of Assault Sorcery and Witchcraft in Amazonia*, edited by Robin Wright and Neil L. Whitehead, 51–81. Durham, NC: Duke University Press.

Viveiros de Castro, Eduardo. 1992. *From the Enemy's Point of View. Humanity and Divinity in an Amazonian Society*. Chicago: University of Chicago Press.

———. 1996. "Images of Nature and Society in Amazonian Ethnology." *Annual Review of Anthropology* 25:179–200.

———. 1998. "Cosmological Deixis and Amerindian Perspectivism." *Journal of the Royal Anthropological Institute* 4(3):469–88.

———. 2001. "GUT Feelings about Amazonia: Potential Affinity and the Construction of Sociality." In *Beyond the Visible and the Material: The Amerindianization of Society in the Work of Peter Rivière*, edited by Laura Rival and Neil L. Whitehead, 19–44. Oxford: Oxford University Press.

Weiner, Annette. 1992. *Inalienable Possessions. The Paradox of Keeping-while-Giving*. Berkeley: University of California Press.

Whitehead, Neil L. 1994. "The Ancient Amerindian Polities of the Lower Orinoco, Amazon, and Guiana Coast. A Preliminary Analysis of their Passage from Antiquity to Extinction." In *Amazonian Indians from Prehistory to the Present: Anthropological Perspectives*, edited by Anna C. Roosevelt, 20–35. Tucson: University of Arizona Press.

———. 2014. "Hambre divina: La máquina de guerra caníbal." *Mundo Amazónico* (S.1.) 4:7–30.

Wilbert, Johannes. 1976. *Metafísica del tabaco entre los indios de Surámerica*. Caracas: Universidad Católica Andrés Bello.

PART THREE

Living Well

CHAPTER SEVEN

Clashing Concepts of the "Good Life"

Beauty, Knowledge, and Vision Versus National Wealth in Amazonian Ecuador

NORMAN E. WHITTEN, JR., AND DOROTHEA SCOTT WHITTEN

"Yachaj awashca," she said, picking up a piece of ancient thin-walled pottery with a smooth, shiny surface. "Mana yachaj awashca, mana sumaj," illustrating her description with a thick-walled, rough-textured shard, a remnant of an old cooking pot. *Yachaj awashca* literally means something made by the most knowledgeable one, therefore master-crafted, well made, and imbued with knowledge. *Mana* is negative; *sumaj* is beautiful. "Mana yachaj awashca, mana sumaj" refers to something not knowledgeably made, and not beautiful; if it is not knowledgeably made, it lacks significance, and if it is insignificant it lacks beauty. (original italics)

—*D. Whitten and N. Whitten,* Imagery and Creativity: Ethnoaesthetics and Art Worlds in the Americas

On his *bancu*, seat of Sungui, [powerful shaman] don Rodrigo chants "sumaj, sumaj, sumaj, sumaj" (beauty, beauty, beauty, beauty). Because he is bottling up his sounds, closing his vowels, and "tightly" releasing his *samai* [breath], it sounds as though he is chanting "tomá, tomá, tomá, tomá." He also chants "taririri ri ri ri" (from the term *tariri* [shaman] in several languages), which demonstrates that don Rodrigo has acquired the killing power of the Jurijuri *supai*, the undersoil, cave dwelling master of monkeys and foreign people, who sends out his *waira samai* (breath of the

> wind) from his mysteriously lighted inner cave and across the mountainous rain forest. (original italics)
>
> —*N. Whitten and D. Whitten,* Puyo Runa: Imagery and Power in Modern Amazonia

The first epigraph comes from an intimate discussion between Sibby Whitten and her *comadre*, Clara Santi Simbaña. Clara shared her insights on knowledge and beauty—ancient and modern—that spanned the Achuar territory, an area that radiates out of Charapa Cocha on the Pastaza River, to the urban site of contemporary Puyo, and its indigenous Quichua-speaking hinterland (the concept of *sumaj* is elaborated in N. Whitten and D. Whitten [2008, 170–72]). Clara is a *sinchi muscuyuj warmi* (a strong visionary woman), whose one-time skill as master potter and storyteller imbued her work and those around her with the quality of beauty, sumaj, which is the core of Canelos Quichua's desirable life. Note that Clara emphasized what was *not* knowledgably made and *not* beautiful. The second epigraph is taken from a Napo Runa *sinchi yachaj*, powerful one-who-knows, who cured a child of a Puyo Runa family at the Napo Runa site of Ahuano where the Arajuno River flows into the Napo River. The power of don Rodrigo exudes sumaj, which resides not only in the power to heal but also in the power to kill.

The 2008 Ecuadorian Constitution

The indigenous people of Amazonia—Canelos Quichua and Napo Runa—had strong and effective voices and played a very active role in shaping many of the sections of the 2008 Ecuadorian Constitution (*Constitución de la República del Ecuador*, http://www.wipo.int/wipolex/en/text.jsp?file_id=178829, accessed April 4, 2012). A large number of the constitution's articles contain the Spanish phrase *buen vivir* as a *right* of all citizens. Many of the articles also contain the Quichua phrase *sumak kawsay* (here rendered as *sumaj causai*), which is a synonym for buen vivir in Quichua.[1] Native *dirigentes* (leaders) of Amazonian organizations, and politicians in the party of the president of the republic, and Dr. Rafael Vicente Correa Delgado, used the two phrases as ideological synonyms. When these Spanish and Quichua tropes are placed next to each other in the texts, they are intended to be synonymous. In their respective languages, however, the two do not carry the same meanings. The former, in Canelos Quichua of Amazonia, means something like "beautiful life" or "beautiful life force," and it incorporates such concepts as *deep knowledge*, especially as revealed in male shamanic gnosis and performance, and the strong visionary creativity of female master potters. The Canelos Quichua concepts of community, conviviality, kinship, integration with nature and supernature, and a shunning of capitalist wealth accumulation are all subsumed under the rubric of sumaj causai.

By contrast, the basic meanings of buen vivir (living well), used literally as the "good life," are based on capitalist wealth accumulation, albeit for a common good. The national strategy for obtaining a good life for all citizens of the republic is bound to the production of wealth through increased petroleum production and the exploitation of gold and copper through mining. This chapter briefly explicates and explores the ramifications of the Amazonian perspective together with the way in which a seeming synonym is currently the root ideological impetus for escalating misunderstanding and open conflict between many indigenous peoples and the executive-led strategies, policies, and practices of "national development" through accumulated capitalist wealth within a framework of "twenty-first-century socialism." This socialism varies in different ALBA countries (Bolivia, Ecuador, Venezuela, Nicaragua) but basically differs from classic socialism because it adopts neoliberal capitalist wealth-accumulation strategies—especially opening mining and petroleum exploitation to private enterprise—to enhance the "common good" regardless of the perceptions and lifeway disruptions of people in a given region or community. Following this explication we turn to the subject of "pubic wealth" to align this analysis with those of other contributors to this volume.

Writing about the Napo Runa of Amazonian Ecuador, Michael Uzendoski (2011) elucidates the fundamental clash subsumed or encapsulated by the juxtaposition of the terms sumak kawsay and buen vivir.

> Capitalism continues to be defined by a destructive essence of surplus-value that relies on contradictory narratives that are a veneer to the deeper realities and contradictions of exploitation. . . . Ecuador's socialist project is a complex and nuanced example of these processes; despite narratives of social well-being and collective progress that seek to reform the negatives of capitalism, the reality of the extractivist economy is contradicting the ideals of the 2008 constitution, the "essence" of a true *Sumak Kawsay*, and the rights of indigenous people to live according to their own ideals. But Ecuador is not alone. All of Western Amazonia . . . has been put at risk by similar processes of development,

> mining, dams, gas, and petroleum exploitation—processes that will bring all or most of Amazonia into the world-economy and open it up for intensive exploitation. (original italics)

Mónica Chuji Gualinga (2009), from Sarayacu in the Canelos Quichua (Pastaza Runa) territory, also explains the fundamental oxymoron of the Quichua and Spanish Carta Magna "synonyms" of the good life.

> Sumak Kawsay is neither a return to the past nor to the Stone Age nor to the epoch of cave life nor negation of modern technology and knowledge as has been argued by promoters of capitalism. Sumak Kawsay is inscribed in the debate about the destiny that should offer a [desirable] future to societies and human beings. For Sumak Kawsay human beings are fundamental, not [capitalist] markets and economic production and growth. . . . The nationalities and indigenous people [communities, pueblos], need to strengthen our self-determination, to deepen and extend the practices of *buen vivir* vis-à-vis [national] society. (N. Whitten, loose translation to convey meaning in English, original italics)

It is important to note here that Chuji Gualinga uses sumak kawsay and buen vivir as her extended goal. In short, sumak kawsay enters the constitution, from her perspective, to crowd out some current meanings of the good life in national society in favor of those embedded in indigenous cosmovision, if not always in practice. Specifically, she writes against the priority of stratified capitalist accumulation embedded in neoliberalism. Once a cabinet member as secretary of communications for President Correa and one of his primary representatives at the extended constitutional convention at Ciudad Alfaro in Montecristi, Manabí, she was recently accused of defamation by this very same president for speaking out against a government official specifically about his "wealth." In November 2011, she was convicted of character assassination for calling a member of the elite "nouveau riche," jailed for one year, and fined $400,000 (Picq 2011). She was subsequently "pardoned."

Our Culture(s) and Other Cultures

By understanding more deeply the cosmology of cultural dynamics among the Canelos Quichua, we can move farther toward an understanding of the juxtaposition of sumak kawsay and buen vivir in what may be the most liberal constitution in the world. Women transmit cultural knowledge and vision to their daughters and daughters-in-law through their mastery of

Amazonian pottery techniques and through their abilities to create beauty in the world (see figure 7.1). In this creative activity, song, storytelling, and historical narration are all important (D. Whitten and N. Whitten 1988). Men transmit cultural knowledge and vision to sons and sons-in-law through shamanic gnosis and, for some, performance (Whitten 1976, 1985). Again, song, musicality, storytelling, and historical narration are all important. Often, as with the Shipibo-Conibo of Amazonian Peru, a man, especially a shaman, "clarifies" a woman's design features of her pottery by naming the patterns. When a shaman in a séance sees a vision coming to him after taking *ayahuasca* (*Banisteriopsis* sp.) and conversing with the *yacu mama* (great boa constrictor), a woman (wife or daughter) snuffs tobacco water and clarifies for the shaman what he is seeing by stating quietly in the first person the very spirit that is arriving: "I am anaconda spirit person," or "I am jaguar spirit person." In the interchange and transmission processes among men and women, and boys and girls, the concept of sumaj is fundamentally important.

The interchange signals a near spiritual movement of understanding between the men as image bringers and the women as image clarifiers. Of equal importance is the concept of *ñucanchi causai* (our life or our life force), which connotes continuity from the life of our ancestors—*old ones*—to and through *us*. In fact, the concept of *quiquin llacta* (one's proper territory) refers to the homeland of a person's father's father's wife

FIGURE 7.1. *Mucawa* (drinking bowl) made by Eva Canelos. It is described as sumaj awashca. Photo by Melissa Sotelo, courtesy of The Spurlock Museum, University of Illinois at Urbana-Champaign.

and mother's mother's husband (D. Whitten and N. Whitten 1988; N. Whitten and D. Whitten 2008).

Canelos Quichua men and women seek to balance *ricsina* (experiential knowledge) with *yachana* (cultural knowledge), and *muscuna* (visionary experience) with *yuyana*, *yuyarina* (learning). Central to the transformative paradigm that involves these critical concepts is the *yachaj*, the "one-who-knows" or "the possessor-of-knowledge." This concept often means *shaman* when applied to males but may also be used to refer to master potters, who otherwise are known as *muscuj warmi* (visionary woman), or sinchi muscuyuj warmi. This paradigm pertains to two realms of existence: one called *ñucanchi yachai* (our cultural knowledge) and another called *shuj shimita yachai* (other cultural knowledge). As shamans and master potters show us again and again, one cannot understand one's own people's perception without understanding something of the lifeways and thought processes of other peoples. This translates perfectly in modern Spanish as *interculturalidad* (interculturality), one of the hallmarks of the contemporary Ecuadorian indigenous movement and a concept now written into the new Ecuadorian Constitution of 2008. Elsewhere (N. Whitten and D. Whitten 2008) we discuss indigenous culture and knowledge—–ñucanchi yachai—as a dynamic template for cultural transformation, and we treat knowledge of other cultural systems—shuj shimita yachai—as an axis for interculturality. A particular paradigm of knowledge, power, vision, and reflexivity does not map readily onto other Amazonian or Andean systems but is reminiscent of many of them when generalized into interculturality. We return to this point in the final section.

Article 1 of the 2008 Ecuadorian Constitution says, "recognizing our millennial roots, forged by women and men in distinct populations (*pueblos*) . . . Ecuador is a constitutional state of rights and social justice, democratic, sovereign, independent, unitary, intercultural, plurinational and secular" (N. Whitten translation and italics). We do not think it is an accident, given the strength of persuasion of Canelos Quichua and other Quichua-speaking Ecuadorians at the constitutional convention, that the terms *unitary* and *intercultural* are contiguous in this strong and dramatic statement about the dynamics and characteristics of the nation-state. By placing buen vivir and sumak kawsay side-by-side in many articles, the unitary and the intercultural are forced one onto and into the other. But with this force comes the clash that has rented the cultural spaces between the indigenous nationalities and the forces emanating from Carondelet—the presidential residence, office, and palace—asunder.

This rending of the increasingly interwoven fabric of cultures in Ecuador became especially apparent in 1990 after the national Levantamiento Indígena (Whitten 1996; 2003a, 6; 2008, 100–101) when then president Rodrigo Borja Cevallos met with leaders of the Organization of Indigenous People of Pastaza in the prestigious reception room of Carondelet to review a document that they had drawn up. The indigenous people thought that, since they were working with the president's own "Indian agent" (and first cousin), Alfonso Calderón Cevallos (their mothers are sisters), and since they were using the very language employed by the president when he ran for office, that an agreement could be reached. Instead, Borja, on all national television stations, excoriated the indigenous people for their arrogance in insisting on self-determination and self-management. This suggests that the "elitist rhetoric (as manifested by Borja at the presidential pinnacle of power of the ethnically entitled white *gente de bien*) is not transformable or transferable to the indigenous (or black) antipode of discourse of the indigenous social movements" (Whitten 1996, 201). It also indicates that "when ideological polarizations, such as *blanco/indio* exist, the text on one side of the contrast takes on the opposite meaning of that which it represents on the other." We could say, following Turner (1974), "that the text itself in its symbolic dimensions oscillates between the official (institutional) pole and the dynamic, agentive (orectic) pole of human discourse and social action" (Whitten 2003a, 6).

In short, there is a clear structural conjuncture in the relationships between President Correa and spokespeople for indigenous nationalities within a social movement, and predecessor presidents and past actors and speakers for indigenous rights, autonomy, and management systems. The president's rhetoric for indigenous rights and justice is negated when indigenous people themselves present the very same rhetoric to him. By placing sumak kawsay in synonymous position with buen vivir in the 2008 constitution, indigenous people highlighted their differences later to manifest in overt clashes with capitalist wealth accumulation through government sponsorship of large-scale mining and petroleum exploitation, even when such activities are said to be undertaken within the ideology and practice of development for the betterment of indigenous (and other) people. Michael Uzendoski and Edith Calapucha-Tapuy, who recently emerged from nearly two full years of sustained field research among the Napo Runa following their previous extended ethnography (Uzendoski 2005), and with Calapucha's native knowledge of the region, make this observation in a complementary manner.

> Through the use of symbols, indigenous people are able to assert their narratives, narratives that oppose the counternarratives that express the perspective of surplus-value. In other words, indigenous narratives

> of the world, which are communicated symbolically in protests and in the social actions of daily life, provide a distinct perspective of the 'good life'; these narratives and symbols contradict the state narrative of social well-being that is grounded in a linear narrative of development and progress. (Uzendoski and Calapucha-Tapuy 2012, 5)

Dynamics of the Clash

On March 8, 2012 (International Women's Day), a Plurinational March for Water, Life, and the Dignity of the Peoples (Pueblos) of Ecuador began in a town of Pangui (*anaconda* in Jivaroan languages) Province of Zamora-Chinchipe. It arrived in the city of Quito on March 22 (World Water Day). The immediate reason for the march, called for by the Confederation of Indigenous Nationalities of Ecuador (CONAIE), was the pending massive strip or pit mining of copper in the Cordillera del Condor, long-time home of and refuge for the Shuar people (Harner 1972), which was or is to take place by the Chinese mining company EcuaCorriente (ECSA). To indicate the scope of Ecuador's national investment in mining, ECSA proposed to invest US$1.4 billion during the first five of a twenty-five-year contract for the Mirador mine. It is estimated that the mine will yield 2.1 million tons of copper, as well as some gold and silver. Ecuador will gain 52 percent in royalties totaling at least $4.5 million as the company invests $100 million in its extensive endeavor.

The march mobilized indigenous people and many other groups nationwide. Speakers for CONAIE proclaimed it a great success. President Correa belittled it, called it a "disaster," and said that it proved that the "twenty-first-century socialism" is what 90 percent or more of the Ecuadorian people want. On March 24, CONAIE trumpeted "¡Por la Tierra, por el agua, por la vida, SUMAK KAWSAY, venceremos! Quito, 22 de marzo del 2012!" (For earth, for water, for life, SUMAK KAWSAY, we shall win [overcome]!)

But the contrast I have just sketched masks the fact that probably as many indigenous people who supported the march also supported a countermarch, which the president and his supporters organized within twenty-four hours. In Pastaza Province, Carlos Antonio Vargas Guatatuca, two-time president of CONAIE, prime architect of the coup that ousted President Jamil Mahuad Witt ([in alliance with past president and then colonel Lucio Gutiérrez] see Whitten 2003b), one-time candidate for the national presidency, and current president of the indigenous Comuna San Jacinto del Pindo south of Puyo, led the countermarch in Quito on March 22. In other words, being "indigenous" is not an indication of where actual indigenous people will be positioned in social movements that resonate to the sounds and rhythms of the clashing concepts signaled here by sumak kawsay and buen vivir.

Further, right before the march the indigenous director of the Instituto para el Ecodesarrollo Regional Amazónico, Carlos Viteri Gualinga, who is from Sarayacu and whose mother is master potter Rebeca Gualinga, gave a speech in Puyo in which he continuously mentioned sumak kawsay in terms of nationalist economic development, and even referred to "the economy of sumak kawsay" (Francesca Mezzenzana, pers. comm.). By so doing Viteri completely contradicted the meaning system that he explicated effectively in his undated blog, "¿Que es el SUMAK KAUSAY?" As with Antonio Vargas, Carlos Viteri has long been a militant advocate for indigenous rights, including indigenous autonomy and management systems. He and Antonio were not "co-opted" by the government as has been reported. Rather, they saw themselves as working within the framework of the constitution to better the lives of indigenous people in the modern, twenty-first-century socialism. Again, this is a socialism that exploits the obvious trappings of neoliberal capitalism for the actual funding of development for the collective, social good life.

We turn now to the Duality of Patterning among the Canelos Quichua people of Pastaza Province to explore this phenomenon of moving in and out of sumaj causai as a beautiful life force and buen vivir as the good life.

Duality of Patterning

In 1972—forty years ago—while residing in the indigenous hamlet of Puma Llacta on the Comuna San Jacinto del Pindo south of Puyo (see Whitten 1976), I (N. Whitten) traveled to Sarayacu with our long-time indigenous collaborator Marcelo Santi Simbaña.[2] The first thing he insisted we do on arrival was to visit Eucebia Aranda, who was an elder relative of his wife, Faviola Vargas Aranda. From the airstrip we crossed the river, moved swiftly across the plaza, and started on the trek to Sarayaquillu, which I had previously visited on two occasions. Half way there Marcelo veered northward on a small trail, and after about twenty minutes we came to Eucebia's house, situated about halfway between the trail from the plaza to Sarayaquillu and the large trail running east–west along a high ridge overlooking the Sarayaquillu River from Shihuacocha to Sarayaquillu. After visiting and drinking her *asua* (manioc brew), and that of her daughters' and daughters'-in-law, she asked if I would like to purchase some of her pottery, and I said I would.

Two of the pieces that intrigued Marcelo the most were very similar. They were originally made for a recent kin festival from which asua was to be served to guests (see N. Whitten and D. Whitten 2008). But Eucebia held them back in order to sell them later to someone like me. She quickly told us that the face on one side of the jar was that of an owl, or more specifically, a powerful shaman self-transformed into an owl while drinking ayahuasca in order to make an attack on an enemy shaman (figure 7.2). This, she said was *sacha runa*, the powerful Canelos Quichua person adept at forest life, and also the master spirit of rain forest dynamics often known as Amasanga.

Marcelo was delighted with this explanation because Virgilio Santi, Marcelo's father, did on one occasion transform himself into a *supai apapa*

FIGURE 7.2. Festival drinking bowl depicting Sacha Runa, made by Eucebia Aranda. Photo by Norman E. Whitten, Jr.

(spirit owl) to do away with a powerful shamanic adversary. On another occasion he battled as a shape-shifted attack shaman with a great owl, killed it, mounted it on a raft, and sent it down the Chingosimi River (Whitten 1976, 152). "Sumaj, sumaj, sumaj," Marcelo quietly said to himself. The combination of the beauty of the festival pot and the analogy to the shamanic prowess of his father nearly overwhelmed him, as he later told me.

After giving Marcelo and me another bowlful of asua in a delicate beautifully painted drinking bowl, Eucebia continued: "the other side of the pot, the one with the arms held out like those of a priest approaching a household or village, represents the *alli runa*, the 'Good Christian Indian'" (see figure 7.3).

The story, as it unfolded, about this festival serving and drinking vessel carries the message that sacha runa and alli runa are one and the same. The former faces and is part of the world of rain-forest dynamics,

FIGURE 7.3. Other side of the same drinking bowl depicting Alli Runa, made by Eucebia Aranda. Photo by Norman E. Whitten, Jr.

including the spirit world in all of its myriad and powerful dimensions. The latter faces and becomes part of the nationalizing modern world, bound up in the union of church and state, to which the Runa must adapt if they are to survive (see Whitten 1976, 218–21; the front and back cover images of this latter book represent this duality).

On our return to Puyo and the Comuna San Jacinto del Pindo, the stylized serving and drinking bowls with sacha runa on one side and alli runa on the other attracted a great deal of attention. The father of Antonio Vargas, Venancio Vargas, took great pains to explain to us the very duality of patterning that we were beginning to vaguely understand. He did this by going over other potteries collected during this trip, and previous trips to other areas, recounting in great detail inner meanings that we might never have grasped. He repeatedly used the term sumaj and spoke at length about the relationships between "our culture" and "other cultural knowledge." Although Venancio was not a shaman, his father, Eliseo, was, in fact, a Zápara shaman from north of Sarayaquillu, who claimed Sarayaquillu as his home prior to moving to the Comuna San Jacinto del Pindo (see N. Whitten and D. Whitten 2008, 25–27). To this day Antonio Vargas regards Sarayaquillu as his quiquin llacta, his proper territory, the region from which his father's father, father's wife, and father's sister all came.

I am sure by now that the reader has grasped the meaning in this discourse: *sumaj causai* is to *sacha runa* as *buen vivir* is to *alli runa*. Put another way, *sacha runa* is to *alli runa* as *sumaj causai* is to *buen vivir*. The concepts, though they represent different, even clashing ideas about life itself, are nonetheless bound to the lived, existential worlds for Amazonian Runa. To conjoin the concepts is to be part of a palpable structure of conjuncture (e.g., Sahlins 2000; Whitten and Whitten 2008, 2011) of dynamic indigenous desirable life and life in a vortex of modern capitalist transformation. We pursue this further with two other examples that for us were quite dramatic and dynamic.

In 1981, the Chango family moved with Marcelo Santi Simbaña, Faviola Vargas Aranda, and others, to establish the new hamlet Cushi Tambo. By this time, roads had cut through the Comuna San Jacinto del Pindo. And many of the Runa, including Alfonso's father, the late Abraham Chango (who is Achuar from the Capahuari River region and is usually known as Rucu Chango, the elder Chango), had incurred a heavy debt to a bank with no way to repay. Just before dawn on June 28, 1981, Rucu awoke in a cold sweat. He dreamt in Spanish about his debt and wrote on the matter: "On that day Challua [pseudonym] 'knew' (*ricsina*) the effect of national control over every aspect of his being, and he felt the sheer force of a new capitalist order of existence" (Whitten 1985, 166). Eight days later, Rucu awoke with a surge of energy running through him.

He had dreamt in Quichua (*sumaj muscui*) and began to perform personal rituals that epitomize power in Canelos Quichua culture (see Whitten 1985; N. Whitten and D. Whitten 2008). He was, he told us, drawing from *yachana*. On hearing this story, I wrote: "he was quintessential human in touch with all of the forces of forest and water, and his wife, Marta [a pseudonym for Clara], was quintessential *chagra mama*, the enduring basis for productive activity" (Whitten 1985, 167). In short, his duality of cultural patterning as manifest in his dream works oscillated on these two pre-dawn events between fear and depression on the neoliberal debt side and optimistic indigenous power play on the indigenous ritual side.

In 1982 and 1983 Alfonso Chango, whose mother, Clara Santi Simbaña, is the daughter of the late powerful shaman (and bancu) Virgilio Santi, volunteered to draw pictures that would clarify for us, and he hoped for many in Ecuador and beyond, the dynamics of shamanism that usually escaped nonindigenous people, Ecuadorians, and foreigners who traveled to the Amazonian region of Ecuador specifically for such knowledge. To be sure he had mastered the proper insights in deep knowledge and thereby be able to teach us through his drawings. He asked his mother to sing beautiful songs about the images he was to create. She in turn took her inspiration for her songs from her shamanic father, Virgilio. During the fall and winter of 1983 we culled the drawings down to a set that we thought would communicate what Alfonso wanted and returned with them to him in the summer of 1983.

He reorganized the drawings, and then wrote, in Quichua and Spanish, the meaning of each image. We put the whole together and did some editing for consistency with Enrique Mayer and Carmen Chuquín Amaguaña. We then took it to Juan Bottasso of Abya-Yala to see if Abya-Yala Press would publish it. The result was a forty-five-page color booklet, *Yachaj Sami Yachachina* (Shaman Class Lessons), published in 1984 and subsidized by Cultural Survival Inc. and the Sacha Runa Research Foundation ([Chango 1984] see figure 7.4). Indigenous people, especially those in the health care field and in bilingual education, frequently referred to this work as *sumaj awashca* (beautifully made) and *yachaj awashca* (knowledgeably made). Something that is beautiful and knowledgeable carries great significance. In fact, Frank Salomon said to us, this "is the most significant work you have done." The booklet was used in a number of bilingual courses in Ecuador that focused on health in the greater Puyo area. It was even used by Kathleen Fine-Dare (pers. comm.) in a course on South American ethnology taught primarily to Native American students at Fort Lewis College in the 1980s and 1990s.

As Abya-Yala expanded, it added priests who were bilingual in Spanish and Quichua to its editorial review board. One *cura*, in particular, who

FIGURE 7.4. *Yachaj Sami Yachachina*, booklet by Alfonso Chango. Photo by Norman E. Whitten, Jr.

hailed from Zumbagua, told Padre Juan Bottasso that he was appalled at this publication because, in many places, the Spanish and Quichua did not say exactly the same thing! Alfonso addressed the same issues of representation in each of his drawings, but he did not try to translate from Quichua to Spanish or vice versa; he wrote about each image in each language. The "bilingual" priest insisted that Abya-Yala withdraw all copies from its bookstore. What the good priest did not understand was the duality of cultural patterning that was pointed out by master ceramist Eucebia Aranda over a decade earlier. Alfonso, quite consciously, was moving in and out of Canelos Quichua culture and national culture in his use of Quichua and Spanish. He was not saying "the same thing" in the two languages because the *significance* of his explanation was different in the two languages. He was writing on paper as a shaman chants in séance, and as a sinchi muscuyuj warmi thinks and decorates as she creates beautiful images in Amazonian pottery and through song. Michael Uzendoski (pers. comm.) points out that this is what Michael Silverstein (1993) calls *metapragmatics* when he states that languages are not simply equivalent but involve all kinds of other social and ideological differences.

We hope that these three examples illustrate the depth and power of a duality of ethnic patterning and power patterning. This patterning, I have argued, is cultural as opposed to analytical. "The trouble with all *analytical* polarities is that they miss the fundamental point of human communication itself—simply put, messages are forever relayed to those capable of reading them by 'debundling' the symbolic text" (Whitten 1985, 213–14). If we in the West take what appears to be a cultural contrast and turn it into an analytical contrast, then we miss the significance of the clashing concepts that we have identified in the first part of this presentation (Whitten 2011, 329–31). We miss the processes involved in interculturality, the very processes written into the 2008 Constitution of the Republic of Ecuador and recently enacted by Amazonian Runa on both sides of the semantic divide.

Sorting Levels of Signification

In 1973, in the introduction to his seminal collection of essays entitled *The Interpretation of Culture*, Clifford Geertz wrote that anthropologists, through application of hermeneutic principles and eschewing the tempting hermetically conceived theoretical constructs, "must descend into detail, past the misleading tags, past the metaphysical types, past the empty similarities to grasp firmly the essential character of not only the various cultures but the various sorts of individuals within each culture, if we wish to encounter humanity face to face" (Geertz 1973, 53). This is a process that he called *sorting levels of signification*. In doing the sorting, one must be sure that the perceived signifier, in this case the tropes sumak kawsay and buen vivir, signify an identifiable set of phenomena (the signified): a life of indigenous beauty and knowledge for the first, and a good life of neocapitalist prosperity, in which the social ends are met by reforming capitalism, for the second. Then, it is up to the analyst to come to an understanding of what Max Weber called the *webs of signification* in which all actors are to some extent ensnared and by means of which human action can and does create transformations of the social and cultural order. Obviously, we have been working toward this point throughout this chapter (see also Geertz 1973, 5; N. Whitten and D. Whitten 2011, 1–7, 187–202).

In *Millennial Ecuador* (Whitten 2003a, 28) I identified the dimensions of modernity within which webs of signification have been embedded in a *longue durée* as follows.

> Modernity emerged out of medieval systems to stress the following components as globalizing ideology: profit seeking; science for economic gain; phenotypic color coding (racializing); concepts of [non-Western] humans as vestiges or relics of an antipodal past; the "growth" of wealth; fetishism of commodities; commodification of land, labor, and humans; ethnic cleansing; the hypostasis of racial fixity; and the power of print languages.

It is these congeries of enduring features against which indigenous spokespersons speak, write, and act, no matter which side of the buen vivir/sumak kawsay clash they may be on in any given moment of dynamic time. *Millennial* is a dynamic by which people challenge their place in modernity. Millennial as used here and elsewhere (Whitten 2003b, x–xi) does not refer to the beginning of a new century or the second coming of Christ. It corresponds very closely to the Quichua concept of *pachacutij* (defined below). Many indigenous Ecuadorians, led by Andean Otavalans, refer to themselves as a *millennial people* (Wibbelsman 2009).

To be on the "government's side" is to insist that the good life brought by neocapitalist development for socialist redistribution can be shared with indigenous kin and comrades without the ideological trappings of Western modernity. To doubt that possibility is to move into the reality of pachacutij, the return of space-time (*pacha*, *ñaupa pacha*—chronotope) of a healthy past to that of a healthy future. Health here is more often than not signaled by the concept of sumaj, beauty, and life, or life force and causai (or living, *causana*). When the semantic dichotomy of the clashing synonymic concept(s) results in clear aggregation of indigenous people contra the state with the aim of fundamental change, then millenarian systems come into play (e.g., Whitten 2003a), though more often than not the surface manifestations are relatively short lived and tied to multiple cultural conjunctures. Early illustrations of the latter phenomenon include the Levantamiento Indígena of 1990 (Whitten 1996; N. Whitten and D. Whitten 2011) and the March for Land and Life of 1992 (N. Whitten and D. Whitten 2008; Whitten, Whitten, and Chango 1997). A more recent example was the "Golpe del 21" in January 2000 (Whitten 2003b), led by Antonio Vargas and Lucio Gutiérrez.

In the introduction and conclusion to *Millennial Ecuador* (2003b), I (N. Whitten) pointed out that "modernity [now with its constitutional concept of buen vivir] and millenarianism [with its constitutional component of sumak kawsay] are inextricably intertwined. They constitute a mutualist dynamic that propels Ecuadorian cultural systems from one historical event to another. The conjuncture that they form is impelling and synergistic; it cannot be unbundled or its elements dissected." Transformative dynamics leading to change, in other words, are bound to a dialectic that leads to dramatic events, such as the aforementioned ones, and many, many more including, most recently, the three-week march from Amazonian Pangui to Andean Quito.

It is to the credit, then, of those indigenous people who managed to insert the clash of concepts into the 2008 Ecuadorian Constitution, that the dynamic of modernity and millenarianism will continue to play out on the ground, in community action, through bureaucracy, within varied rhetorical performances, and in legal circles, and that the clashing concepts will be sustained on all sides of oppositions as they wax and wane. There are many things of great significance in the new Ecuadorian constitution. One of them is the phenomenon of sumak kawsay and its clashing Spanish gloss of buen vivir. Indigenous people at one level find great significance in the beautiful life force that is knowledgeably constituted; others try to insert this into a framework that is imbued with neoliberal capitalist wealth accumulation to be applied to socialist and humanist goals. The one thing that seems certain at the moment is that placing a clash of tropes of life into the constitution, the dialogues, debates, manifestations, conflicts, and social movements and their suppressions will not lack for a semantic base at every level. We are drawn to the statement made by Jaime Roldós Aguilera, the first president to speak publicly in Quichua during his inaugural address some thirty-three years ago. "Only the clash of ideas can ignite the light of truth" (*El Comercio* January 27, 1979, A-1, A-15; Whitten 1981, 776).

Public Wealth Among the Canelos Quichua

In 1985, I published *Sicuanga Runa: The Other Side of Development in Amazonian Ecuador*. Soon after opening, I discussed the myth of Sicuanga Runa, "toucan person," who frees two lovely women, red woman (*Bixa orellana*) and black woman (*Genipa americana*), from a spiny bamboo cage in which they were placed by evil monkey (foreign person) Machin Runa. The women then turn their liberator into the beautiful toucan bird and go on to create beauty in the world for humans to enjoy (see figure 7.5).

FIGURE 7.5. Festival drinking bowl depicting Sicuanga Runa, made by Alicia Canelos. Photo by Norman E. Whitten, Jr.

This beauty, and the power emanating from it, was considered the "wealth" of the "other [indigenous] side" of (Western, state, national, Ecuadorian) development. After reviewing the literature on the Central Amazon and the Amazonian rim, I turned to an emblematic proclamation carved into the cement façade over Davenport Hall at the University of Illinois, where the Departments of Anthropology and Geography are housed. The sign reads (to this day): "The Wealth of Illinois is in her Soil, and her Strength lies in its Intelligent Development." I went on to write, "whereas my colleagues in developmental agriculture think of the integrity and richness of soil per se, and strive to protect it and enhance its vital nutrients, indigenous Amazonian people think of the integrity and richness of the *forest*. It is the combination of forest and hydrosphere—rainfall and river activity—that provides the basic features of soil itself in Amazonia" (Whitten 1985, 30).

To understand the Runa side of life, within a framework of Western capitalist development, we must go back to the Canelos Quichua concept of ñucanchi yachai introduced above. Within "our culture" there exists what we call a dynamic template for cultural transformation. This template is bound to a paradigm of ecological imagery (Whitten 1985), which in its entirety and with all of its specificities and variations (described in Whitten 1985; N. Whitten and D. Whitten 2008) constitutes what many authors in this book refer to as "public wealth" (especially Guzmán-Gallegos, chapter 4; Micarelli, chapter 6; and Santos-Granero, chapter 3). This wealth is grounded in concepts and praxes of usufruct, defined by Santos-Granero as the "totality of value things—whether material or not—over which a collectivity claims to have rights of usufruct." Among the Canelos Quichua of Amazonian Ecuador, usufruct is subsumed by a paradigm well known to all. It is embedded in images evoked especially in female Amazonian pottery making and male shamanic vision and performance, and it is projected through song, convivial play, myth telling, and discussions of geocosmography.

To condense a complex system of ecological imagery that constitutes the dynamic template, the symbolic and metaphorical framework for the cultural dimensions of public wealth, let us think of four spheres (N. Whitten and D. Whitten 2008, 47–50). In the outer sphere we have the entire hydrosphere, the ultimate source of power. The Canelos Quichua condense the dynamics of this power source as spirit master Sungui, who is male, female, and androgynous first shaman, and whose corporeal manifestation is the anaconda. Sungui nourishes the dynamics of the next (inner) sphere, that of the tropical rain forest, whose male, female, and androgynous spirit master is Amasanga, also known as Sacha Runa. Amasanga, in turn, controls the power of Sungui and keeps the hydrosphere from going wild and creating floods, landslides, and other disruptions. The third inward sphere is that of the indigenous swidden garden, which is nourished by forest dynamics and feminine skill and knowledge. It is overseen by master spirit Nungüi, who is strictly feminine and whose manifestation is a small, deadly, black coral snake with a mouth too small to bite humans. The rain forest itself is controlled by chagra dynamics, for it is through female human volition and knowledge that rain forest diversity is increased and nourished.

And finally, at the core of the four spheres is the human household where the human male-female procreating couple maintains and projects *ayllu* continuity. This continuity is symbolized mythically by the indigenous fundamental root metaphor that the anaconda of the macrocosmic water (hydrosphere) domain *is* the procreating penis in the male-female microcosmic household domain (N. Whitten and D. Whitten 2008, 50–51).

Not all Canelos Quichua people, of course, are fortunate enough to be in interpersonal and ecological systems in which their lives would be characterized by themselves or by others as sumaj causai, but most would consider their situation to be in the realm of *alli causai* (good life). Beyond goodness lies bad situations and evil, both of which are subsumed by the concept *manalli*. In the context of usage in this book, we could call such situations states of "poverty." *Waccha* is the condition of being without crucial aspects of a minimal social unit. It applies to orphans, widows, and widowers. Whereas adult men may find another wife, sometimes one much younger, and restore the basic male-female household unit, and whereas most children are either adopted or sent out of the system to work in households, widows are in a particularly vulnerable situation, even when they have many relatives around. To be in a state of waccha is manalli, and the individuals fall outside of the good life, even when those around them enjoy such a position.

Another condition of a bad life lies with those who have been bewitched, cursed, or ensorcelled. They, too, in the context of this work are in a condition of poverty. Such people must have access to effective shamanic expertise and must recover by the curing ministration of a shaman or shamans, as well as by retaliatory mechanisms against evil ones. In other words, the male-female pair at the center of the household must control the female dynamics of the garden, and the dynamics involved there must control the male-female dynamics of the rain forest, which in turn must control the male-female dynamics of the hydrosphere. These ecological and imageric processes, which have been elaborated elsewhere, rest on the combination of usufruct and social support, as suggested and demonstrated by most of the chapters in this excellent book.

The wealth bound to cosmos, rivers, forests, and gardens (see Guzmán-Gallegos, chapter 4, and Sarmiento Barletti, chapter 5) shared by the collectivity is found in this paradigm, which then in terms of the thrust of this book, translates to a system of public wealth for the Canelos Quichua of Amazonian Ecuador. This paradigm of "our cultural knowledge" complements those of adjacent peoples, such as the Achuar and Napo Runa, and it contrasts with the public wealth of capitalist prosperity. The axis of interculturality that we mention above—shuj shimita yachai—is bound to complementary cultural systems, as well as contrasting cultural systems. Sumaj causai is a trope of the complementary systems and buen vivir that of contrasting systems. But both signal systems of public wealth that operate in the lifeways of the contemporary people.

The relationship of the complementary system is this: neither the Napo Runa nor the Achuar express their cognate public wealth paradigm as do the Canelos Quichua. Both have other ways of presentation and explication at cosmological, social, and individual levels. Nonetheless, Napo Runa and Achuar peoples can and do understand Canelos Quichua expressions of such a symbolic-ecological template, just as Canelos Quichua people can and do understand Napo Runa and Achuar systems.

Relationships and articulations to the contrasting, or clashing, system of public wealth bound to success in the capitalist market may be harder to grasp. There is a tendency in anthropology to maintain a cultural contrast as an analytical contrast (Whitten 2011), and in so doing we may fail to see the inherent relationships that apparently led to the placing of sumak kawsay and buen vivir as synonyms in the Ecuadorian constitution. In her chapter for this volume, Giovanna Micarelli analyzes the relationship between the contrasting systems for the multiethnic, linguistically diverse, but culturally unified People of the Center of southeastern Colombia. "Money is the linchpin where *lo de afuera* (the external world of radical alterity) and *lo de adentro* (the internal world of shared substances) swing into each other." A statement that complements Micarelli's perspective and insights, and deepens ours, was made by Michelle Wibbelsman (e-mail communication to author, August 13, 2012). In a review of the penultimate draft of this chapter she writes,

> your analysis seems to maintain the tension and purity of two different, and in fact clashing, systems where any space that exists in between may well imply openness to listening, understanding, learning, appreciating, but not necessarily reconciling. Reconciliation would potentially be equivalent to compromise—not knowledgeably made [see first epigraph to this chapter]; responsive to immediate circumstances, pressures, desires, but not enduring principles, and which, if carried to its eventual conclusion would be neither sustainable nor productive.

Following Sahlins (1999), Micarelli (chapter 6) also writes of the "indigenization of modernity," a subject to which I have given considerable attention in my 2008 article in *Tipití* and that we again address in *Histories of the Present* (N. Whitten and D. Whitten 2011, 163–85). In that article and in the more recent chapter, we argue, "indigenous modernity has clear millennial proclivities" (Whitten 2003b) and that "the intertwining of modernity and its indigenization, the genesis of alternative modernities, and emerging culture generate a myriad of intercultural systems to which, it is hoped, more and more ethnographers will turn their attention" (N. Whitten and D. Whitten 2011, 184).

It is with great pleasure then, that I close this chapter by noting that my hope is nourished by many of the outstanding chapters in this book. By focusing on public wealth as an indigenization of modernity—as Micarelli and the other analyses herein have finely articulated—ethnography of greater Amazonia is enhanced and, *mutatis mutandis*, world ethnography is enriched.[3]

Acknowledgments

Dorothea (Sibby) Scott Whitten passed away on August 8, 2011. Nevertheless, almost everything in this chapter pertains to data we collected and analyzed jointly, and some of the insights, translations, and interpretations come directly from her indefatigable work, especially with women's ceramic creativity and song. She is in all ways joint author. We thank Alfonso Chango for procuring a copy of the print version of the 2008 Ecuadorian Constitution and discussing its meanings with me, Norman Whitten, in 2008. During the months of March and April 2012, e-mail communications I exchanged with Francesca Mezzenzana in Puyo clarified many aspects of the clashing concepts with which we deal. I am very grateful to her for taking time from her own productive field research to provide such information and interpretation. We also appreciate many years of collegial exchange of information and interpretation with Mike Uzendoski. In addition, Mike read an early draft of this chapter and made very valuable contributions, including the observations that this analysis fits very well with what is taking place among the Napo Runa. Rachel Corr and Kathy Fine-Dare also read this chapter and made some comments that led to significant change and clarification, for which I am grateful. Fernando Santos-Granero made excellent recommendations for the final draft and helped me develop the final section. Beth Conklin presented the short paper at the panel organized by and chaired by Fernando Santos-Granero at the International Americanist Congress in Vienna. Thank you Beth! In reading the penultimate draft, Michelle Wibbelsman made trenchant comments that allowed me to pull together the significance of this work and understand that even in a structure of conjuncture, criteria of sharp contrast may not only apply but also be nurtured as they are transformed.

Notes

1. In this presentation sumaj causai pertains to the local-level semiotics of beauty (connoting knowledge, vision, and power) from our ethnography with the

Canelos Quichua indigenous people of Pastaza Province, and sumak kawsay pertains to the concept paired with buen vivir in the 2008 Ecuadorian Constitution and its subsequent entry into a sustained literature found in all media from indigenous protest and national development through press releases and scholarly discourses.

2. The first-person plural is used in most of this chapter because of our joint work on it or subjects that pertain directly to it. In some instances, such as this trip to Sarayacu with Marcelo Santi, the first-person pronoun is used because I (N. Whitten) went alone, while Sibby worked on other materials in Puyo and/or the Comuna San Jacinto del Pindo. In the latter part of the chapter, I use the first-person singular when I range into areas that Sibby and I had never discussed.

3. An anonymous reviewer for this chapter submitted this comment, which certainly deserves attention. "My only critique of this chapter is that the authors' discussion of sumak kawsay shows that perhaps modernity tries to indigenize to neutralize the indigenization of modernity—perhaps the logics of domination today are precisely those that seem the most liberating? Thus the duality of power patterning has changed historically . . . now with capitalism attempting to co-opt the logics of interculturality itself."

Back when we began our research in 1968 and increasingly throughout our first period of ethnography in 1970 and 1971 and then for the years 1972–1973, the government of Ecuador, then under military dictatorship, was determined to destroy indigenous culture. The first lines of *Sacha Runa* (1976) state, "just east of the Andes, in clear view of spectacular snow-capped peaks, live two of the largest concentrations of tropical forest [indigenous people] in central Ecuador. . . . The policy of the contemporary Ecuadorian military government is to destroy their way of life" (Whitten 1976, 3). The transformation from forced assimilation to co-optation of indigenous concepts of interculturality leaves room for more maneuvering by indigenous actors than ever before, even though, under the present regime of President Rafael Correa, the idea of assimilation is again being promulgated in a very disturbing manner. For example, Carmen Martínez Novo recently observed "for the Ecuadorian case indigenous rights have suffered a reversal. There has been an expansion of some legal rights, but the legislation is contradictory and difficult to implement, as no serious attempt has been made to implement it. The regime is appropriating indigenous symbols and demands, but is not recognizing indigenous peoples as actors. The neoliberal emphasis on participation has also been reversed. Finally, there has been a resurgence of prejudice against indigenous peoples" (Martínez Novo 2014, 108).

The nationalist indigenous concept of sumak kawsay is under consideration for incorporation into a bevy of systems throughout Ecuador, just as the indigenous concept of sumaj causai is brought increasingly to the forefront of discourse among indigenous people. These discourses, diverse though they may be, underscore the points about the duality of power patterning discussed in this chapter.

References

Chango, Alfonso. 1984. *Yachaj Sami Yachachina*. Quito and Cayambe: Abya-Yala.

Chuji Gualinga, Mónica. 2009. "Modernidad, desarrollo, interculturalidad y Sumak Kawsay o Buen Vivir." Fundación Regional de Asesoría en Derechos Humanos. Ponencia presentada en el Foro International sobre Interculturalidad y Desarrollo; Uribia, Colombia, May 23.

Geertz, Clifford. 1973. *The Interpretation of Culture: Selected Essays*. New York: Basic Books.

Harner, Michael. 1972. *The Jívaro: People of the Sacred Waterfalls*. New York: Natural History Press.

Martínez Novo, Carmen. 2014. "Managing Diversity in Postneoliberal Ecuador." *The Journal of Latin American and Caribbean Studies* 19(1):103–25.

Picq, Manuela. 2011. "Using Courts to Harass Ecuador's Dissidents." LASA e-mail, November 14, 2011 to Ecuadorianist subscribers.

Sahlins, Marshall. 1999. "What is Anthropological Enlightenment? Some Lessons of the Twentieth Century." *Annual Review of Anthropology* 28:i-xxiii.

———. 2000. *Culture in Practice: Selected Essays*. New York: Zone Books.

Silverstein, Michael. 1993. "Metapragmatic Discourse and Metapragmatic Function." In *Reflexive Language: Reported Speech and Metapragmatics*, edited by John A. Lucy, 33–58. Cambridge: Cambridge University Press.

Turner, Victor. 1974. *Dramas, Fields, and Metaphors: Symbolic Action in Human Society*. Ithaca: Cornell University Press.

Uzendoski, Michael. 2005. *The Napo Runa of Amazonian Ecuador*. Urbana: University of Illinois Press.

———. 2011. "Indigenous Amazonian Peoples, Surplus-Value, and the End of Capitalism." Paper presented at the annual meeting of the American Anthropological Association. Montreal, November.

Uzendoski, Michael, and Edith Felicia Calapucha-Tapuy. 2012. *The Ecology of the Spoken Word: Amazonian Story Telling and Shamanism Among the Napo Runa*. Urbana: University of Illinois Press.

Viteri Gualinga, Carlos. n.d. "¿Qué es el SUMAK KAUSAY? ¿Existe el concepto de desarrollo en la cosmovisión indígena?" Accessed April 3, 2012. http://www.intiraymi.org/sumak-kausai.htm.

Whitten, Dorothea Scott. 2003. "Connections: Creative Expressions of Canelos Quichua Women." In *Crafting Gender*, edited by Eli Bartra, 73–97. Durham, NC: Duke University Press.

Whitten, Dorothea Scott, and Norman E. Whitten, Jr. 1988. *From Myth to Creation: Art from Amazonian Ecuador*. Urbana: University of Illinois Press.

———, eds. 1993. *Imagery and Creativity: Ethnoaesthetics and Art Worlds in the Americas*. Tucson: University of Arizona Press.

Whitten, Norman E., Jr. 1976. *Sacha Runa: Ethnicity and Adaptation of Ecuadorian Jungle Quichua*. Urbana: University of Illinois Press.

———, ed. 1981. *Cultural Transformations and Ethnicity in Modern Ecuador.* Urbana: University of Illinois Press.

———. 1985. *Sicuanga Runa: The Other Side of Development in Amazonian Ecuador.* Urbana: University of Illinois Press.

———. 1996. "The Levantamiento Indígena of 1990 and the Epitomizing Symbol of 1992: Reflections on Nationalism, Ethnic-Bloc Formation, and Racialist Ideologies." In *History, Power, and Identity: Ethnogenesis in the Americas, 1492–1992*, edited by Jonathan D. Hill, 191–217. Iowa City: University of Iowa Press.

———. 2003a. "Introduction." In *Millennial Ecuador: Critical Essays on Cultural Transformation and Social Dynamics*, edited by Norman E. Whitten, Jr., 1–42. Iowa City: University of Iowa Press.

———, ed. 2003b. *Millennial Ecuador: Critical Essays on Cultural Transformation and Social Dynamics.* Iowa City: University of Iowa Press.

———. 2008. "Interculturality and the Indigenization of Modernity: A View from Amazonian Ecuador." *Tipití: Journal of the Society of Lowland South America* 6(2):3–36, 47–48.

———. 2011. "Ethnogenesis and Interculturality in the "Forest of Canelos": The Wild and the Tame Revisited." In *Ethnicity in Ancient Amazonia: Reconstructing Past Identities from Archaeology, Linguistics, and Ethnohistory*, edited by Alf Hornborg and Jonathan D. Hill, 321–34. Boulder, CO: University Press of Colorado.

Whitten, Norman E., Jr., and Dorothea Scott Whitten. 2008. *Puyo Runa: Imagery and Power in Modern Amazonia.* Urbana: University of Illinois Press.

———. 2011. *Histories of the Present: People and Power in Ecuador.* Urbana: University of Illinois Press.

Whitten, Norman E., Jr., Dorothea Scott Whitten, and Alfonso Chango. 1997. "Return of the Yumbo: The Indigenous Caminata from Amazonia to Andean Quito." *American Ethnologist* 24(2):355–91.

Wibbelsman, Michelle. 2009. *Ritual Encounters: Otavalan Mythic and Modern Community.* Urbana: University of Illinois Press.

CONTRIBUTORS

Beth A. Conklin is Associate Professor of Anthropology at Vanderbilt University (Nashville, Tennessee). She has done long-term research with the Wari' in Rondônia, Brazil, and has written on a variety of issues, including the anthropology of the body, environmental discourse and indigenous rights, visual and performative politics, and medical anthropology. Her book, *Consuming Grief: Compassionate Cannibalism in an Amazonian Society* (2001), is a study of Wari' ritual as a nexus of bodily experience, sociality, emotion, memory, and human-animal relations that challenges Western theory and preconceptions. Her chapter "Amazonia" in *The Handbook of Sociocultural Anthropology* (2013) highlights Lowland South America's ongoing contributions to cultural critique. Her current research explores indigenous community museums, food politics, consumption, and climate change in the United States and developments in Brazil in the two decades since she and Laura Graham published "The Shifting Middle Ground: Amazonian Indians and Eco-Politics" in *American Anthropologist* (1995).

María A. Guzmán-Gallegos is a senior researcher at Fafo (Institute for Applied International Studies), Oslo, Norway. She has done extensive fieldwork in Amazonian Kichwa communities in Ecuador and has been involved with indigenous organizations and nongovernmental organizations working with territorial issues in Peru and Brazil. Her theoretical interests center on personhood and gender, kinship, interethnic relations, indigenous political organization, indigenous movement, and socio-environmental conflict related to oil extraction. She has published the books *Para que la Yuca Beba Nuestra Sangre* (1997) and *Conflicting Spatialities: Networks, Mediation and Alterity in the Making of Indigenous Territories in Ecuadorian Amazonia* (2010), as well as several articles and book chapters. Among these are: "Identity Cards, Abducted Footprints, and the Book of San Gonzalo: The Power of Textual Objects in Runa Worldview," in *The Occult Life of Things: Native Amazonians Theories of Materiality and Personhood*, edited by Fernando Santos-Granero (2009).

Giovanna Micarelli is Associate Professor of Anthropology at the Pontificia Universidad Javeriana of Bogotá, Colombia, and researcher at the Center for Social Studies of the University of Coimbra, Portugal. She has worked with the Shipibo Conibo of the Ucayali region in Peru, the Tikuna of the Amacayacu River, and the indigenous peoples belonging to the supra-ethnic cluster Gente de Centro (People of the Center of southeastern Colombia) at the periphery of the Colombian town of Leticia. She has published several articles and book chapters, the most recent of which is: "Pensar como un enjambre: redes indígenas en las márgenes de la modernidad" in *Perspectivas antropológicas sobre la Amazonía contemporánea*, edited by M. Chaves and C. Del Cairo, (ICANH/Universidad Javeriana, 2010). She has also edited the bilingual Spanish-Muinane book *Taagai Búuamïsi jïïbegeejï* by Aniceto Nejedeka Kajutne (ICANH 2012). Her book *Weaving a New Basket: Indigenous Networks at the Margins of Development* is forthcoming with Editorial Javeriana, Bogotá.

Fernando Santos-Granero has a Litentiate degree in anthropology from the Pontificia Universidad Católica del Perú (1980) and a PhD in social anthropology from the London School of Economics (1986). He has done ethnographic research in Yanesha and Ashaninka communities of Central Peru and historical research on Upper Amazon regional economies and tropical American regimes of slavery and servitude. At present he is a senior staff scientist at the Smithsonian Tropical Research Institute in Panama. He is the author of *The Power of Love: The Moral Use of Knowledge Amongst the Amuesha of Central Peru* (1991) and of *Vital Enemies: Slavery, Predation, and the Amerindian Political Economy of Life* (2009). He is the editor of *The Occult Life of Things: Native Amazonian Theories of Materiality and Personhood* (2009) and coeditor, with Jonathan D. Hill, of *Comparative Arawakan Histories: Rethinking Language Family and Culture Area in Amazonia* (2002). With Frederica Barclay he has coedited the six volumes of the *Guía etnográfica de la alta amazonía* (1994–2007), and coauthored the books *Selva Central: History, Economy, and Land Use in Peruvian Amazonia* (1998) and *Tamed Frontiers: Economy, Society, and Civil Rights in Upper Amazonia* (2000). He has also published numerous articles and chapters on indigenous leadership and philosophies of power, notions of personhood and people making, history and landscape, theories of materiality, shamanism and witchcraft, and conceptions of the body and its senses.

Juan Pablo Sarmiento Barletti has a PhD in anthropology from the University of St. Andrews. At present he is Lecturer in Anthropology at Durham University. He has done extensive fieldwork among groups of Ashaninka people throughout Peruvian Amazonia and their political federations since 2007. His research centers on the Ashaninka experience of the Peruvian internal war and the process of reconciliation in its wake. He has published the article "Les enjeux politiques du 'bien-vivre' en Amazonie autochtone" (*Recherches Amérindiennes au Québec*, 2012) and is in the process of publishing his dissertation "Kametsa Asaiki: The Pursuit of the "Good Life" in an Ashaninka Village (Peruvian Amazonia)" (University of St. Andrews, 2011).

Anthony Seeger is an anthropologist, ethnomusicologist, archivist, record producer, and musician. He has taught at the Museu Nacional/UFRJ (1975–1982), Indiana University (1982–1988), and the University of California Los Angeles (2000–2012). From 1988 to 2000 he was Curator of the Folkways Collection and Director of Smithsonian Folkways Recordings at the Smithsonian Institution. He has authored or edited six books and over one hundred articles and book chapters on anthropological, ethnomusicological, archival, intellectual property, and Indigenous rights issues, as well as served as executive producer of more than two hundred and fifty CDs and other media projects. His research on the Kïsêdjê (formerly known as the Suyá) in Mato Grosso, Brazil, resulted in three books: *Os Índios e Nos; Estudos sobre sociedades tribais brasileiras* (Editora Campus 1980); *Nature and Society in Central Brazil: The Suya Indians of Mato Grosso* (Harvard University Press 1981); and *Why Suyá Sing: A Musical Anthropology of an Amazonian People* (2nd edition with CD, University of Illinois Press 2004).

Norman E. Whitten, Jr., and Dorothea Scott Whitten met as graduate students (Dorothea sociology, Norman anthropology) at the University of North Carolina, Chapel Hill, where they graduated (Dorothea MA 1960, Norman MA 1962, PhD 1964). They began joint research with the Canelos Quichua in 1968. At the University of Illinois at Urbana-Champaign, where they spent most of their career, Norm was professor of Anthropology and Latin American Studies, and both of them became curators of the Spurlock Museum in 2000. Together they have published *Sacha Runa: Ethnicity and Adaptation of Ecuadorian Jungle Quichua* (1976); *Sicuanga Runa: The Other Side of Development in Amazonian Ecuador* (1985); *From Myth to Creation: Art from Amazonian Ecuador* (1988); *Puyo Runa: Imagery and Power in Modern Amazonia* (2008); and *Histories of the Present: People and Power in Ecuador* (2011). They have also published more than one hundred and fifty articles and book chapters and curated thirty museum and gallery exhibitions in the United States and Ecuador.

INDEX

abundance, 4, 8, 10, 15, 24–26, 65, 93, 97–98, 102, 126, 130, 144, 173–74, 177–81; of food, 25, 61, 121, 176, 179; of land, 13, 104; of public wealth, 90–91; of resources, 11–12, 136; of vitality (life), 15, 26–27, 110, 181
accumulation, 11–12, 15, 24, 29, 62, 78, 99, 133–34, 136, 147–50, 157, 162, 173; capitalist, 146, 193–94, 197, 207; material, 8, 14–15, 28, 30, 74, 142, 147, 150; wealth, 3, 6, 15, 24, 27, 29, 60, 63, 72, 78, 133, 150, 154, 193
affects, 21, 26, 181
alterity, 18, 80, 162, 177, 211. *See also* Others

beauty, 27–28, 54, 70, 121, 191–92, 195, 201, 205–8, 212n1
biopolitics, 60, 78, 83
biopower, 8, 15
blood, 18, 22, 67, 72–73, 80
body, 8, 17–18, 22–23, 38, 40, 44, 51, 55, 65, 71–72, 79–81, 100, 102, 109, 126–28, 131–33, 135, 143, 147, 152, 171, 174–75, 178, 184n17; and affects (habits), 26, 52, 178, 181; and embodiment, 8, 72, 84n2, 126, 153, 183n8; gendered, 118, 128, 178; painting, 44–45, 51, 55, 70, 72
breath, 21, 51, 92–93, 98, 109, 126, 168, 178, 191
buen vivir, 6, 156n2, 192–94, 196–97, 199, 202, 205–7, 210–11, 213n1. *See also* living well

capital, 4, 9–10, 25, 61, 78, 146, 155–56; human, 16, 63, 78
capitalism, 3–4, 9, 11, 43, 53, 64–64, 84, 137, 193–94, 199, 205, 213; millennial, 4
care (caring), 15, 16–23, 25–26, 28, 30, 62, 67, 72–74, 83–84, 90, 108, 124, 126–28, 132, 135, 140–44, 149–55, 157n12, 168. *See also* nurture
ceremonies, 17, 37–38, 41, 43–52, 55–56, 56n1, 97–98, 173; collective (communal, public), 19, 21, 26–27, 39–40, 45, 49, 53, 55, 99; and ceremonial centers, 92, 96–97; and ceremonial groups, 41, 44, 48, 50; as public wealth, 39
chiefs, 16, 19, 21, 23, 66, 75, 77, 92, 103–4, 110, 168–70. *See also* leaders; leadership
children, 20–21, 23, 37–38, 43–44, 47, 50, 66–67, 75, 78, 82–83, 95, 97, 117, 121, 124, 126, 128, 131–32, 147, 149, 152–53, 173, 177–78, 210; as wealth, 15, 18, 27, 61, 108
coca, 24, 100–101, 167–68, 170, 183n2, 183n6
collectivity, 10, 12, 14, 18, 20, 27, 42, 52, 90–91, 99–100, 110, 125, 134, 173, 175, 181, 209–10
commensality, 18, 72, 143–44, 176, 179
commodities, 10–11, 28, 65, 71, 80, 82, 206
community, 8–9, 11–13, 15, 17, 19, 20, 22, 25–27, 40, 42, 44, 51, 53–54, 57n8, 60–61, 66–67, 73–75, 77–78, 80, 83,

community (*continued*)
91, 103–5, 131, 140–41, 151–54, 156n2, 158n19, 164–66, 175, 182, 183n5, 193, 207; sense of, 13, 17, 154
compassion, 15, 18, 30, 90, 108
competition, 17, 29–30, 70; for land, 13, 70; for resources, 142, 145; for status, 73, 81; for vitality (life forces), 16, 22, 30, 91, 95, 110–11, 122, 153
conflict, 31, 65, 67, 79, 95, 105, 145, 152, 156n5, 158n19, 164, 168, 193, 207; and witchcraft, 27, 54
consumption, 3, 6, 30, 61, 71, 81, 118, 134, 143, 151, 155, 166; and consumerism, 31, 82
conviviality, 8, 15, 17–18, 27–28, 67, 80, 108, 142, 147, 149, 153, 169, 172, 177, 193
cooperation, 17–18, 22, 71, 81, 105, 144
cosmologies, 30, 43, 63, 77, 119, 122, 162, 170, 194; and cosmological competition, 122; and cosmological levels (domains), 13, 90, 108, 165, 211; and cosmological perceptions (views, understandings, concerns), 118, 122, 124, 163, 168; and cosmological relations, 67; and cosmological reproduction, 55

dance, 17, 19, 21, 38–44, 46–48, 50–52, 55–56, 57n5, 70, 99, 167–68, 171–72, 176, 179–80
death, 23, 43, 46, 52, 72–73, 79–80, 93, 102, 104, 135, 142; rituals, 44
distribution, 4, 19, 29, 63, 78, 94, 152–53, 157, 169–70, 206. *See also* redistribution

economies, 3–4, 61, 63–64; Amazonian (indigenous), 30, 74, 169, 175; capitalist, 29–30; market, 64, 66, 77
education, 3, 63, 84n1, 118, 120–21, 123, 126–27, 130, 134–36, 155, 163–64, 173, 203
egalitarianism, 29, 62, 71, 73–74, 140, 142, 153, 155
epidemics, 62, 70, 79–82, 96–97, 110
equality, 4, 152–53
euphoria, 17, 21, 26–27, 38–39, 41, 46, 50–55, 156; as wealth, 17, 26, 39, 53
exchange, 10–11, 14, 16, 22, 24, 26, 48, 55, 65, 71, 81–82, 98–100, 124, 157n14, 162, 165, 169–70, 172, 174, 176–77, 181–82, 183n9

family, 20, 35, 37, 46, 50, 54, 61, 65, 67, 70–71, 73, 78, 82–83, 95, 100, 103–5, 120–23, 128, 130, 132–33, 142, 144–45, 147, 152, 158n18, 192; extended, 77, 121, 144, 150; leaders, 133; nuclear, 90, 144, 147; places, 20, 121, 123, 128–30, 135
fertility, 21–22, 25, 60–61, 67, 98, 165
food, 11, 15, 25, 27, 47–48, 51, 60, 62, 66–67, 71, 73–74, 77, 82–83, 90, 97–98, 101–2, 120–21, 124, 127, 131, 143–44, 147, 152, 169, 178; abundance of, 25, 27, 61, 121, 176, 179; insecurity, 25, 61, 73
forest, 6, 20, 24–25, 29, 65–66, 77, 81–82, 94, 99, 102, 119–22, 124–25, 128, 131–32, 134–37, 147, 157n11, 180, 178, 192, 200–201, 203, 208–10, 213; and deforestation, 29, 54, 65–66; protected, 65; resources, 17–18, 20, 90, 122–23
friendship, 16–17, 21, 80–81, 90, 108, 145, 152, 167, 177

gardens, 20, 44, 51, 96–97, 110, 124, 128, 135, 146, 152, 154, 209–10; and gardening, 84, 94, 120–21
gender, 17, 26, 39, 41, 46, 51, 55, 178; and gendering, 22, 118–19, 126–28, 132, 135, 178
generosity, 15, 30, 71, 143, 146. *See also* sharing
gods (divinities), 19, 21, 89–93, 95–99, 101, 108–10, 111n2, 111n5, 173, 182; creator, 16, 27, 89, 93, 95, 99, 102, 108, 168, 171, 182
good, common (public), 4, 29–30, 38, 45–46, 53–55, 60, 174, 193
goods, 15, 21, 48, 53, 63, 71, 82, 123, 128, 132–34, 152, 156, 157n14,

161–62, 169–70, 173, 176; material, 4, 8, 28, 151, 157n16; public, 22, 62, 65, 153, 155
greed, 4, 15, 31, 94, 110
growth, economic, 4, 29–30, 194, 206

happiness, 4–6, 12, 17, 26–28, 30, 39, 41, 51–55, 60, 143, 155–56
health, 3, 5–6, 8, 14–15, 18, 21–22, 25–28, 30, 60, 62, 66–67, 72–73, 80–81, 91, 97, 118, 120–21, 131, 136, 145, 164–65, 172, 178–79, 181, 183n8, 203, 206; collective, 61–62; ill, 25, 61, 79, 172; individual, 62; as wealth (well-being), 8, 25, 60–63, 79, 81, 83–84, 125

identity, 17, 22, 44, 61, 63, 71–72, 83, 131, 133, 140–41, 154–55, 162, 168, 177–79, 182
ilths, 30–31, 62–64
incorporation, 8, 21, 127, 133, 135, 163, 177
interculturality, 12, 31, 82, 164, 175, 196, 205, 210–11, 213n3
interethnic relations, 12, 44, 62, 79, 162, 164

jealousy, 92, 143, 145, 149, 153, 173
joy, 27, 42, 52–53, 60

kin (relatives), 16, 18–21, 25, 48, 50, 61, 67, 72–75, 77–80, 82, 84, 90, 118, 121, 123, 126–28, 130, 132–35, 140–42, 144, 148–49, 156n3, 199–200, 206, 210
kinship, 17, 22–23, 25, 27, 38–39, 44, 55, 72, 118–19, 121, 124–25, 127, 131–32, 134–35, 140, 142, 144–45, 148, 152–53, 156n3, 193
knowledge, 20–21, 26, 28, 47–48, 71, 78, 83, 91–92, 99, 102–3, 109–10, 124, 126, 128–30, 136, 143, 153, 156n2, 162, 168, 172–74, 179–80, 181–82, 183n12, 191–94, 196–97, 203, 205, 209, 211, 212n1; cultural, 17, 135, 175, 194–96, 202, 210; life-giving; 15–16, 19, 23, 109–10; transformative, 20, 26, 174, 181

labor, 9–10, 16, 22, 26, 30, 53, 60, 63, 70–71, 83, 122–23, 133, 135, 139, 144, 146–48, 150, 175–76, 206
land, 9–11, 13, 15, 17, 18, 20, 25, 29–30, 38, 54, 64–65, 70–71, 89–91, 95–97, 103–9, 111n9, 118–23, 125, 128, 130–37, 140, 145, 167, 181, 206; communal, 20, 105, 110; titles, 91, 103–7, 109, 111n9, 120–21, 132, 136, 140–41, 147, 153, 169; as wealth, 122
landscapes, 65, 70, 163, 169
leaders, 8, 15–16, 21, 23–24, 27, 39, 45, 47, 91, 95, 103, 104–5, 110–11, 117–19, 123, 129–37, 141, 150, 153, 157n12, 165, 169–70, 172–73, 175, 192, 197; community, 15, 104, 151, 166, 183n5; priestly, 16, 19, 21, 23, 89, 91–92, 97, 99, 109–11. *See also* chiefs; leadership
leadership, 8, 23, 61, 75–77, 104–5, 117–19, 123, 129–31, 135, 137, 162, 164, 168, 172, 175. *See also* chiefs; leaders
life, 13, 16, 18–19, 22–26, 30–31, 41, 60–61, 66, 72, 74, 80, 82–84, 89, 93–95, 100, 121–22, 127, 135, 150, 152–53, 165, 168, 170–74, 177–82, 192, 198, 200, 202, 205, 207–8; art of, 4; beautiful, 15, 17, 25, 27, 193, 199, 207; ceremonial (ritual), 43, 46, 55; everyday (daily), 13, 20, 37, 40, 47, 57n9, 67, 144, 148, 150, 152, 154, 166, 174, 198; harmonious (peaceful, tranquil), 21, 91, 108, 145, 148; potentialities of, 127–28, 137; quality of, 4–5, 62, 74; social (community), 21, 41, 44, 52, 54, 108, 145, 165, 199; ways of (lifeways), 3–4, 17, 24–25, 29, 84, 109, 119–20, 124, 129, 135, 193, 196, 210, 213. *See also* life, good; vitality
life, good, 3, 4–8, 12, 21, 24–27, 30–31, 41, 50, 55–56, 61, 91, 125, 127–28, 134, 143, 156n2, 181, 191, 193–94, 198–99, 205–6, 210. *See also* buen vivir; living well
life force, 15–17, 21–22, 27, 91, 94–95, 98, 122, 125–26, 135, 147, 153, 168, 182, 193, 195, 199, 206–7. *See also* vital force

living well (live well), 6, 25–26, 136, 140, 142, 147–48, 150, 153–56, 193. *See also* buen vivir; life, good
love, 21, 25, 28, 30, 47, 74, 98, 127, 143, 149, 152

maize, 22, 61, 67, 70, 72–73, 77, 94, 121; and beer (chichi), 67–68
manioc, 71, 94, 97, 117, 121, 124, 126–27, 146, 176; and beer (brew, chicha), 22, 48, 98, 109, 117, 131, 144, 147–48, 151, 153, 168, 183n2, 199
market, 12–13, 28, 31, 63, 89, 92, 147, 150, 157n11, 194, 211; economies, 64, 66, 77
meat, 22, 67, 72, 97, 100, 117, 121
money, 4, 12, 15, 18–19, 22, 24, 28, 61, 65–66, 71, 81–83, 109, 120, 127, 146–49, 151–52, 154, 161–65, 169–71, 173–77, 184n16, 211
morality, 22, 67, 110, 150, 157n12, 168
music, 15, 21, 37–44, 46–48, 50–53, 55–56, 57n5, 57n9, 67, 69–70, 75–77, 91, 98–99, 109, 153, 156, 195

nongovernmental organizations, 19, 122, 130, 133, 140, 151, 164
nurture (nurturing), 16, 21, 26, 67, 132, 181, 212. *See also* care

objects, 16, 20, 57n4, 93, 100, 109, 128, 143, 148, 154; material, 14–15, 47; sacred, 61; valued, 25, 126–27
organizations, ethnopolitical (ethnic, indigenous), 12, 23, 66, 120, 123, 129–30, 133, 137, 154, 192
orphans, 25–27, 75, 110, 126, 168, 180–81, 183n5, 183n10. *See also* poor; poverty
Others, 8, 16–19, 23–24, 105, 109–10, 118, 122–24, 127–28, 130, 132–33, 135–36, 169–70, 177, 181. *See also* alterity
ownership, 20, 108, 128–29, 141; and owners: 19–20, 25, 30, 48, 94, 108, 111n4, 118, 124, 167–68, 173

patrimony, 8, 20, 64, 174, 179
people-making (fabrication of, production of), 15–17, 20–23, 25–26, 118–19, 121–22, 125, 132, 135–36, 141, 143, 153, 168, 177–78. *See also* personhood
personhood, 8, 61, 84n2, 118–19, 129. *See also* people-making
political economy, 9–10, 16, 30, 89, 122; classical, 9; of life, 16, 81, 89, 91–92, 175; of people, 16, 175
poor, 4, 11–12, 26, 28, 60, 74, 82, 95, 126, 146–47, 149–50, 180–81. *See also* orphans; poverty
possessions, 10, 12, 25–26, 71, 73–74, 78, 146, 148–49, 173, 176–77
poverty, 8, 11–12, 24–28, 61, 63, 82, 110, 146–48, 155, 180–81, 210. *See also* orphans; poor
power, 10, 24, 27, 42, 52, 62, 65, 73–75, 78, 80, 84, 90–91, 93, 95, 98–99, 105–6, 110, 122, 125, 129, 133, 148, 155, 168–72, 180, 191–92, 196–97, 203, 205–6, 208–9, 212n1, 213n3; bio-, 8, 15; generative, 99, 180; political, 28, 38; state, 82, 161; of thoughts, 19, 90; transformative, 8, 31, 52, 162, 172; of wealth, 84n1
predation, 8, 17–18, 22, 24, 30, 57n4, 91, 93–93, 166, 170, 172–74, 177, 181; and prey, 24, 93–94, 124, 171–74
privatization, 10, 20, 28–29, 62, 64, 83, 123
production, 3, 6, 11, 14, 18, 71, 81, 176
productive capacities (skills), 15–17, 20–21, 25, 82, 118, 122, 124–27, 133, 135
project, development, 14, 19, 117, 120, 131–32, 134, 140, 146, 157n15, 162, 165–66, 169, 173–74, 177–79; funds, 14–15, 18, 75, 162, 164, 166, 170–71, 174–75
property, 8, 46–47, 61–63, 65, 70–74, 78, 108, 120, 124, 134–35, 141–42, 169, 182; collective (common, public), 8, 19, 39, 77–78, 90, 120, 135; inalienable, 20, 174; material, 77; personal, 8, 19, 23, 99, 109; private, 19, 46, 53, 70, 73, 77; rights of, 12, 19–20, 28

prosperity, 10, 12, 23–24, 41, 71, 73, 83, 165, 205, 210
public, 9–10, 13, 19–20, 22, 39, 50, 64, 78, 139, 143, 150, 154; definitions of, 10, 12, 140, 182; space, 46, 49–50, 53, 55, 140; sphere (domain); 13, 20, 28, 132, 140

reciprocity, 18, 20, 128, 144, 149, 162, 172, 176
redistribution, 140, 142, 151, 157, 162, 173, 206. *See also* distribution
reproduction, 14, 16, 18, 24, 81, 94, 118, 166, 174; social, 8, 17, 45, 55–56, 91, 119, 136, 155, 163, 181
resources, 16–17, 20, 23, 28–30, 44, 60, 64–65, 70–71, 79, 118–19, 121, 123–25, 128, 130, 132–34, 136–37, 142, 144–45, 152, 165, 169, 173–74, 182; forest, 17–18, 20, 90; natural, 4, 10–11, 15, 28, 122–23, 139, 151, 157n11; public (communal, common, collective), 14, 20, 64, 70, 84, 182; scarce, 10, 12, 16, 19, 28, 65, 70, 77–78, 89, 91, 94, 120, 122, 125, 134–35, 157n14, 174. *See also* scarcity
riches, 9–10, 25, 60, 63, 95, 173; collective, 10–12
ritual, 18, 21, 27, 42, 44, 46, 48–50, 52, 54–55, 73, 80, 98–100, 110, 121, 152, 158n19, 162, 168, 173, 175, 179, 183nn6–7, 203; death (funerary), 44, 81; experts (leaders), 26, 47, 168; initiation (puberty), 21, 56, 100; musical (dance), 42, 52, 167–68, 171–72, 176, 179–80; owners, 48; paraphernalia, 44, 61; protection, 21, 100, 102, 109; seclusion, 22, 80–81; space, 46; substances, 163, 179, 182n2; techniques (practices), 16, 19, 23, 90, 110

sacred: fires, 99, 109; landscapes, 163; objects, 61; sites, 61; songs, 91, 109
scarcity, 9–10, 13, 53, 70, 119, 122, 128, 144. *See also* resources, scarce
seduction, 17, 24, 169–71
selfishness, 4, 15, 23–24, 29, 94
sexuality, 22, 67, 72, 81, 95
shamans, 16–17, 19, 21, 23, 43, 53, 56, 68, 91–92, 95, 100–101, 103, 109–10, 126–30, 133, 166–67, 170–71, 177, 191, 193, 195–96, 200–203, 205, 209–10
sharing (share), 12, 14–15, 19–20, 23–24, 26, 29–30, 44, 47, 67, 71, 73, 78, 82, 90, 93, 98–99, 127, 136, 140, 143–44, 148, 150, 152, 157n7, 179, 210. *See also* generosity
sociality, 16, 67, 72, 74, 80, 82, 90, 153, 163, 181
societies: Amazonian (indigenous), 5–6, 13–16, 29–30, 39, 56, 57n4, 71, 118, 122, 154, 178; capitalist, 4, 8, 12, 28–30, 74; kin-based, 3, 8, 11, 73–74; national, 13; non-state, 11; risk, 61–64, 78, 83, 84n1; state, 11, 65; tribal, 11
solidarity, 30, 64, 74, 84, 173, 175
songs, 15, 19, 37–38, 40–41, 44, 47, 49, 51, 55–56, 78, 91, 98–99, 109, 168, 172, 195, 203, 205, 209
sorcery (sorcerous), 93, 97, 100, 170, 184n16
spirit, 16–17, 39, 41, 55, 72, 91, 93, 95, 99–102, 110, 124–25, 128, 130, 133, 163, 166, 171, 173–74, 183n11, 184; animal, 47, 77, 101, 103, 124, 178, 195, 201; blood, 18, 22, 80; evil (malevolent, wicked), 95, 100–102, 110, 174, 180, 184n16, 210; forest, 124; owners (masters), 19, 94, 130, 167, 179, 200, 209; worlds, 21, 23, 26, 67, 118, 124–25, 130, 132, 172, 178, 181, 202; water, 95, 100, 102, 124, 128
status, social, 25, 48, 52, 61, 63, 67, 71, 73, 75, 80–81, 83, 84n1, 168
stinginess, 26, 143, 147–50, 174
subsistence, 11, 71, 74, 108; means of, 11, 17, 110; resources of, 44, 70; struggle for, 4
substances, 16, 18, 22–23, 44, 72, 143, 162–63, 166, 171, 176, 179, 182n2, 211; alien (foreign, exogenous, enemy),

substances (*continued*)
8, 18, 21, 80–81, 12–17, 166, 173–74; life-giving (vitalizing, health-enhancing), 15, 18, 21–22, 72, 80–81, 118, 122, 133, 135, 181–82; pathogenic, 24, 170

territory, 54, 64, 70, 74, 77, 81, 90, 92, 97, 103, 118, 131, 133, 136, 139–41, 144, 151, 154–55, 156n5, 164, 167, 179, 181–82, 192, 194–95, 202; and territorial rights, 163, 168–69
things (goods, items, objects): intangible, 8, 14–15, 28, 38, 57n5, 71, 109, 147; tangible, 15, 18, 57, 67, 70–71, 73, 108–9, 147, 166
tobacco, 11, 21, 23, 24–25, 100, 163–64, 166–68, 170–73, 176, 178–79, 183n2, 183n4, 183n6, 195
trust, 134, 144; and mistrust, 152

usufruct, 12, 29, 47, 70, 174, 209; rights, 19–20, 28, 78, 90, 134–35, 139–42, 151, 209

value, 13–15, 19, 22, 25, 28–29, 31, 60, 62, 64, 66–67, 73–74, 81–84, 95, 103, 139, 145–51, 155–56, 157n14, 161, 173, 175–77, 179, 193, 197; exchange, 10–12, 14–15, 28, 77; theory of, 14, 148; use, 10, 12, 28
vital force (energy), 17, 21–22, 24, 26, 126, 128, 165, 173, 175, 181. *See also* life force
vitalities, 21, 93–95, 101–2, 110, 127
vitality, 8, 15–18, 21, 23, 25, 28, 60–61, 66–67, 72, 81, 91–94, 97, 99, 122, 135, 181; circulation of, 16, 22, 30, 72, 80–81, 100; struggle (competition, strife) for, 27, 30, 89, 91–92, 95, 110–11; as wealth, 8, 15–18, 21, 28, 60–61, 110, 181. *See also* life; life, good

wealth, 9–10, 12–15, 20–21, 26, 28–30, 60–65, 71, 73, 77–79, 81, 83–84, 84n1, 99, 118–19, 121–25, 128, 132, 134–35, 139, 145–47, 149–51, 155–56, 157n15, 162, 164, 173–74, 181–82, 194, 197, 206, 208, 210; accumulation of, 3, 6, 15, 24, 27, 29, 60, 63, 72, 78, 133, 149–50, 193, 207; circulation of, 117, 145; collective (common), 3, 8, 40, 70, 90, 135–36; convivial, 18, 21, 27, 90–92, 108–9; definitions of, 10–12, 14, 19–20, 24–25, 38, 41, 53, 139; distribution of, 4, 29, 63, 142, 152; environmental, 27, 90–92; generative, 18, 21, 27, 91–92, 95, 108–11; material (tangible), 11, 14–15, 61, 63, 74, 81, 147–50, 152, 154; national, 9, 65, 90, 191; personal, 29–30, 40, 135–36, 174; private, 9–10, 28, 39, 53, 56; production of, 11, 16–17, 23–25, 30, 135, 193; public, 3–4, 8–10, 12–13, 15–30, 39–40, 46, 49–50, 53, 55–56, 60, 62, 64–65, 69–70, 82, 84, 90–92, 99, 103, 106–11, 118–19, 125, 134–35, 139–43, 151–55, 156n2, 157n11, 174, 181–82, 193, 207, 209–10; theories of, 39
welfare, 10, 30, 155
well-being, 3–6, 8, 10, 12, 17, 21, 25–28, 31, 39, 50, 60, 67, 73, 83–84, 91, 118–19, 121, 125, 128, 133–36, 142, 146, 149, 154–56, 162–63, 166, 168–69, 179, 181–82, 193, 198; anatomy of, 3, 24; collective, 8, 25, 27, 61, 66, 110, 136, 154, 166; indicators of, 5–6; individual (personal), 8, 61, 136, 155
white people, 15, 18–19, 21, 24, 66, 91, 94–98, 103–6, 109–11, 143, 150, 156n6, 163, 165, 169–70, 174, 177, 197
witchcraft (witches), 15, 19, 27, 29, 43, 47, 54, 110, 149, 153, 172, 210
work, 4, 16, 18, 20–22, 24, 26, 28–30, 67, 70, 72, 74–75, 77, 81–82, 95, 108, 117–18, 120–21, 127–28, 130–33, 135, 143–45, 147–51, 153–54, 157nn11–12, 166–68, 171–79, 181–82, 184n17; collective (communal), 67, 127, 144, 151, 167–68